A GRAPHIC DESIGN STUDENT'S GUIDE TO FREELANCE

A GRAPHIC DESIGN STUDENT'S GUIDE TO FREELANCE

PRACTICE MAKES PERFECT

Ben Hannam

WILEY
JOHN WILEY & SONS, INC.

Copyright © 2013 by John Wiley & Sons, Inc. All rights reserved.
Published by John Wiley & Sons, Inc., Hoboken, New Jersey.
Published simultaneously in Canada.

For general information on our other products and services, or technical support, please contact our Customer Care Department within the United States at 800-762-2974, outside the United States at 317-572-3993 or fax 317-572-4002.

Wiley publishes in a variety of print and electronic formats and by print-on-demand. Some material included with standard print versions of this book may not be included in e-books or in print-on-demand. If this book refers to media such as a CD or DVD that is not included in the version you purchased, you may download this material at http://booksupport.wiley.com.

For more information about Wiley products, visit our Web site at http://www.wiley.com.

Library of Congress Cataloging-in-Publication Data:
Hannam, Ben.
A graphic design student's guide to freelance : Practice makes perfect / Ben Hannam.
pages cm
Includes index.
ISBN 978-1-118-34196-4 (pbk.); ISBN 978-1-118-39621-6 (ebk); ISBN 978-1-118-39623-0 (ebk);
ISBN 978-1-118-39704-6 (ebk); ISBN 978-1-118-39705-3 (ebk); ISBN 978-1-118-39731-2 (ebk)
1. Commercial art—Vocational guidance—United States. I. Title.
NC1001.H36 2012
741.6023—dc23
2012011012

Printed in the United States of America
10 9 8   7   6   5   4   3   2   1

Book Cover Designed by FourDesign
FourDesign is a faculty-led, student-run digital and print design agency at Virginia Tech, within the Visual Communication Design department in the School of Visual Arts. FourDesign specializes in corporate branding, print design, signage development, advertising, and basic web and interactive design. For more information visit www.wearefourdesign.com. Cover concept and illustration by Drew Ellis.

Contents

GENERAL INFORMATION

ADVANCED LEVEL

LANDING A JOB

EPILOGUE

Accessing Digital Files Online

There are several business forms that you can access online and use to help protect yourself, manage your work flow, and prepare a budget. You are free to modify these documents to fit your needs. However, before using these documents you should consult with a business attorney to make sure they provide you with ample legal protection for your region. To access these forms, you must go to www.wiley.com/go/graphicdesignstudentguide

Files Available For Download

Job Proposal Form
InDesign CS3+

Monthly Budget
Microsoft Excel 2008+

Proof Approval Form
InDesign CS3+

Job Jacket
Adobe Illustrator CS3+

Invoice of Services
InDesign CS3+

Model Release Form
InDesign CS3+

Time Sheet
InDesign CS3+

Vendor Contract
InDesign CS3+

Master Client List
InDesign CS3+

Retainer Client Contract
InDesign CS3+

Master Job Tracking List
Microsoft Excel 2008+

Request For Proposals
InDesign CS3+

Archive Your Work
Apple Macintosh OS X

Preface

For the last four years I've required the students entering my Introduction to Graphic Design class to work with a paying freelance client. I'm one of those annoying teachers who love seeing their students achieve more than they thought possible, and I'm okay with pushing my students beyond their comfort zones.

I was pushed hard at Virginia Commonwealth University, and while it was occasionally painful, it was a time when I experienced tremendous growth as a graphic designer. Sometimes we have to be reminded to work outside our comfort zones because it's easy to become complacent and only embrace the opportunities that are easy for us to complete. It doesn't matter if the change takes the form of writing your first book, experimenting with a new design methodology, or working for your first freelance client. These are all opportunities for growth.

In order to get outside of our comfort zones, we occasionally need a little nudge from behind or must gather our courage and take a running start. Just like entering a cold pool on a warm summer day, once we acclimate ourselves to the initial shock of entering the chilly water, we adjust quickly to our new conditions. As a student in a graphic design program, the question you need to answer is, "Are you ready to try something new, or do you want to maintain the status quo?"

This book is written for students who are willing to try something new and who are interested in learning more about working as a freelance designer. Throughout this book I have tried to strike a balance between encouraging you to work outside your comfort zones and helping you to minimize your chances of a less than successful outcome. The bottom line is that while I can help you lay out a strategy to work with clients, you have to provide the common sense, motivation, and work ethic. For many of you success will be determined by the amount of energy you are willing to put into your freelancing endeavor.

I asked my students how they felt when they learned that they were going to have to work with a client; 50 percent of the class said they felt nervous, 40 percent said they felt confident, and 10 percent said they were ambivalent about the idea. Strangely, it's the students who said they were ambivalent about the idea who worried me the most. Working with a client isn't something to be taken lightly, and a measured amount of fear is to be expected. Similarly, being confident in one's abilities can help a student power through indecision and lead to success. It's the "not caring" mentality that I believe is the biggest predictor of a less-than-successful outcome.

I can offer encouragement for those students who are intimidated by working with clients, and I can help those who are ready to hit the ground running understand why it's important to develop a plan before leaping into action, but I can't make someone who is ambivalent suddenly begin to care. No matter how hard I try, I can't push a rope. But I can certainly use one to rein in motivated students. Without self-motivation, you will be dead in the water.

Chances are good that working as a freelance designer isn't going to be as traumatic as one might think. When I polled my class to see if I should continue to require classes to work with a client over 90 percent of my students said "Yes, absolutely!" Not a single person replied "No." It's clear by this response that my students valued the experience, but their response certainly didn't mean their experience was problem-free. In fact, 80 percent of my students described working with a clients as "problematic at times, but successful overall," and I think this is indicative of the design profession as a whole. Rarely have I ever worked on a project where I did not run into some kind of snag. As students gain more work experience they realize that there are times when they will need to be firm, times when they need to be accommodating, times when they need to accept constraints, and times when they just need to break all the rules. Perhaps one of the most difficult lessons to learn is when to fight for something and when to give in.

It can be incredibly difficult, without actually working with a client, to develop the sensitivity to know when you should dig in your heels and when you should be flexible. The small nuances of the designer/client relationships simply can't be learned in the artificial reefs of academia. While academia provides students with the freedom to take risks and fail with minimal repercussions, there is a great deal you can learn through the firsthand experience of working with a client. Business is about relationships, and business relationships are difficult to fabricate in academia and remain authentic. It's important to realize that a school and a design agency have very different goals. While the school's goal might be to equip students with knowledge, an agency's goal is to make a profit. When organizations have different objectives, it is not uncommon for them to take different paths to reach their goals—which is why there is a gap between academia and professional practice.

Many graphic design programs try and bridge this gap by requiring you to complete an internship or by offering a Professional Practices class. These are fantastic opportunities that you should take advantage of, but when you freelance, you are working as a professional, and you must weigh the risk versus reward scenarios before you act. There is no safety net, no umbrella of academic protection, and no Command + Z to press if you get in over your head—your successes and failures are yours alone. While there may be plenty of people you can turn to for advice, the decisions are yours to make. If you make good decisions, then you will reap the rewards, but if you make bad decisions, then you will feel the consequences. It's extremely difficult to create this type of experience within the walls of academia.

I've worked as a consultant, a creative director, a graphic designer, a small-business owner, and an educator. I've hired and fired interns, graphic designers, illustrators, writers, photographers, and computer programmers, and I've learned that there is a big difference between my expectations as a teacher and my expectations as a business owner. By choosing to freelance, you help close the gap between your academic experiences and your professional experiences, learn more about the disconnect between academia and the design profession, and make yourself a better designer in the process.

I want you to succeed in both your academic and freelance endeavors because both will help you understand the design profession better. I tried to write the type of book I wish I had read when I was still a student in college, one that is encouraging, and yet realistic with its goals. I remember how proud I felt when I walked around town and saw my freelance work in restaurants and local businesses. I hope you get to experience this feeling of accomplishment for yourself.

I tell my students that if they can work with a client once, then they can do it again. Every time they work with a client (even if they fail), they'll learn a bit more about the design profession—and a bit more about themselves. I have no doubt that this experience can yield the same results for you. Good luck!

Acknowledgments

I would like to express my sincere thanks and gratitude to the many individuals who have made this book possible. Many of my views about graphic design and life have been shaped by my conversations with friends, family, colleagues, and students, and I am deeply grateful for your hard work, kind words, constructive criticism, and encouragement.

I owe Michele Domenech a debt of gratitude for convincing me that I should write this book, and for coaching me through the process—thank you for your help.

I count myself very lucky to have such awesome colleagues to work with. Dr. Troy Abel and Meaghan Dee have become extended family and sources of encouragement and inspiration. I would also like to thank Somiah Muslimani and Darin Hagerman for their friendship, contributions, and support. You guys kept me laughing, and I hope to work with you again soon.

There would be no book without the help of Margaret Cummins, Amanda Miller, Mike New, David Sassian, and the entire team at John Wiley & Sons. Thank you for your hard work and support of this project.

I would like to take a moment and thank the Radford Small-business Development Group, John Wallace, Cole Harven, Greg Justice, Anne Graves, Jack Davis, Virginia Tech, the School of Visual Arts, and all of the students who submitted examples of their freelance work. I appreciate your contributions and kind words.

Finally, and most importantly, I would like to thank my beautiful wife Julie, daughter Ruby, and son Beckett for their love, patience, and support—I am most grateful for you. My family has always encouraged and supported me through both my successes and failures and have given me the courage to "Go big, fail big." Mom, Dad, Matt, Whitney, and Sarah, I appreciate and love you all immensely. Thank you for your love and support.

Introduction

My first job after graduating college was at a local printing company. They hired me to prepare files for printing and to do some graphic design work when it was needed. I remember being nervous, but feeling confident that I'd do well. In fact, I felt so confident in my graphic design abilities that I was already calculating ways I could approach my boss to talk to him about giving me a raise. I hadn't even made it through my first day, and I was already thinking about strategies to convince my boss that I was worth a lot more money.

When I arrived on my first official day of work, the secretary gave me a quick tour of the facilities, introduced me to everyone as the "new guy," led me to a computer station, and wished me luck.

My job was simple enough. People sent in their files to get printed, and my job was to open the files on the computer and print out color separations on a special printer, which printed on film instead of paper. As film came out of the special printer, it spooled into a light safe canister, and it was my job to take the canister of film to a darkroom and run it through a processor to develop the film. After the film had been developed, I gave the film negatives to a person called a "stripper," who registered the cyan, magenta, yellow, and black separations to make an impression on a metal plate that was treated with a light-sensitive coating. After the metal plate had been "burned," it would get delivered to the printing press operator, who would prepare the printing press.

Eager to make a good impression, I tried to work quickly, but within minutes I was informed that I had done the job incorrectly. The stripper told me that I had forgotten to include "traps" and that I would have to fix my error and reprint the job correctly. I blushed as I confessed to the stripper that I didn't know what a "trap" was. She sighed loudly and stared at me indignantly.

"Trapping," the stripper explained, "is an overlap that prevents the appearance of tiny gaps of white space, which are caused by small misalignments on the printing press." I had never heard of this term before and asked the stripper to explain it again slowly. The stripper sighed and said, "You have to set your traps in your computer document before your print them out. There is a window in QuarkXPress that lets you set them, but I don't know where to find this window. Didn't they teach you this in school?"

I spent the next several hours with my nose buried in a QuarkXPress manual trying to learn about traps. I felt humiliated that I had dropped the ball. Production came to a halt as everyone waited for me to figure out what I was doing, and I felt like crawling under a rock! The stripper's comment "didn't they teach you this in school?" kept going through my mind.

When 5:00 p.m. finally arrived, I walked out to my car and began to replay the day over again in my mind. "So much for asking for a raise," I thought to myself, and I was angry that my teachers hadn't covered something as fundamental as trapping color in any of my graphic design classes. I began to wonder what else they hadn't told me and hoped that this was an isolated incident. The feelings of confidence that I felt on the drive into work were gone, and I thought long and hard about quitting and never returning. If my bank account hadn't been dangerously low, I probably would have quit that day. But there's nothing like desperation to keep you motivated.

Sometime later that evening, I decided that I was going to stick with the job and learn from the experience. Even if I got fired, at least I'd learn something new about the printing process.

Filling in the Gaps in Your Education

The truth is, no matter how hard your teachers try, they aren't going to be able to cover everything you need to know about graphic design in four years of school. Now that I'm a professor, I can see firsthand how difficult it is to prepare my students for the many challenges they will face as graphic designers. There is a Chinese proverb that states, "Give a man a fish, and he eats for a day. Teach a man to fish, and he will eat for the rest of his life." That's why I'm writing this book. I want to help you create your own freelance graphic design business, so you can use this experience to fill in the gaps in your education. I'm going to show you how to find clients and earn a little extra money while you're in school. It's my

> *"How do I fill in the gaps in my education when I'm not really sure what they are?"*

hope that through this process you'll continue to learn about the graphic design profession and help you identify your personal goals.

Before you get freaked out or too fired up about the idea of starting a free-lance business, you need to do a little planning to make sure that you don't get in over your head. Starting a business can be risky, and I am going to try to help you minimize your chances of a less-than-successful outcome. It's important to strategize and understand your role as a business owner and freelance graphic designer and to get a feel for the business environment you're planning to enter.

I hope you're a tiny bit uncomfortable with starting your own freelance business, because it's not something to be taken lightly. But with planning, discipline and patience, you can do it! Let's face it. You're going to have to do some "outside the classroom" learning anyway, so why not dictate the pace of these lessons and make a little money on the side?

Most graphic design programs seem to either try to cover the most important aspects of graphic design and then touch upon specialties that might interest you, or they focus on a particular aspect of graphic design and help you become extremely proficient in this one area (e.g., website design, print design, advertising design, typography). In either case, you're going to have to tackle some self-initiated projects to deepen your graphic design skills. You might be thinking to yourself, "How do I fill in the gaps in my education when I'm not really sure what they are?"

Reading books and magazines about graphic design can be helpful in determining which techniques and skills you might want to hone. Internships can be a great way for you to bridge the gap between academics and real world experience. Professional organizations like the American Institute of Graphic Arts (AIGA), the Graphic Artists Guild (GAG), and the Art Directors Club (ADC) can also be great resources for information, trends, and inspiration. Both internships and professional organizations give you an opportunity to meet professionals in the graphic design community and can provide a variety of learning experiences that you can add to your résumé. However, I've always learned the most by rolling up my sleeves and getting my hands dirty. While I recommend that you secure an internship sometime during your college career and become active in a professional design organization, I think it's important for you to freelance as well.

Freelancing is a great way for you to test the waters for a career in graphic design, to make a little money, and to fill in the gaps in your education. The key is to keep it simple, start slowly, and build momentum over time. By starting your own business, you'll gain experience and begin to understand how the projects you're working on in school have been designed to prepare you for problems you are likely to encounter in the profession. It's my hope that you will bring your freelance experiences back into the classroom and share them with your professor and peers in order to enrich everyone's academic experience.

This book is written to serve as a guide on your graphic design journey, but you need to realize that there are many paths to success. Running a freelance company can be anything but formulaic. The best advice I can give you is to keep an open mind, to be honest with yourself about your strengths and weaknesses, and to seek the advice of people you trust along the way. Ultimately, the decisions are yours to make. But taking the time to look at your business through the eyes of people whose opinions you respect can be invaluable.

What Is Freelance?

A freelance graphic designer is someone who is self-employed and not committed to an employer for the long term. A freelancer designer sells his or her services and generally enjoys a greater variety of projects than the typical company employee, although a freelancer's income may fluctuate more than a company employee's does. The uncertainty of your income is perhaps the biggest drawback of working as a freelance designer, but having the ability to choose when you work, the projects you work on, and the rates you charge your clients are perks that many designers appreciate and take advantage of when possible.

Don't Wait until You Graduate

While it might be tempting to wait until you graduate before you begin to freelance, there is no reason why you can't start now. In fact, starting a freelance business while you're in school will help you develop your business skills and establish a few industry contacts. If you start freelancing now, then by the time you graduate college, you'll potentially have less debt, an established client base, and a more thorough understanding of the graphic design profession. Freelancing isn't suited for everyone, so reading this book might be able to give you an idea about what you can expect and help you make a more informed decision about whether freelancing might be a good option for you.

Having a diploma in your hand and four years of college under your belt isn't a magic formula for success, so don't be afraid of getting started sooner rather than later—the risks are virtually identical no matter when you start. Business is essentially about relationships, and you're going to be ahead of the game if you begin to build these relationships while you're still in school. Having a degree and training in graphic design does have its advantages, but the strongest relationships are forged over time. Don't wait for the perfect moment before you jump in and get started—you might find yourself waiting a really long time before you feel ready.

The truth is, I can't recall a time where I felt that I had it all figured out. Part of your role as a graphic designer is to problem-solve and figure out solutions to a variety of problems. There are no shortage of problems that will stump, frustrate, confuse, and terrify you, but they can be solved through creativity, ingenuity, and perseverance. Overcoming these problems (and your fears) is part of the adventure and are reasons why I think it's so much fun to be a graphic designer. I am always exploring ways to be more efficient with my time, to communicate my ideas more clearly, to become more creative with my solutions, and to grow as an individual.

Businesses want to work with people who will help make them be more successful, so it's important to know your strengths and weaknesses. It's a good idea to make sure you focus in areas where you are strong, while working to improve your self-identified weaknesses. Basically, you are going to start simple, do a great job with a small project, and add in complexity only when you feel comfortable doing so. As the jobs you get become more complex, the amount of money you make will increase, but it's extremely important to start slowly and make good decisions along the way. It's important to not agree to work on jobs that are too big, have deadlines that are too tight, or have clients who are difficult to work with—it's not just about the money you can make. Keep in mind that each business endeavor is a marathon, not a sprint. You're going to want to underpromise and overdeliver instead of the other way around.

A few years ago I brought a client into my classroom to work with my class. The client described his needs, and each student developed several concepts as a potential solution. One by one each student presented their concepts to the client, and the client shared his feelings about the designer's direction. Two weeks later we met with the client again, but I gave the next round of presentations an interesting twist—I gave the client permission to fire the student designers.

If the student designer had ignored the client's feedback or did not produce enough work between Round One to Round Two, then the client had the option to fire the designer and the student would have to write a research paper instead. After announcing this change to my students, I noticed that they seemed more worried than usual about the critique. I wondered out loud if it was because they didn't want to write a research paper or if they hadn't given the project their full attention and were about to be called out on their lack of effort.

Almost half of my class was fired by the client, and my students suddenly felt the gravity of being ill-prepared for this particular meeting. One of my students who had been fired by the client wrote in her paper, "Throughout this whole process, the designer should guide the client in decision making. Designers have the upper-hand in the visual world and should offer the client advice on what is visually appropriate and what design will be the most effective. This diminishes the chances of a disastrous outcome and helps the process run smoothly."

As I read through my student's papers, I discovered that the common theme from students who had been fired was regret. My students regretted not being prepared and didn't want to make the same mistake again. I didn't want my students to get fired by the client, but I wanted them to understand that if they didn't do their job correctly, they would have to deal with undesirable consequences.

The experiences you gain through freelancing will help you understand the graphic design profession better, challenge you to work more efficiently, and help you realize how important it is to establish boundaries. Just like my student who was fired and suddenly realized that she had a few areas that she could improve, you will undoubtedly know your strengths and weaknesses much better by having worked as a freelance designer. You shouldn't be afraid of failing, you should be afraid of "not trying." I hope that you have discovered a profession that will be rewarding, fulfilling, and challenging to you—as well as respect.

About This Book

The information in this book is divided into four different sections. Each section is color coded, so that you can find the information that is most relevant to you quickly and easily. Information that is helpful to all levels of students is red, information for Beginner designers is green, information for Intermediate designers is blue, and information for Advanced designers is purple. These color bars are located on the outside margins of this book.

Since this book is written for students, it makes sense to divide the book into sections that correspond to particular skill levels. The goals and expectations at the Beginner level are easier than those at the Advanced level because you must first establish a foundation and develop a healthy work ethic and good habits that you can build upon later. As you build upon this foundation you will begin to add in complexity as you feel comfortable doing so. Work within your comfort zones at first and mix in more complex projects slowly over time.

Foundations are important. If the foundation of a building is laid incorrectly, there is a good chance that when the building is completed it will be plagued by problems. Similarly, it would be easy to skip over the Beginner sections of this book and begin with a chapter that has a more rewards. But don't do it! What you skip in the pages of this book are the curve balls that your clients will throw at you later on. Everyone's freelance graphic design business experience will be different, so don't try to keep up with your peers. Execute your own game plan instead.

There are several great books available to help you set up a freelance business, but there aren't many books that have been written to help students navigate the freelance experience. I've seen students get taken advantage of by clients because they wanted to freelance but weren't sure how to protect themselves, so I wrote this book in order to assist you and make your freelance design experience go a little more smoothly.

I receive many e-mails that say "I need a designer. Can you recommend someone? This would a great project for a student portfolio." My past experiences have led me to believe that this roughly translates to "I need a designer, and I don't want to pay for their services." My response to these types of requests are always "What's your budget? Because my students get paid for their graphic design services," and it becomes apparent which of these requests are legitimate and which are simply from people looking for someone to work for free.

The skills you are learning in school are valuable, but you may not be sure what they are worth yet. In fact, you may be pleasantly surprised to discover what people are willing to pay for your services. In the Beginner through Advanced chapters, I've included some examples of freelance work that other students have completed. You will be able to see from these examples how much they charged their clients and hear about their freelancing successes and frustrations. I hope that you can use this information to your advantage. Learning from the successes and failures of students in your situation may help you make informed decisions when it comes to freelancing.

"You can pick your clients as well as the projects you work on. Don't overcommit yourself or let your academic work suffer."

I tend to be relatively conservative when it comes to financial and business matters, so I try to minimize my risk and avoid promising a client more than I can realistically deliver. Fear is one of the biggest enemies of the creative mind, and fear is extremely hard to compartmentalize.

If freelancing begins to stress you out, then these feelings may also creep in and effect your academic work. Instead of creating a situation in which there is no place you can turn, slow down and work at a slower pace until you feel more comfortable. Another way to alleviate feelings of stress are to work on smaller, more manageable projects.

The point is that you can pick your clients as well as the projects you work on. Don't overcommit yourself or let your academic work suffer. If you use common sense and try to keep your academic and freelance commitments in balance, you're going to have a great experience. You'll look back and be amazed how far you've come.

Why Should You Freelance?

2

Balancing Creativity and Commerce

Getting paid and bartering for your services is great, but there are also other reasons why freelancing is a good idea. Learning to balance creativity and commerce is a skill that is valuable, but one that can be difficult to learn outside of a business setting. Learning to work creatively while accepting certain financial constraints is a way in which you can stand out in a sea of designers who are vying for an employment opportunity.

Creativity often ebbs and flows. Commerce gets right to the point and often focuses on the bottom line. Absolutely every company I've worked for has its own formula for the amount of time spent on creative pursuits versus maintaining a profit margin. Graphic designers act as problem solvers in many cases and need the freedom to experiment and fail. Failure can be difficult to bill a client for (they tend to want results), but it is a critically important component of the designer's creative process. Generally speaking, creativity doesn't follow a direct path to a solution. Finding good solutions requires a designer to experiment, play, engage, question, challenge conventions, and sometimes fail. Many business models are highly structured, time-tested, and financially sound, but they have been known to stifle creativity. I'm convinced that the key to success is to strike a balance between being a creative designer and a shrewd business person. A great way to learn to achieve this balance is by running your own freelance design business.

When you work as a freelance designer, it won't take long before you begin to develop your own recipe for creativity and financial stability. You'll discover that you need to be both left- and right-brained in order to be successful. When you are able to integrate business concepts like Return On Investment (ROI) and time management with conditions of graphic design like creativity, cleverness and innovation there will be no limit to your business' potential. Clients will hire you because of your ability to generate creative solutions, and you will probably want to be compensated for your time and efforts. Therefore, it's up to you to determine where your priorities lie and to develop your own formula for blending creativity and commerce.

Many design programs try to integrate business principles into their curriculum by offering a Professional Practices class. These classes can be extremely helpful in teaching you more about the business side of graphic design and can also help you familiarize yourself with the local design scene. In these classes you'll usually learn to read and write contracts, discuss ethical issues, learn about copyright and trademark law, and other common business practices.

When you are already freelancing, Professional Practices classes become more lively and fun because the discussion is no longer purely academic in nature, and you can bring the sticky situations that you encounter while freelancing to class to discuss with your teacher and peers. You'll quickly discover that sometimes there are no black and white answers, but shades of gray that are influenced by your morals, ethics, and personal beliefs. Sometimes there isn't a "right" answer to your question, and it can be helpful to look at your question from many angles. Being able to talk about scenarios and tactics with your peers can be helpful because you might discover viewpoints that you hadn't previously considered.

Employers want designers who can make creative and financial decisions that will improve the company's profit margin. When you're showing your portfolio to a prospective employer they may ask you a question like "Why did you choose this paper for your letterhead?" If you reply, "Well, I really liked the matte paper from Mohawk, but I found a paper that was very similar and cost 30 percent less," you are subtly communicating that you can balance creativity and commerce. It's rare that young designers demonstrate that they have awareness about the business side of graphic design; many portfolios are only focused on the work and not the process one takes to get to a solution. Demonstrating that you can work within constraints can be a great way to capture an art director's attention.

Escaping the Project Mode Mentality

You may still be in the process of discovering your visual voice, not to mention learning about what will be involved with making a living as a graphic designer. More than likely, you don't have much professional experience at this point, which

> *"School allows you to test the waters, practice, and hone the skills you will need to begin your career as a graphic designer."*

is part of the reason why you're in school—to gain more experience. School allows you to test the waters, practice, and hone the skills you will need to begin your career as a graphic designer.

It's easy to lose focus when you're in school, and occasionally students have been known to take the path of least resistance to finding a solution for a project. After a lecture, I am sometimes asked, "Is this going to be on the test?" Hearing that, I get a little worried because I'm afraid the student is missing the point. The test is designed purely to gauge understanding of a particular concept or idea; the real trick is being able to recall that information when you need it. Grades are simply a by-product of your work rather than being the point of your education.

Every semester I receive a few e-mails from alumni who remember a lecture I gave, but can't recall the specifics. For example: "Do you remember when you told us about nondisclosure agreements, and you told us to find out if we could use the work we did for our clients in our portfolios ahead of time? Well, I just received a letter from their lawyer because I posted the work I did for them on my website. What do I do?" I try to answer these questions as best I can, but once you graduate, you may not have full access to all the support structures you enjoyed as a student. It's important that you learn the lessons you are taught in school and know where you can go to find answers on your own.

What teachers sometimes forget is that students are looking to them to create projects in an academic environment that will help them prepare for scenarios that they are likely to encounter in the profession. Lists of do's and don'ts can be good to learn, but sometimes they are easily forgotten because they lack the context of when you are likely to face these types of situations in your professional work. Without some sort of context for the lessons you are learning, it is likely that you will forget how to react when a similar situation presents itself.

By going to school and running a freelance business, you will be grounded in reality, and you help create a context for the lessons you are learning. Freelancing helps you prioritize information and validate the wisdom that your teachers are trying to share with you. Having a little street smarts will help you determine which lessons and principles are the most applicable to your situation.

I love it when students bring their experiences to a discussion in the class-room. It makes teaching so much more fun because the discussion is relevant to my students' success and not just a theory without an application. These types of interactions help me connect with my students in a meaningful way and are help-ful in evaluating their trajectory toward success. A small correction or adjustment at the early stage can have a significant impact on them down the road as they develop their visual voice, design methodology, and graphic design skills.

In my experience, there are three areas in particular that seem to snare young designers. These three areas are superficial research, a resistance to sketching, and a lack of attention to detail. Your teachers know you are trying to balance your time and energy throughout your classes and hopefully leave some time for fun. But it's important that you don't get caught in a "project mode mentality."

Project mode is a term I use to describe a mentality that you sometimes adopt where you begin to think of me (your teacher) as the client and try to reverse en-gineer a graphic design solution that you think I will like. At first glance you might think working this way is more efficient and will save you time. But what you are really doing is establishing a personality-dependent method of problem-solving rather than stretching your wings as a designer. To contrast this, when students work with real clients (especially clients they don't already have a relationship with), they are less likely to cut corners because they are getting paid for their services.

I'd like to share a few examples of the traps that students sometimes fall into. But before I do, I want to be clear that my purpose in doing so isn't to embarrass former students. I simply want to analyze a situation, after the fact, and identify where things might have gone wrong—in the hopes that you (the current student) will learn from their mistakes. Hopefully, these examples will give you a set of filters to use to look at your own problem-solving and research methods and to show you how important it is to stay engaged and pay attention to the details. After all, there are no dead ends in the creative process, only new possibilities for you to explore.

As you read through the following examples, think about the amount of effort that you put into your own research. How much time do you put into identifying what's important to your client and their audience? Do you throw out everything you know about your audience or do you assume that everyone holds the same opinions as you? Sometimes, taking all the information you know about your cli-ent and throwing it all out is the best way to start because it helps you to identify the issues without bias. Remember that your goal as a designer is to identify and solve problems, not simply to recontextualize the information that your teacher or client has already provided. If you don't understand what the problem you're being asked to solve is, how can you come up with ideas about how to solve it?

SUPERFICIAL RESEARCH

Project: Create a kinetic (moving) icon

Brief: Choose three companies that you like or feel particularly inclined to work with. Research the companies (go beyond just going to their website) and write an analysis of what these companies do or sell. Determine what kind of message they are trying to deliver to their audience. How has this message been received? Who are their competitors, and what strategies do these companies take to differentiate themselves from the competition?

Once you have finished your analysis, pick one of these companies and make their logo move and sound in a way that reinforces the myth that the company is trying to project. Companies often try to project an image (i.e., myth) to distinguish themselves from their competition. Apple Computer's myth is that it is one of the most creative and innovative companies in the world, while FedEx is a company that is dependable and can be trusted for all your shipping needs. What criteria does one use to determine who is the most dependable company? Is CNN really your most dependable source for news? These and many other companies have shrouded themselves in myth in order to stand out in the consumer's mind. The goal of this project is for you to identify the myth about the company and reinforce it by making their logo behave in a certain way. Your goal isn't to redesign their logo but to translate it in a time-sensitive format.

In order to successfully complete this project, you have to actually know something about the company you chose to work with. Let's pretend that you chose BMW as one of your companies to research. You are excited because you like their cars, and you go to Google and type in "BMW" and learn that the blue and white parts of their logo refer to a time in World War I when BMW made fighter plane engines. "Huh? I didn't know they made planes," you think to yourself. "I've only seen their cool looking cars and motorcycles."

After a little more digging, you learn that fighter planes had their propellers painted blue and white, so the pilots could see through them more clearly, and this is part of the reason why BMW's logo has the blue and white checker pattern on it.

"Ta-da!," you think. "My research phase is over! Now it's time to make the blue and white areas of their logo spin like an airplane propeller and play an aircraft engine sound and collect my good grade." In truth, you've only scratched the surface of what you could learn about BMW before attempting to start working on your solution, and you have completely missed the myth the company is trying to communicate to its clients.

While everything you've just found out about BMW is true, the big question is "Has the information you gathered been enough to justify ending your research phase?" What I want to see, as your teacher, is that you have ample research under your belt so that you can begin to make smart design decisions. So I begin asking you questions about BMW like the following.

- What is BWM doing now that many automobile manufacturers have started downsizing their cars to make them more environmentally friendly?
- What is BMW's vision for the future? Is the company heading in any new directions? How does it respond to shifts in the market?
- What is the myth BMW is trying to project?
- Who are BMW's biggest competitors?
- Who is BMW's customer base?

What you initially discovered about BMW making aircraft engines in the early to mid 1900s is fascinating, but it may not be relevant to the company's current mission or goals. Without a doubt BMW's past has helped shape its future, but you haven't convinced me that you've identified BMW's current marketing strategy.

Google is a great tool, but sometimes it's relied upon too heavily. It provides quick and superficial answers and cannot be relied upon as a substitute for good old-fashioned research. Sometimes nondigital means of gathering research can provide unexpected results. For instance, what if you drove down to the local BMW dealership and talked with a salesperson? What kinds of things might he say to convince you to buy a BMW? Chances are, he'll never mention World War I, airplane engines, or blue skies, but he'll talk with you at length about performance and owning a piece of "German Engineering." What if you took a car out for a test drive? How might that influence your solution? Maybe you'd feel cooler or even a little bit elite?

Research is necessary in order to create a solution that will hit the mark. When you're freelancing, you have to talk to business owners about their needs

> *"Sketching is generative, and since there is such a small investment in time, sketches can be discarded without remorse if a better solution is identified."*

and get to know them. You will talk with them about their plans for the future and what things keep them up at night worrying. You'll help them articulate which audience they are trying to reach, as well as the message they should project. These kinds of discussions are essential for you to be involved in because they provide clues about potential solutions. The work that graphic designers produce isn't only about making something visually appealing. Its roots are in communication, and knowing what needs to be communicated, and to whom, is a big part of our job.

Knowing which messages are the most important and delivering them to the appropriate audience is the foundation upon which graphic design is built. When your research is anemic, you are missing out on the true power of graphic design. It stands to reason that if research is the foundation of good design, then sketching and ideation are some of the most important tools in the designer's toolkit, and it's another aspect of the design process worth investing in.

RESISTANCE TO SKETCHING

Working quickly, being creative with limited resources, and being efficient with your time aren't bad traits for a designer to have, but sometimes you just have to roll up your sleeves and grind it out. Lately, I've noticed a resistance from my students when I asked them to sketch ideas (using a good old-fashioned pencil and paper), and I'm surprised at their aversion to do so. I suspect that many of my students consider sketching to be an inefficient use of their time, but they couldn't be further from the truth.

I consider sketching to be the equivalent of attaching the movement of a pencil to your thoughts. Sketching provides a designer the freedom to make marks that are lively, bold, quick, and ephemeral. Sketching is about letting yourself explore and not worrying about what the outcome is going to look like. The goal is to get your thoughts out of your head and into a physical form. Sketching is a means for rapid concept development and a means to generate ideas quickly with little self-editing. Sketching is generative, and since there is such a small investment in time, sketches can be discarded without remorse if a better solution is identified. The time you spend developing potential solutions can add up, so working quickly is important because it allows you to cover the most conceptual ground. If you get bogged down trying to sketch a particular idea, jot down a few key words to remind yourself of the idea you were exploring, and move on.

Sketches allow you to show your freelance clients where some of your time (and their money) has been spent and gives you an opportunity to teach them about your creative process. I've talked clients through my sketches on numerous occasions, describing what I was thinking and demonstrating how my sketches have influenced my solution. To this day, I've never had a client tell me he or she thought my sketches were a waste of time—in fact, I've noticed that clients tend to feel better about the solutions I present because they feel I've really taken the time to understand their needs, attack the problem from different angles, and come up with several viable solutions.

The first time I showed a client my sketches was because the client received an invoice that he thought was too high. While my client liked the solution, he wanted me to itemize my bill and justify where I had spent my time. I immediately produced pages and pages of sketches and walked him through my visual research and ideation. When I had finished, there was no question about the validity of where my time had been spent. In fact, the client actually said that he felt better about the solution I gave him because he could see the amount of work and attention that I devoted to his project.

I think some of the resistance my students feel regarding sketching comes from a lack of understanding about the sketching process. Sketches are quick gestures and marks that convey ideas, not drawings that are shaded and carefully drawn. Sketches are a way to get ideas out of your head and show them to other people and get feedback about the potential success of an idea.

I know you probably think that sketching on the computer is quicker than sketching with a pencil, but it isn't. I believe the computer adds in a psychological element to the equation because the sketches are too refined too early in the process. When I sketch out something typographic with my pencil I have a different experience than when I sketch out something typographic with my computer. On the computer I begin thinking about what typeface to use, it's size, the tracking, its weight, and so on. But when I sketch with a pencil, I am less concerned with details. This means I can continue sketching and generating more possibilities instead of getting bogged down with small decisions while I am on the computer. When you work on the computer, you get psychologically invested in making a particular sketch work, even though there are so many other possibilities to explore.

The next argument I get is "Well I have a Wacom tablet that lets me sketch on my computer. What about that?" My answer is—it depends. Prospective employers often like to look at a designer's process work and sketches in order to get a glimpse of the designers problem-solving tendencies and abilities. If you can work quickly, without getting bogged down with details like color, typeface selection, or brush selection, and your computer is charged up, and your battery won't die, and your Wacom tablet is working properly, and....

My time-tested advice for you is to simply use a pencil. Unless you run out of lead or paper, you're good to go. Don't make sketching any more complicated than it needs to be. When you sketch, you want to focus on getting your ideas out of your head and down on paper. It's that simple.

Once your sketches have provided you a framework for working, it's time to switch gears and pay more attention to the finer points of your design. This is where attention to detail and the principles of design really come into play. You have to know what you want to say, shape your message effectively, and then deliver a solution with impact.

LACK OF ATTENTION TO DETAIL

Often it's the small, seemingly insignificant details that are the difference between a good solution and a great solution. Everyone makes mistakes, but there are plenty of habits that you can adopt to minimize your errors. One mistake that's incredibly easy to fix is to run a spell-check before you output a job. I embarrassingly misspelled "calendar" on an advertisement that was printed 40,000 times before the mistake was caught.

Simple tasks often get overlooked because they seem insignificant or because we forget to proof our work. Other times we make mistakes when we're trying to perform a task quickly. This is why getting into a routine to check for potential problems before turning in a project or submitting a proof to a client can be a worthwhile practice. No matter how many times you are reminded, you'll probably forget to put your name on your work, convert your fonts to outlines, set your bleeds, convert your color mode to CMYK—there are just so many things to remember!

Try to get into the habit of going down a mental checklist at the end of each project you work on in order to catch whatever small details you have a hard time remembering. Taking a little extra time up front can help you avoid the embarrassment of making a mistake and save you the time and money of having to fix it.

Working for Money

There are so many reasons to start your own freelance company and only one reason not to—you might fail. That's right. You might mess up, or something might go wrong. To be honest, you are assuming risk by starting a business, and you will be accountable for both your successes and failures. But let's take a moment to discuss what you might gain.

Perhaps the most obvious perk is that you can make money or barter your graphic design work in exchange for goods or services. In addition, freelancing allows you to bring in money while fine-tuning your business and graphic design skills. College is expensive, and being able to pay down or eliminate some of your debt as you go along may help you to establish financial security and stability.

There is nothing wrong with waiting tables or working at other types of jobs as you go through school; I worked at Outback Steakhouse during graduate school. But wouldn't it be great to put your education to use and work more creatively? Working for a client can be a lot of fun, and sometimes it doesn't seem like work. There are a lot of people and businesses out there who need help reaching their audience and would love to hire someone to help them achieve their goals. Why not help these people out and make some money for yourself in the process? As long as you're careful about choosing your clients and the projects you work on, you'll find freelancing to be enjoyable, educational, and lucrative. Making money isn't the only reason you should consider freelancing, but it certainly doesn't hurt!

SETTING YOUR RATES

Most graphic designers usually bill their clients for their services by using a flat-rate or hourly-rate system. It's important to realize that each method for billing has advantages and disadvantages, and it's common to use the best billing plan for the job rather than simply picking one method and using it for all your clients. Just make sure that your client is informed about the billing method you will be using in advance and agrees to your terms *before* you begin working on the project.

Both billing methods are based on gross amounts, meaning that taxes haven't been withheld, and you will be responsible for paying all your business expenses out of the money you collect. As a general rule, you should set aside approximately 30 percent of your revenue for taxes and pay off all your vendors and business expenses as you go. It's always a good idea to talk with a Certified Public Accountant (CPA) who specializes in business accounting if you have questions.

DESCRIPTION	08:00 - 08:15	08:15 - 08:30	08:30 - 08:45	08:45 - 09:00	09:00 - 09:15	09:15 - 09:30	09:30 - 09:45	09:45 - 10:00	10:00 - 10:15	10:15 - 10:30	10:30 - 10:45	10:45 - 11:00	11:00 - 11:15	11:15 - 11:30	11:30 - 11:45	11:45 - 12:00	12:00 - 12:15	12:15 - 12:30	12:30 - 12:45	12:45 - 01:00	01:00 - 01:15
Monday, Jan. 16																					
Client meeting					X	X	X	X													
Audience research									X	X	X										
Sketching												X	X	X	X	X	X	X	X		
Tuesday, Jan. 17																					
Sketching		X	X	X	X	X	X	X	X												
Refining concepts									X	X	X	X									

It's a good idea for you to fill out a time sheet for the projects you work on in school so that you can begin to see trends in the amount of time it takes you to complete certain types of tasks.

Geography and competition can also be a factor in setting your rates. If you live in a rural town with one stop light, chances are the cost of living is lower than in a metropolitan city. Your rates should reflect this difference. Similarly, if there are a slew of freelance designers in close proximity and in competition with each other, you might need to lower your rates to stay competitive.

FLAT RATES

Charging a flat rate for large projects or projects that repeat (i.e., a newsletter) is a common practice for many designers. Flat rates work best when the designer can accurately estimate the number of hours the project will take to ensure that the job won't be completed at a loss. One of the big advantages of using a flat rate is that you are guaranteed a specific amount even if you finish the job quickly, and it also allows you to account for the inherent value of your work. For example, logos generally have a high value regardless of the time it takes you to complete them. The reason they have a high value is because they are used frequently and are highly visible. For this reason, I prefer to use a flat rate (instead of an hourly rate) when I create a logo for a client. The value of a logo is generally greater than the number of hours it took me to complete it, multiplied by my hourly rate.

Flat rates are easy for your clients to understand and budget for because they pretty much know how much money a project will cost them. However, you can get burned if you don't accurately predict the number of hours it will take you to complete the job. I've found that it's usually smaller tasks that begin to eat into my flat-rate profits. It's a good idea to include information about your hourly rates in your contract, even if you're using a flat rate, in case additional work is required that is outside the scope of your agreement.

When you're writing your contract, make sure to quote enough time for client meetings, small changes to the scope of the project, e-mail correspondence, and other time-consuming tasks when you prepare your flat-rate fees. So both you and your client will be on the same page, it's also a good idea to specify the number of proofs you will deliver, the number of client meetings you will attend (and where), and the number of revisions you are prepared to make. You can certainly provide more proofs or attend more client meetings, but your contract should specify that these are outside of the scope of your agreement and that these extras are at the client's request and may be added to their bill.

Setting up a flat rate can be a trial-and-error process unless you have an idea of how long it takes you to complete certain types of jobs. I ask all my students to keep a time sheet for each project they complete in my classes, but I don't use their time sheets as criteria in determining their grade. When I grade their work, I calculate the amount of time it took each student to complete the project and give the class averages back to my students along with their project grade. This way my students can see how quickly they completed the project, compared with their peers, and identify areas in which they could improve their efficiency and make adjustments if they need to.

When you are setting up your time sheet, make sure to include what phase of the design process you are working on under the "Description" column, and record the amount of time you spend on each phase in fifteen-minute increments. Rounding the time you spent working on a project to the nearest fifteen-minute increment makes your time easy to calculate. While keeping track of your time to the nearest fifteen minutes might seem a little ridiculous at first, you will begin to see trends emerge over time and begin to get a better sense of how long it takes you to complete certain types of projects. You can compare the time it takes you to complete a project with the time it takes your peers to complete a similar task in order to gauge your speed and how quickly you are working. The faster you are able to work, the greater your potential to make a profit. Conversely, if you take a long time to complete a project, you can lower your rates in order to stay competitive.

> *"One of the most challenging aspects about using an hourly rate is how much to charge per hour because there isn't a one-size-fits-all answer."*

HOURLY RATES

Similar to charging a flat rate, using an hourly rate to bill your clients for your services is a perfectly acceptable practice. Hourly rates are a great way to bill for projects that will have lots of revisions, changes, or updates. Hourly rates are usually a smart choice for small projects or when it may be too difficult to estimate a flat rate accurately.

Work billed using an hourly rate does not take the intrinsic value of the project into consideration; it is simply a reflection of your time multiplied by your hourly rate. You will be paid for the actual number of hours that you worked, but determining the cost to complete the job can be difficult before the job has been completed and the total number of hours have been accounted for.

One of the most challenging aspects about using an hourly rate is how much to charge per hour because there isn't a one-size-fits-all answer. There are several variables (unique to your business) that need to be taken into account, such as the number of billable hours you are able to produce, your desired profit margin, local competition that might drive your price down, the average rate for similar services in your geographic location, your overhead, and the speed at which you are able to work. If you are just getting started, you might start off with a low hourly rate and then increase your rate as you gain experience.

More than likely, you are going to have low overhead (expenses), a low number of billable hours, and a reasonable profit margin (10 to 15 percent). With these factors in mind, I imagine your hourly rate will most likely be between $15 and $50 per hour. This means that if you have a job that will take ten hours to complete, you could potentially make between $150 and $500.

There is a big discrepancy between charging $150 and $500, so how do you know which rate to charge? If you charge too little, you might feel that you're being taken advantage of—or worse yet, that you might not be profitable! On the flip side, if you charge too much, you might have a hard time finding clients. This is where having access to professional organizations and connections in the graphic design community can really pay off. To help you make an informed decision, talk with other local freelance designers about their rates.

> *"Many freelancers reduce their hourly rates if their clients agree to pay to retain their services each month."*

Whatever information these designers share with you, use it ethically! Do not use this information to undercut them or to approach their clients—this is unethical. Instead, use the information they share to help you accurately reflect the value of the services you offer for your region and to gauge what niches are not currently being serviced by your competitors. There are times when you will be in direct competition with other designers. But make sure you maintain the moral high ground and act responsibly.

RETAINER FEES

A retainer fee is a fee that a client pays in advance for a predetermined amount of work or time. Retainer arrangements can benefit both designer and clients. Retainer fees are guaranteed income for you, and clients knows that they have consistent access to you. Many freelancers reduce their hourly rates if clients agree to retain their services each month. For example, if your normal hourly rate is $25 per hour, you might approach your client and tell them that you are willing to reduce your hourly rate by $5 per hour if they retain your services for five hours each month. This means each month you will receive a check from your client for $100 and you owe them five hours of work. Some months they may not need your services at all, but you will still receive the $100 per month retainer fee. Other months they may need you for five or more hours, and the client will save $25.

You will have to negotiate with your client about the terms of your retainer fees. For example, for months that they do not use their allotted hours, you will need to decide whether that time can be rolled over into other months or lost. When your client needs more time than what is in your retainer agreement, what will your hourly rate be? In many cases a freelance graphic designer's income is sporadic, so having a retainer client can help you stabilize your income. At the very least you will have a small income to count on each month.

I recommend that you avoid working with retainer clients at the Beginner or Intermediate levels. You can get into some sticky time-management situations when working with retainer clients, and your priority should be on your education at this point. Remember that while you might be operating on an academic calendar, your client may not. This means if you were to enter into a retainer agreement with a client they would probably expect you to work through your semester and summer breaks. I don't want you to get in too far in over your head at first, so make sure you're up for the challenge before entering a retainer agreement with one of your clients.

Working for Trade

It's understandable if you're a little intimidated about setting your rates and billing clients at first. Working for trade can be a good way to ease into the freelance experience. While living in North Carolina, I realized that trading my services for goods could be a lot of fun and lucrative when a friend agreed to barter her graphic design services for a sailboat. My friend's client said that he had an old sailboat he would trade her in exchange for her help on a project. She agreed, and when the project was complete, she met with her client to pick up the sailboat.

Her jaw dropped when she saw a twenty-four-foot sailboat with a bathroom, outboard engine, and two sets of sails. She could practically live on it! The client, who was getting older and having difficulty taking care of his boat because of his declining health, felt glad that his boat would be appreciated. And he got some really great graphic design work without having to pay cash for it. The idea of bartering appeals to many small businesses because their cash reserves are often low.

My friend got lucky finding someone interested in trading her services for a sailboat, but she took a risk by not knowing what kind of sailboat it was or its condition. Luckily, she came out ahead in the deal, but if the client gave her a radio-controlled sailboat, she might not have been so happy about the deal.

If you decide that you want to barter for your services, make sure that you and your client share the same expectations. If you don't communicate your expectations clearly, there is a good chance that one of you may walk away from the deal feeling unsatisfied. Never assume that you and the client are on the same page, and always write out a contract (including specific details) regarding what products or services will be exchanged, along with their monetary value.

It feels great to go into a restaurant and not have to pay cash for your meals because you designed the restaurant's menus, or to learn to hang glide for free because you designed the company's website. Moments like these make you feel connected to the people in your community and can be a means of creating new adventures and experiences for yourself. I've bartered my services for a new surfboard, gym memberships, plane rides, free camping, and all kinds of fun things!

> *"The work you do while freelancing has the potential to become work in your portfolio that is unique, and will help your portfolio stand out…"*

If a business is reluctant to pay you for your services and they have a product or service that interests you, then talk to the manager or owner and suggest that they trade you for your services instead. It's a good idea to keep records of the items and services you barter for, and their intrinsic value, because you are supposed to report this income on your taxes.

Enhancing Your Portfolio

When you graduate and begin searching for your first job, you will be in competition with other designers. You never know who will interview for the same job that you are applying for. You could be competing for a job against one of your classmates or even an alumnus from your school. One of your goals will be to make yourself and your work stand out in order to leave a positive impression with the employer. I've interviewed many young designers, and there is a pattern in academia that you should be aware of.

Although you might not realize it, professors sometimes recycle projects from year to year because the project may be very effective in teaching a particular design principle. This recycling of projects makes many student portfolios look almost identical, and unfortunately, very forgettable.

I remember going to a job interview early in my career, and the art director who was interviewing me looked at my portfolio and said, "Ahh, I see you had Professor McCullough. I remember doing this same brochure project for him when I was in his class…not much has changed has it?" Immediately the art director began to mentally compare my brochure to every other brochure he had seen from over the last fifteen years. Talk about pressure! I didn't end up getting the job, but when I returned home I removed the brochure from my portfolio and began working on a replacement portfolio piece.

The work you do while freelancing has the potential to become work in your portfolio that is unique, and will help your portfolio stand out from your classmates. It is perfectly fine to have student work in your portfolio; nobody expects you to be an accomplished graphic designer overnight. But your work in your portfolio needs to stand out from the work of your peers. By adding some quality freelance work to your portfolio, you make the work in your portfolio unique and show that you can work with clients and see a project through from start to finish.

When I review a young designer's portfolio, I get a better sense about his strengths and weaknesses by looking at his freelance work. One of the most undervalued benefits of school is having peers and faculty available to critique your work. Many times they give you advice about how to improve it.

Generally speaking, there are far fewer "voices" giving you feedback when you're working on a job for a client. When I see a young designer's freelance work, I get the feeling that I'm seeing his abilities in a more raw and unedited light and less of the inherent support systems of classmate and teacher input. When I look through student portfolios I'm looking for mistakes, poor decisions, and inconsistencies. I'm not trying to be a jerk and say, "Haha! You made a mistake." But I am trying to determine the degree of the designer's eye for detail. I want to see if he can create and follow a system, and I'm looking for evidence that he understands and can use the principles of design.

It's important to realize that every designer has strengths and weaknesses, so don't fixate on your imperfections. Take advantage of feedback when you can get it. I've found that in many cases when a classmate puts his work up for a critique, it's far easier to critique his work than it is to critique your own work. This is because you get too close to your own work and can no longer see it objectively. That's why graphic designers sometimes say, "I need someone with 'fresh eyes' to look at this and tell me what they think." The designer recognizes that he or she is too invested in the work and needs someone who can look at it objectively.

Everyone makes mistakes, so don't feel bad that you're not perfect. Nobody is. Simply do the your best, learn as much as you can along the way, and keep trying to grow and improve your skills as a designer.

Learning to Fail

Perhaps one of the most counterintuitive lessons that a designer needs to learn is how to fail. The fear of failure is one of the biggest obstacles in the creative process. The more comfortable designers become with rejection and failure, the more likely they are to continue taking risks, shedding constraints, and developing nontraditional and highly creative solutions for their clients. Unfortunately, one doesn't just decide to become brazen and will oneself immune to the effects of criticism and peer pressure. Your resilience is developed slowly over time. Failing has unfortunately become viewed as a negative experience, but one could argue that failing is a necessary step in the creative process. Many times failure leads to new and better solutions. It seems so contradictory in nature to include failure as a benchmark of success, but I believe it's a good barometer for the strength and healthiness of your creative process. I have to remind myself that I believe this when I find myself out on a limb taking risks. Every year I share my mantra of "It's better to beg forgiveness than ask permission" with the students I teach, and I have to remind myself that it's okay for teachers to take risks too.

I received an interesting lesson in failure at age fifteen while I was taking kung fu. Looking back years later I realize that my interest in martial arts was probably influenced by my love of karate movies. I remember being eager to learn martial arts so that I could learn to fight like my heroes in the movies that I loved to watch.

To my surprise, the first few weeks of kung fu class were devoted to learning how to fall. As our class learned the mechanics of falling safely, we were also being taught that being thrown off balance wasn't the equivalent of losing the fight. Recovering from being thrown off balance and remaining uninjured is as important as landing a punch and not injuring your hand. Everyone in our class was required to spar with someone much larger, and we were all thrown off balance at some point. We were taught to think of being thrown to the ground not as "losing" but as a technique that we needed to master.

Similar to my experience in martial arts, taking creative risks are necessary parts of the creative process. While most people can embrace the concept that being thrown to the ground in martial arts isn't the equivalent of losing, fewer people view taking creative leaps that might not pan out as key components of the creative process. Without these creative leaps of faith, we rely purely on luck to identify solutions that exceed our clients goals.

There is a better than average chance that you will eventually miss your mark, be unable to meet your client's expectations, or find an acceptable solution that fits within your client's constraints. Graphic design isn't a hard science, and there are many variables that you must account for. Occasionally, despite your best efforts, you will fall short of success. However, learning to handle yourself in these situations determines whether you retain your client's trust or lose it.

> *"Owning a business while you're still a student will make you think about how the lessons you are learning in school might apply to a business context."*

We rarely seek out opportunities to fail, but a college education allows us to take huge risks and leaps of faith with very few negative consequences. If we take risks when freelancing, there might come a time when we might have to fix a mistake at our expense, but life will still go on. In the end, what matters is that our client gets what he needs and that we've learned from the experience. Giving ourselves the opportunity to fail can provide tremendous lessons for those with the constitution to take creative leaps. I can think of no other way in which you can grow as quickly as when you take a creative risk and fail.

For many, the fine line between failure and success is part of what makes owning a business exhilarating. The decisions you make as a small-business owner can lead your business down a path of success or failure, and not knowing what's around the next turn can be as exciting as riding on a roller coaster. If your business doesn't work out, look at the lessons you will have learned. If your business is wildly successful, imagine how good you'll feel. Don't be afraid of failing. There's too much to gain by not rolling up your sleeves and jumping in.

Experience the Thrill of Owning a Business

Owning your own business can be very exciting! Being a business owner is a great feeling, and for many it's the epitome of the American dream. You are the boss. You make your own rules. You determine the hours you work and how much you will be paid. You make the decisions about which clients to work with and what projects to work on. The sky is the limit, and if your company does well, it's probably because you've done a good job planning and are determined to see your company succeed. Sometimes people don't understand what graphic designers do, but almost anyone can wrap their head around the notion of being a business owner. There is a certain amount of respect that is often extended to entrepreneurs and small-business owners, and having people acknowledge your leap of faith and ask how things are going can make you feel great.

Owning a business while you're still a student will make you think about how the lessons you are learning in school might apply in a business context. We are all guilty of having tunnel vision at times, and sometimes it's helpful to look at our current situation through an unfamiliar set of filters. It can be very easy to get caught up in the routine of school and forget that you're being equipped with a set of tools to help you succeed as a professional.

When I was still in school, I felt that I needed to graduate before I began working as a freelance graphic designer. However, looking back I wish I had started my freelance career earlier. I was afraid I would do something wrong or mess something up, and I didn't know where to find my clients. In hindsight, all I really needed to know was where to begin and how to minimize my risks so that I wouldn't get in over my head. Looking back now those were all easy problems to solve and certainly shouldn't have kept me from starting to freelance.

Over the next few chapters I will walk you through the planning stages of starting your freelance graphic design company. I will discuss how to write a business plan, minimize your risk, identify potential clients, protect yourself legally, and make your business sustainable. Your first goal will be to grow more comfortable with the idea of owning your own company. In order to do so you're going to start slowly and warm up to the idea.

I firmly believe that you can start a successful freelance business while you're getting your college degree—and hopefully make a little extra money in the process. In fact, my first-year graphic design students made over $5,000 in 2010, and I believe that with a little planning and luck, you can make some money for yourself, too. I want to stress once again that opening a freelance graphic design business isn't just about making money. It will also help open your eyes and give you context for your entire college education. For the last five years my freshman students have been required to work with a paying freelance client, so I know you've got all the tools you need to do it also. The first thing we have to do is to come up with a plan for what your company will look like and who your customers will be. So take a deep breath and roll up your sleeves because your life is about to get a little more exciting!

Planning Your Business

3

You probably think that starting a company is too expensive, too complicated, or too risky. To be fair, there are expenses, complications, and risks that you will have to accept, but you are capable of handling these and other issues as they arise. This is part of the reason why I recommend that you begin this journey by writing out a business plan. You will eventually run into problems, and your business plan will help you keep your bearings.

Writing a business plan forces you to think about many aspects of running a business. A good business plan basically becomes a road map for you to follow. The more time you spend working on your business plan, the more detailed your map will become. Writing a successful business plan requires you to consider your needs, the types services your business will offer, who your clients will be, and external factors that may have an effect on your business. A good business plan makes you think about your constraints you'll have to work around and helps you identify a path to reaching your goals. While it might be tempting to jump in and start making money right away, taking the time to plan your business will improve the likelihood of your success.

According to the U.S. Small-business Administration, around 70 percent of new businesses that began in the year 2000 survived at least two years, and 51 percent survived five or more years. This data suggests that careful, methodical, strategic planning and hard work are necessary in order for your company to survive. Many small businesses fail because of fundamental errors in their business planning. Needless to say, it's important to be honest when identifying your strengths and weaknesses, to seek input from a variety of sources, and to ask a lot of questions. Your business can be as simple or complex as you make it, so it should go without saying that your business plan is likely to be similar in terms of its complexity.

Writing a Business Plan

Your business plan is a living document that will grow and change over time. It's a road map of where you began, your current position (relevant to your goals), and the direction your company will go in the future. Your business plans can be unique and don't have to follow a particular format. However, there are several standard components that you will need to address.

I started a business called Accomplish Studios, LLC in order to walk through the various steps involved with starting a company. There is an example of my business plan and a SWOT analysis later in this chapter, so you can see how these documents might be written. You can edit these documents to reflect your own ideas for your company, but sometimes having a model to follow can help you understand what information may be important for you to consider.

BUSINESS PLAN OUTLINE

I. Strategic Planning
   1. Company mission: A concise statement defining your business.
   2. Definition of the company's goals and objectives: List of quantifiable and precise objectives.
   3. Identify external threats and opportunities that are influenced by your local environment.
   4. Identification of your internal strengths and weaknesses.

II. Business Plan Components
   1. Executive Summary
   2. Company History
   3. Business Summary
   4. Definition of Products and/or Services
   5. Marketing & Sales Strategies
   6. Operational Plan

III. Summary

This is where your understanding of your business venture is most apparent. You need to write a brief description of your company's goals, strategies, successes, and financial position.

IV. History of the Company

This is where you provide information about the company: when it was founded, organizational structure, major successes, and weaknesses.

Performing a SWOT Analysis

SWOT is an acronym that stands for Strengths, Weaknesses, Opportunities, and Threats and can provide insight into identifying and understanding the variables that may affect your company's success. When you write your business plan, you'll want it to be detail oriented and very thorough. When you write your SWOT analysis, you'll want it to be painfully honest about your strengths and weaknesses. Your business plan and SWOT analysis are designed to give you a competitive advantage by helping you match your company's goals and strengths to the opportunities you've identified in the marketplace.

Performing a SWOT analysis usually takes thirty to forty-five minutes, and you will need a pen and four sheets of paper. In big bold letters at the top, label your first page "Strengths," the second "Weaknesses," the third "Opportunities," and the last "Threats."

- **Strengths:** Internal attributes that are helpful in achieving your objective(s).
- **Weaknesses:** Internal attributes that are harmful to achieving your objective(s).
- **Opportunities:** External conditions that are helpful in achieving your objective(s).
- **Threats:** External conditions that could do damage to your objective(s).

Starting with "Strengths," brainstorm keywords, phrases, and ideas that best describe your company's strengths. Items on this list could include unique services that you offer, cost advantages, your technological skills, business relationships you may already have lined up, your low overhead, and your ability to make quick business decisions. Basically anything that could potentially give your company an advantage in the business world should be listed as a strength.

Once you have finished listing your company's strengths, move on to the "Weaknesses" page. Here you will identify aspects of your business that could be improved. Items on this list could include a lack of name recognition, your lack of business experience, the location of your business, or other items. Listing your weaknesses can be a humbling experience, but it's important that you're honest with yourself and that you are able to identify areas where your company could improve before you even launch your business.

On your "Opportunities" sheet, you'll want to identify strategies and venues for generating business. In this list you'll identify items like competitor vulnerabilities, unfulfilled customer needs, industry and social trends, potential partnerships with other businesses, developing markets (such as the Android and iPhone marketplace), emerging technologies, and other areas that could be profitable for your company. Once again, it's important to be honest with yourself. If you aren't capable of designing iPad applications, even if you want to learn how, it's best to leave it off your list for now. When you reach a point where you can realistically add it to your list of services that your company can legitimately offer, then revise your document to determine how this new skill might affect your business.

The final page is "Threats," and your goal is to identify factors that can prevent you from achieving your business goals. On this list you might identify factors like a new competitor moving into your market, competition or price wars, new or higher taxes, technological advances that might make your services obsolete, chances of a bad economy, situations that would make you unable to pay off your debts, and rising costs in technology. The purpose of this list is to identify potential problems before you have to deal with them and to avoid being caught off guard once you've started your business.

Once your four lists are complete, it's time to analyze the results and to put together an action plan for your company. Here are some suggestions:

- **Strengths:** These are attributes that you're good at now. Maintain these qualities, build upon them, and leverage them in the marketplace.
- **Weaknesses:** These are attributes that are bad or counterproductive and need to be stopped, avoided, or remedied. Look for ways to fix or neutralize these problems, so they don't impact your business negatively.
- **Opportunities:** These attributes are good to follow up on for future successes. You'll need to prioritize your goals, optimize your time, and try to incorporate these opportunities into your business plan.
- **Threats:** These are attributes that are bad for business and should be avoided when possible. If these attributes are unavoidable, then you need to develop a strategy to counteract any negative impact on your business.

Your action plan will be unique to your business because each business has different strengths and weaknesses. Your plan should be broken down into a series of steps and prioritized in order of importance. It's a good idea to give yourself a deadline for accomplishing these goals in order to stay on track and remain focused. Remember that it's going to be better for you to be proactive rather than reactive, so devote some quality time developing an action plan.

Accomplish Studios

B L A C K S B U R G ,   V A

The following analysis was created for Accomplish Studios, LLC, the company I launched in 2010. My company is a small business in every way and brings in less than $5,000 per year. I thought it might be helpful to show you how I structured my business plans in order to give you an idea of how you might create your own. Feel free to adapt and modify my business plan to meet your needs.

SAMPLE SWOT ANALYSIS

Strengths

- I have an extremely low overhead (I work out of my home) and I have no business debt. I don't need an open line of credit for my business. I can use Square (www.squareup.com) to allow clients with credit cards to make payments and charge them a 2.75 percent convenience fee to recover my expenses.
- I am willing to work with clients that have unique constraints and objectives.
- There is very little competition for low- and mid-level clients in my geographic region. I also have good connections to subcontract work that I cannot handle or don't want to do myself.
- I am willing to barter my services, and I can offer both print and web design.

Weaknesses

- I am the only designer, and I could get bogged down if I accept too much work at once or overcommit myself to a project.
- My company is just getting started, and I don't have good name recognition within my community—this will improve over time.
- Due to zoning issues, I cannot meet clients at my house, display a sign outside my residence, or advertise my business on my vehicle.
- I do not hold regular business hours.

Opportunities

- The local design agencies in Blacksburg have traditionally focused on landing larger accounts. I have many friends in these firms who may be willing to send me clients whose jobs are too small to be of interest to them, and in return I can send them clients whose jobs are too large for me to handle by myself.

- I grew up in this area, and I have many local contacts who could potentially become clients. I also have a good network of family and friends in this area who are willing to help me promote my business and make more business contacts.

Threats
- I may occasionally be in competition with students who freelance. They will probably be able to undercut my prices.
- I have to be careful about "conflicts of interest" when working with Virginia Tech clients and vendors.
- The local tax structure may change over time, and a business license is required to operate in Montgomery county.

Action Plan for Accomplish Studios

I will maintain a low overhead by working out of my home and keeping my business expenses to a minimum. By requiring a 50 percent deposit when I enter into an agreement with a client, I can use this money to offset any costs I incur while working on their project and refrain from opening lines of credit. I will use Square to allow clients with credit cards to make payments to me via iPhone, iPad, or Android device and charge them a 2.75 percent convenience fee to recover my expenses. Otherwise clients will have thirty days to pay by check and settle their outstanding balance.

I will have to carefully balance my time and the number of clients I work with, so that I will not overcommit my time. I will always try to deliver solutions that exceed my client's expectations because positive feedback and referrals are crucial to the success of my business. I want my clients to know that the success of their business is important to me and to know that I will go out of my way help their business succeed.

I will create a time line for each project as a component of my contract. A project may require the client to provide content, give approval, or evaluate a concept, and I will make the client aware of the importance of meeting these deadlines and when deadlines can be expected.

Sample Business Plan for Accomplish Studios

I. STRATEGIC PLANNING

Mission Statement: Accomplish Studios, LLC, is a freelance graphic design agency that provides high-quality graphic design and consultation services to local, regional, and national clients.

Goals and objectives: Accomplish Studios, LLC, desires to work with clients who are financially secure and recognize the inherent value of graphic design and visual communication. I seek clients who have a vision, who have the ability to respond quickly to market trends, and who need help reaching their target audience. I want to work with clients who are open-minded and receptive to my input. I want to create award-winning work for my clients and promote my studio through word of mouth, self-promotional material, and the Internet.

External threats and business environment: Blacksburg, Virginia, is a relatively untapped market for freelance graphic design clients. The students at Virginia Tech tend to pick up low-budget work, and bigger agencies tend to pick up larger jobs. This leaves mid-level work in the $1,000 to $15,000 range relatively underserviced and creates an opportunity for Accomplish Studios, LLC, to service these needs.

Accomplish Studios' most immediate business competition is Venveo, a Web design company started by a former Virginia Tech student, as well as local freelance graphic designers and agencies in the Roanoke Valley.

Strengths: Accomplish Studios' strengths are that it has a low operating budget; an ability to produce high-quality graphic design work; years of hands-on work experience in the graphic design profession; previous experience working as a business consultant; a strong commitment to servicing clients' needs; a mission to exceed our clients' expectations; and a willingness to take on project with unique and challenging constraints.

Weaknesses: Accomplish Studios' weaknesses are that it is a small agency and cannot handle a large influx of work. Occasionally, I may have to subcontract out some programming to a third-party vendor, and I will not hold standard 9 a.m. to 5 p.m. business hours.

II. BUSINESS PLAN COMPONENTS

Executive summary: Accomplish Studios, LLC, is a freelance graphic design agency and works with a variety of clients and is not considered an employee of its clients. I am hired to help clients by providing graphic design and consultation services. I bill clients by the hour, using a flat-rate fee or by being put on a retainer by a client.

Company history: Accomplish Studios, LLC, was recognized by the Virginia State Corporation Commission as a Limited Liability Company on May 17, 2010.

Business summary: Prior to entering into an agreement with a client, Accomplish Studios, LLC provides a client with a written estimate of the projected costs for completing the project. This estimate can fluctuate as much as 15 percent in some case and are valid for thirty days. If the client agrees to the terms of the agreement, he signs the contract and a 50 percent deposit is due.

I will then work on the client's project until it reaches a point where client feedback is necessary to continue, or the objectives of the project have been achieved according to the terms of the contract, or the project is terminated by the client and a "kill fee" will be applied to their bill for my services.

Typically, when a job nears completion I contact the client and provide him with a proof to review and give him a Proof Approval Form to sign. If the client signs the Proof Approval Form, he agrees that the project is complete and he accepts responsibility for any errors in the content. If the client wants to make changes when I give him the Proof Approval Form, he will be asked to provide information regarding this change and a new mock-up or proof will be delivered. This process is repeated until the client agrees that the project is complete or is in accord with the terms specified in the contract. Once the client signs the Proof Approval Form, I will deliver the product and send the client an invoice for the remaining 50 percent balance along with any incidental costs accrued throughout the project. Payment is due within thirty days.

Definition of products and services: My design process is research-based, and a good deal of time is spent researching the audience and the client's message and determining the best course of action. Once my research phase is complete,

I typically sketch many ideas in order to generate many possible solutions before choosing the best ideas and refining a concept. At this point, client feedback is critical, and I try to meet with the client to narrow a few select ideas to a single solution. I then work until with the client until a final solution is found and the client's needs are met.

Marketing and sales strategies: I do not require a vigorous marketing and sales strategy to maintain profitability. Customer referrals, seasonal promotion material, and the Internet will be my primary means of generating business leads.

Operational plan: Since I am the only employee, and I will not be taking out any loans or lines of credit, no bank representation is required, I am able to make decisions quickly and act on them immediately. Occasionally, Accomplish Studios, LLC, may have to subcontract portions of a job, but those business relationships will be considered work-for-hire and recovered from the client.

III. EXECUTIVE SUMMARY

Accomplish Studios, LLC, is a freelance graphic design agency that works with a variety of clients. I am hired to provide graphic design and consultation services. I bill clients by the hour, using a flat-rate fee or by being put on a retainer by a client.

Accomplish Studios' goals are to remain profitable while carefully selecting the clients and jobs I choose to work on. My core principle is to underpromise and overdeliver high-quality graphic design work to my clients and to be a company that my clients can trust. My goal is to provide solutions to the problems that keep my clients up at night worrying.

My primary means of marketing is through word of mouth, self-promotional items and the Internet, and my initial goal is to bill for $1,000 worth of graphic design work my first year and increase this amount each year as my client base grows. There is no sales team at Accomplish Studios, LLC, so doing a great job and exceeding client expectations is crucial to my success. In order to receive recommendations from my clients, it's critically important that I maintain a superior level of client satisfaction by solving my clients' problems and exceeding my clients' expectations of what working with Accomplish Studios, LLC, will be like.

It is extremely important to me that I do not accumulate debt, which is part of the reason why I choose my clients and jobs carefully. When I am hired by a client and collect the required 50 percent deposit, this money will remain in an account to pay for incidental expenses like copywriting, photography, programming, or other third-party product or service. This allows me to pay my vendors in a timely manner and recoup all of my expenses when the client's job is complete.

IV. HISTORY OF THE COMPANY

Accomplish Studios, LLC, was recognized by the Commonwealth of Virginia Corporation Commission as a Limited Liability Company on May 17, 2010. Prior to launching Accomplish Studios, Ben Hannam had been freelancing since 1993 and received numerous design awards at the local, regional, national, and international levels. In addition, his work has been published in a variety of graphic design books, as well as in *Design Behaviors: International Design Research Journal*.

Ben believes that graphic design is an instrument of organization, a means of relating objects to people, a medium for persuasion, and a way to cope with the complexity of everyday life. Design is rooted in communication, and Ben's approach to practicing graphic design, both professionally and academically, stems from this belief.

Ben received his BFA from Old Dominion University in 1996 and his MFA from Virginia Commonwealth University in 2002. In 2003 he left the United States to teach overseas in Qatar at Virginia Commonwealth University in Qatar and returned in 2006 to teach at Virginia Tech in Blacksburg, Virginia.

Ben Hannam
Accomplish Studios, LLC
Proprietor

Identifying External Factors

Looking internally and defining your company's mission and goals is certainly important, but so is looking outward and identifying some of the external factors that may have an effect on your business. External factors that can affect your business may be things like social and cultural trends, technical tendencies, political and legal issues, economic movements, and competition in the marketplace.

Understanding how these factors might affect your business can be the difference between being prepared and getting caught off guard. By understanding how external factors can affect your business, you may be able to minimize any negative effects, while also positioning your company to take advantage of opportunities when they arise.

Most of the documentation you've gathered for your business thus far is designed to help you look at your business from various angles, but now it's time to take a hard look at some of the elements that may exist outside of your control. Some of these external factors are opportunities in disguise that you can take advantage of, while others are perils which should be avoided.

SOCIAL AND CULTURAL TRENDS

How old were you when you got a smart phone, and did it change the way you shop? In April 2011, Score Data Mine reported, "Nearly half (48.7 percent) of smart-phone owners in the U.S. were between the ages of twenty-five and forty-four, with those in the twenty-five to thirty-four year-old demographic making up the largest segment of the smart-phone population." What does this mean to graphic designers? Well, as location-based marketing grows in popularity, it means that it might be a good idea to familiarize yourself with websites and applications such as Foursquare, Facebook Places, and Gowalla. You might be able to service a niche market in your area by identifying a social trend like the increased use of smart phones and brushing up on a few strategies for location-based marketing.

By adding location-based marketing to the services you offer, you might attract a client who wants to offer this feature to his clients, but needs help shaping his message. Location-based marketing probably won't be a silver bullet that solves all of your client's needs. However, it may be a perfect way to bring up the idea of developing a larger marketing campaign for your client and a means of getting your foot in the door.

Social and cultural trends can be viewed at both the micro and macro level, meaning that while 48.7 percent of *American* smart-phone owners are between ages twenty-five and forty-four, perhaps only 30 percent of the men and women in that age group in *your town* own a smart phone. One could argue that there might be a small home-field advantage to working with a local designer rather than working with an outside firm—the local designer may be more in touch with the social and cultural trends of the area. Observing social and cultural trends can often give designers ideas about nontraditional avenues for communication and how to craft messages that are likely to be positively received by the intended audience.

TECHNICAL TENDENCIES

When Apple released the iPod touch, iPhone, and iPad, it created a new market for developers. When an application is sold through the App Store, 70 percent of the profits go to the developer and 30 percent goes to Apple. Over three billion applications have been downloaded from the App Store since it opened in 2008 and have generated a lot of income for developers willing to jump in. AdWhirl reports that iPhone applications that crack the Top 100 downloads chart have traditionally made between $400 and $5,000 per day. To put this into perspective, the iPhone application 5800+ Drinks and Cocktail Recipes made over $1,500 per day, the iFart Alert application made over $2,000 per day, and the Sound Grenade application made over $3,000 per day—that's a lot of money!

As a business owner, you should ask yourself, "How can I position my company to benefit from the next technological breakthrough?" It goes without saying that paying attention to changes in technology might create opportunities for your business, but technology can also reduce your profitability. Author Daniel Pink comments:

> Automation is also changing the work of many doctors. Much of medical diagnosis amounts to following a series of decision trees—Is is a dry cough or a productive one? Is the T-cell count above or below a certain level?—and homing in on the answer. Computers can process the binary logic of decision trees with a swiftness and accuracy humans can't begin to approach. So an array of software and online programs has emerged that allow patients to answer a series of questions on their computer screens and arrive at a preliminary diagnosis without the assistance of a physician.[1]

[1]Daniel Pink, *A Whole New Mind: Why Right-Brainers Will Rule the Future* (New York: Riverhead Books, 2006), 45.

As a business owner, you will need to make yourself aware of technological advances that might undercut your services or remove you from the equation altogether.

ECONOMIC MOVEMENTS

Economic changes can have an effect on your business, and many graphic design agencies have felt a pinch since the economic recession began in 2007. When clients tighten their financial belts many advertising, design, and marketing campaigns are abandoned and work can become more scarce.

If you find yourself in the middle of an economic recession, it doesn't necessarily mean that it's a bad time to start a business; in fact, there are a few perks for starting a business in a down economy. Usually, recessions are a time when the cost for starting a business is lower, more people are looking for jobs (although I recommend you don't take on employees at this point), and advertising costs are typically reduced. General Electric, Walt Disney, Microsoft, and Google were all started during hard times, so there's plenty of precedence for success.

When the economy is good, clients tend to need more design services to advertise in order to distinguish themselves from competitors, and suddenly you may have more work than you can handle! Regardless of the economic environment in which you find yourself, there are some very good deals you can take advantage of if you know where to look.

Navigating economic movements is remarkably similar to buying winter clothes in the spring when merchants are trying to get rid of their inventory in order to make room for their summer clothing. When the market expands, you should contract and not worry as much about promoting your business and internal jobs. Work on jobs that are profitable and bring in a healthy income. Conversely, when the market contracts and jobs get tougher to find, that is a great time to streamline your business and look for new ways to promote yourself. Take on charitable and pro bono work to keep your business name out there, and avoid accumulating as much debt as you can.

You can watch the news or look in the newspaper and find a number of major market indices listed. For example, the S&P 500 Composite Stock Price Index is an index of five hundred stocks from major American industries. Many investors track the performance of a particular index and use it as an indication of the strength of a particular market. If you can project where a market is going, you can make better decisions on whether to expand or batten down the hatches.

POLITICAL AND LEGAL REQUIREMENTS

Just like economic movements, political and legal requirements can also have an impact on your business. If your city favors business development, your tax rate will probably be modest, and your city will generally have more relaxed environmental concerns. On the other hand, if your city is concerned with safety or environmental issues, there may be lots of rules and regulations that you need to follow, and your taxes could be higher in order to enforce these rules.

Rules and regulations can have a significant influence on the costs associated with running a business. It's a good idea to know who your local and state officials are and how their plans might affect your business. A good way to do this is to talk with other owners of small businesses in your area and ask them about their concerns and frustrations. They will probably be happy to talk you, and you are likely to learn a lot about politics and legal issues in the process.

COMPETITION

Researching companies that you will be competing with is a necessary step in the planning stages. Not only is competition something that is found in nature between living organisms, it's also often a common occurrence in the business world as well. As a business owner you'll need to know who your business rivals are and what distinguishes your company from theirs. You'll have to determine what services you offer that they don't? Whose business is the most prompt and efficient? How much promotion and publicity does your company get, compared with your competition?

Similar to nature, businesses also have to compete for resources and mates (or in your case, clients). Occasionally, competition can lead to duplicated or wasted efforts or increased prices, but competition can also benefit a company by making it focus and become more efficient in delivering its product or services to the client. Competition is a double-edged sword that has the potential to strengthen a company or stress it and potentially put you out of business. It's important not to fear competition, but to try and understand its effects on your business. In most cases, small shifts in services or niche markets can alleviate direct competition with other companies.

Your goal should be to find out as much about your competition as you can, in order to find a niche and develop a profitable business strategy. A good place to start is by talking with your potential competition in person, visiting their website, and talking to potential clients.

I Have A Business Plan.
Now What?

Choosing a Business Name

If you haven't already decided on a name for your business, it's time to do so. It's important that you don't duplicate the name of a company that already exists in your state. You'll have to check with your local or state agencies to make sure that your idea for a business name is still available. Each state keeps track of business names a little differently, so you may have to check with the Chamber of Commerce, your state's Small-business Development Center, or the Secretary of State's office to see if your business name is still available.

In Virginia, we are asked to contact the Clerk's Office Call Center, using their toll-free number, 1-866-722-2551. However, if your business isn't in Virginia, you should be able to identify the right agency to talk to by searching the phrase "Available LLC names in <your state>" online and sorting through the results. You're looking for the name and contact information of the state agency that is responsible for managing and recording business names.

Picking a name for your business is the beginning of branding your company. The name should be memorable and create positive emotions with your clients. It's worth spending some time thinking about your business name before committing to one. There are a few key points in the following sections that you should consider before finalizing a business name.

CREATE AN EMOTIONAL RESPONSE

Think about how you want clients to feel when they first hear about your business. When I first began thinking about names for my business, I really liked the name "Method" a lot because I was thinking about all the different methods and strategies that I could use as a designer to help solve my clients' problems. When I

> *"Keep in mind that your company name may be the only thing that a prospective client sees."*

tested the name with friends, colleagues, and students, it was received poorly, and I got comments that the name was not descriptive enough and that it reminded some people of a popular soap. While almost everyone liked the concept behind the name, they insisted that I needed to give them a better sense of what kind of work the company would do. I liked the name "Method," and it took me a long time to accept that it wasn't going to work for my business.

If you find yourself stuck, create a list of words to describe your business. Once you've exhausted your initial ideas, add in related words and phrases that evoke the kinds of feelings and emotions that you want your clients to have when they work with you.

Sometimes simple shifts in the words you use can have a big impact on how your audience will perceive your business. For instance, consider the words "Mommy" and "Mother." Both can be used to describe the same person, but the positive emotional impact of "Mommy" is generally much greater than "Mother."

Your mommy kissed your boo-boos and cut the crust off of your peanut butter and jelly sandwiches, while your Mother sent you to your room without supper when you misbehaved. It's important to understand that small shifts in the words you use can have a big impact on the feelings they invoke.

DESCRIBE WHAT YOUR BUSINESS DOES

Keep in mind that your company name may be the only thing that a prospective client sees. It's hard to see your business through your client's eyes, but you'll want a name that gives a client an idea of what type of work your business does. Clearly, the name "Method" failed to communicate the idea that my business was a graphic design studio.

You don't have to be blatantly obvious, but make sure your name doesn't communicate something too broad or obscure either. Words like studio, agency, creative, and interactive can help hint about the type of work you specialize in, while more complicated phrases like "visualization experts" or "new media specialist" are more open ended with their meanings and will require more explanation. Add words to your list that describe your business, the type of work you do, and how you want your company to be perceived five years from now.

The exception to the "Describe what your business does" rule is to make sure that you don't eliminate any potential business by being too narrow with your business name. If you intend to work with clients on Web and print projects, a business name like "Dots & Coms" might fool potential clients into thinking you only do work for websites. Your business name should give clients an idea about the services you offer, but still be open-ended enough that you will not quickly outgrow the name.

It's easy to experience a feeling I call "paralysis by analysis" at this point because you're trying to come up with the perfect business name, and you might feel like you're banging your head against the wall. Instead of tackling this task head on, let's try to outflank the problem and approach it from a different angle.

USE SYNONYMS, TRANSLATIONS, AND WORD ASSOCIATIONS

Sometimes looking words up in a thesaurus, translating words into different languages, or creating a word map can be helpful for generating ideas. Go online to www.thesaurus.com and look for synonyms for some of the words up on your list. Remember how the words "Mommy" and "Mother" essentially have the same meaning, but have different connotations? Look for synonyms for words on your list that have a positive emotional response and add them to your list.

Similarly, look up words on your list using an online language translator like www.translate.google.com and add interesting sounding words to your list. You might find a French or Greek word that sounds interesting or sparks an idea. By continuing to add words to your list, you're giving yourself options. You'll begin to refine your results soon enough, but keep generating ideas for now.

EXPERIMENT WITH PARTS OF WORDS

As your list of words grows have some fun mixing and matching words and parts of words together. You can break words up phonetically or look at their root words and origins and experiment.

When Zach Williams chose the name "Venveo" for his business, he created the name by combining excerpts of the Latin words: *inverventus*, meaning media, and *promoveo*, meaning to propel. Venveo then began to brand themselves as "Venveo: Media that moves" and created a niche for themselves by specializing in designing websites, online games, and iPhone applications for their clients.

You can break words down from their syllables or by their root words. Zach broke the words *inverventus* and *promoveo* into their root words to create the name

Venveo, whereas Bittbox, a website that provides free images for designers to download, combined the words "bit" and "box" to create their name. When you break down Bittbox's name, there are some clever components at work. First, the repetitive "B" sound and short name makes the name memorable. Second, the use of "bit" (the basic unit of measurement of a computer) and "box" (a container or storage device) helps create an idea about the type of services Bittbox provides. You don't have to be overly descriptive with your business name, but you shouldn't be obscure for the sake of being obscure, either.

GROUP SIMILAR IDEAS TOGETHER

By now you should have a larger list of possible business names, and you probably have a few ideas that you are starting to like. Now it's time to begin refining your list, by going through all of your names and grouping similar names together on a fresh sheet of paper.

Perhaps there was an idea that you just couldn't get away from, so that you have several variations of the same word on your list. Grouping these words together allows you to see if one version stands out in the pack. Mark your best ideas with an asterisk (*) and continue on. Remember how attached I was to the name "Method"? Grouping ideas like Method Studios, Method Mill, Method Made, and many other variations together helped me to feel that I had explored the concept. This process allowed me to eventually move on to other ideas and to avoid getting stuck on a particular idea.

If you've allowed yourself to explore freely, you will have a wide variety of groups of names to choose from. If you only have a few groups of names, it means you probably got stuck on an idea and couldn't let the idea go. If this is the case, go back to the drawing board and generate more ideas. You want many options to choose from before beginning to sort and narrow down your list.

REFINE YOUR LIST

You're going to want a business name that is short and memorable, so if you have lengthy names or names that are difficult to spell (or pronounce) cross them off your list or find an alternative.

When clients are typing in your Web address or giving you a referral, a short and memorable name will serve you much better than a longer, more descriptive name. In addition, it's generally a good idea to avoid names with geographical descriptions in them. These types of names can make your business appear small and local, and unless you only want to service local clients, they may be outgrown quickly. If you live in the town of Springfield and call your business "Springfield Graphic Arts," will the people living in Hendersonville feel that you're there to service them also?

GIVE IT A PROFESSIONAL LITMUS TEST

Your business name should sound professional, not campy. If your business is called Web Whirks, you have communicated two things to clients: you have something to do with the Internet and you're a bit campy. Playing with words isn't a bad idea, but you still have to exercise good judgment.

While you might think the play on the word "whirks" is a more creative way to spell "works," think about how it will be perceived by others. When your client is paying you to work on their project they don't want you to "whirk" (aka play around) on their dime. They are paying you to do a job for them and to do it right!

Look through your list and cross off the names that don't sound like a place where clients would want to spend their hard-earned money. While it's great to be creative, you'll also want to give the impression that your company can get the job done and deliver amazing results.

DISTINGUISH YOURSELF FROM THE COMPETITION

It is a good idea to familiarize yourself with your competition in order to help distinguish your business name from theirs. If there are any names on your list that sound similar to your competitor's names, cross them off your list. Additionally, if you have any names that sound similar to nationally known companies' names, like "Yahoo Graphics" or "The Nikon Studio," this could expose you to possible legal action and should be crossed off your list of names.

CHOOSE THE BEST OPTION

At this point you should have generated a long list of possible names and then begun to thin your list. You should check with your local or state agency to make sure that the names that are on your list are available, and check that an Internet domain name is available.

Trying to get a domain name after the fact can cost you a lot of money and be difficult. Don't set yourself up for a big hassle or risk losing visitors because you didn't plan ahead. Use a registry like www.godaddy.com, and search for available domain names before you finalize your business name.

> *"The key to choosing your business name is patience and persistence—don't rush the process."*

Typically a ".com" or a ".net" extension is the most sought after extension, but it might require you to be a bit creative in order to find an available domain name. It's smart to include finding an available domain name as a consideration of choosing your business name because it's an important component of your brand. I prefer domain names without a dash in them, but if I were unable to get a .com or .net website address, I would probably use the dash rather than a more unfamiliar extension like .us, .biz, or .me.

Sometimes a business name may sound really good to you, but other people may not share your excitement. While everyone does not have to like your business name, the majority of the people you ask should not dislike it either. By now you've been staring at a list of names for a long time and are probably beginning to go a little cross-eyed. It's time to get feedback from people you trust and who have an understanding about the type of work you'll be doing.

This may be the first time you've shared your business name with others, so prepare yourself to receive a lot of feedback. There is a better than average chance that the people you show your list to will try to throw out some "better" business name suggestions for you. The key here is avoid getting upset. Refrain from stopping them from being silly, and don't get defensive and shoot their ideas down. Just be a good sport and write down their suggestions. Once they've emptied their tank, go back through the list of names they suggested and look for interesting ideas.

Sometimes a close friend or family member will offer up a suggestion based on a quality or observation that you don't see in yourself and might lead you in a new and unexpected direction in your search for a business name. These insights are a gift and can really help you understand how you and your work are perceived. A lot of times your friends and family members will share a mental association with you that can be incorporated into your business' name.

The key to choosing your business name is patience and persistence—don't rush the process. Seek out other people's opinions, but be aware that there isn't one business name that everybody will like. Take your time, generate as many ideas as possible, refine your list, and then test a few select names with close friends and family. You'll be fine!

Talk to a CPA and Fill out Your LLC Paperwork

Now that you have a plan, it's time to take it and put it into action. You're about to be a business owner so get ready. The first thing you'll need to do is talk with a Certified Public Accountant (CPA) because you want to make sure that you don't run into any unforeseen problems setting up your company.

There are many types of CPAs, so you will have to look in the phone book (look under Accounting). Find a CPA who specializes in business development or bookkeeping. Once you've found a CPA, call him or her up and your conversation should sound like:

> *Hello, my name is (insert your name), and I'd like to make an appointment with (insert the CPA's name) to discuss setting up a limited liability company. I want to start a freelance graphic design business, and I was wondering if you could help me choose the right type of business entity and help me get started?*

The reason I recommend that you talk with a CPA is because they are like Sherpas when it comes to navigating the terrain of setting up a small-business. Similar to how a Sherpa would help you through the wilderness and avoid swollen streams that might impede your progress, a CPA will help you avoid obstacles that might impede the success of your business. Tax laws and regulations change, and a good CPA can help you find the most efficient way to set up your company and avoid unnecessary expenses.

SOLE PROPRIETOR LLC

When it comes to setting up a business entity, there are many ways to do so. Every option has its advantages and disadvantages that vary from state to state, but I recommend that you talk to your CPA about a Sole Proprietor LLC because it's extremely easy to manage. This is when talking to a CPA who is familiar with the business terrain in your area will pay off.

The benefits of choosing a Sole Proprietor LLC is that filing taxes involves a simple self-employment income tax form, no fees or registration requirements, and no payroll set-up. It requires you to set up a business banking account for quick and easy accounting and tax purposes. However, a sole proprietorship makes you personally liable for all debts and incidents that are a result of your company. This means that if your company goes bankrupt or incurs excessive debt, everything will show up on your personal credit report and records. Needless to say, you have to be careful about accumulating debt, but the simplicity of setting up and running a Sole Proprietor LLC makes it one of my favorite business entity options.

After you've run your business for a bit and have begun to establish a client base, you can switch your Sole Proprietor LLC to an LLC if you feel that you need more protection from debt. Some of the advantages of an LLC is that you are personally protected from business debt. Your bottom-line profit is not considered earned income, so it does not incur self-employment tax.

If this sounds like mumbo jumbo, then you have realized why talking to a CPA can be a good idea—he or she can help you get your bearings and decide which business entity is right for you. It's important to pick an entity that fits your needs, so that you don't end up making things more complicated than necessary or paying too much in taxes. Your CPA can give you the forms you'll need to fill out to register your business or tell you where to find them online. Then you can print them out and send them in yourself.

SEND IN YOUR LLC APPLICATION

Once you and your CPA have identified the type of business entity that's right for you, begin filling out the paperwork and send in the processing fee (if applicable). Contacting a CPA and filling out your paperwork is the first step to officially starting your business, and I hope you are beginning to get excited about the idea of owning your own company!

Once you've sent in the paperwork, your state agency will send you back a certificate that says your company is recognized as an official business entity and that you are authorized to transact business in accordance with state laws. You are not quite finished setting up your company yet, but you are getting very close.

Apply for an Employer Identification Number

Now that you have received confirmation from your state agency stating that your business has been officially recognized by the state, you need to apply for an Employer Identification Number (EIN) from the IRS.

An EIN, or Federal Tax Identification Number, is used to identify a business entity and is used to identify the tax accounts of employers. The IRS uses the number to identify taxpayers who are required to file various business tax returns. Applying for an EIN is a quick and free process. Simply go to www.irs.gov and click on the "Businesses" link. On the left hand side is an "Employer ID Num-

COMMONWEALTH OF VIRGINIA
STATE CORPORATION COMMISSION

LLC-1011
(07/06)

ARTICLES OF ORGANIZATION OF A
DOMESTIC LIMITED LIABILITY COMPANY

Pursuant to Chapter 12 of Title 13.1 of the Code of Virginia the undersigned states as follows:

1. The name of the limited liability company is

_____.
(The name must contain the words **limited company** or **limited liability company** or the abbreviation **L.C., LC, L.L.C.** or **LLC**)

2. A. The name of the limited liability company's initial registered agent is

_____

   B. The registered agent is **(mark appropriate box)**:

   (1) an <u>INDIVIDUAL</u> who is a resident of Virginia **and**
   ☐ a member or manager of the limited liability company.
   ☐ a member or manager of a limited liability company that is a member or manager
      of the limited liability company.
   ☐ an officer or director of a corporation that is a member or manager of the limited
      liability company.
   ☐ a general partner of a general or limited partnership that is a member or manager
      of the limited liability company.
   ☐ a trustee of a trust that is a member or manager of the limited liability company.
   ☐ a member of the Virginia State Bar.
                                            OR
   (2) ☐ a domestic or foreign stock or nonstock corporation, limited liability company or
       registered limited liability partnership authorized to transact business in Virginia.

3. The limited liability company's initial registered office address, including the street and number,
   if any, which is identical to the business office of the initial registered agent, is

   _____,VA _____,
        (number/street)   (city or town)   (zip)

   which is physically located in the ☐ county **or** ☐ city of _____.

4. The limited liability company's principal office address, including the street and number, is

   _____
        (number/street)   (city or town)   (state)   (zip)

Organizer(s):

_____   _____
        (signature)   (date)

_____   _____
        (printed name)   (telephone number (optional))

SEE INSTRUCTIONS ON THE REVERSE

Filling out the paperwork to register your Sole Proprietor LLC with your state is relatively easy once you find the correct form. You can find this form yourself by doing a little digging, or your CPA can give you a copy of and help you fill it out correctly. Most states require you to pay a small fee to process this form. Each year you will have to pay a small fee to keep your business registered with your state.

> *"I can't stress enough that you should not use your personal checking account because it is a sure fire way to get audited."*

bers" link that will take you to the EIN page, where you can apply for an EIN online. After reading the information and following the prompts, you will be asked a series of questions and will be immediately sent an EIN.

Print this document out and keep a copy of it and the business certificate you received from your state agency in a safe place. You will need to bring both of these documents with you when you open your business account at the bank.

Opening a Business Checking Account

Opening a business checking account will make it much easier for you to track your financial transactions rather than using your personal checking account and trying to keep track of business and personal expenses. I can't stress enough that you should not use your personal checking account because it is a surefire way to get audited. Opening a business checking account is simple and often is a service that your bank will provide at no cost to you.

Bring in your Business Certificate and your EIN with you when you go to open your business checking account, and ask the manager if he can supply you with some temporary checks. My business account does not have a minimum balance and does not charge a monthly fee. Deposit $20 to $100 into your account, so that you have a positive balance and a little money in your account in case you need to make a purchase for your business. After a few days you should receive a debit card in the mail with your name and your business name on it. Make sure that you use your business account only for business purchases. Don't withdraw cash from your business account—instead write a check or use your debit card. This includes paying yourself for all your hard work. This way you have a record of where all the money in your business account goes. Remember, don't pay cash and keep all your receipts because you will need them in when it comes time to report your expenses and taxable earnings to the government.

As long as you keep track of where all the money in your business account goes, and practice some common sense when it comes to financial decisions, you should be okay. Your CPA can advise you on ways to avoid paying more taxes than you need to by keeping track of your mileage, writing off business expenses, and other tricks of the trade. If you ever have a question, be sure to pick up the phone and call your CPA to make sure that you avoid getting yourself into hot water!

Getting a Business License

You will need to contact your local city hall or courthouse to see if you need to apply for a business license to legally conduct business in your town or district. There may be fees in doing so, but they are usually minimal.

Depending on where you live, there may be requirements that you will need to meet before your business license is approved. For example, your district may have a zoning compliance or permit to work out of your home. For the type of business you are starting, you shouldn't run into too many problems with your application. Most likely you will not be allowed to put up a sign for your business, have clients visit you at your home, or advertise your business on your vehicle, but these aren't huge deal-breaking obstacles in most cases.

You may have to estimate what your income will be in some cases, and your fees will be based on this estimate. If you exceed the amount you specified on your application, you will be assessed a small fee for every dollar you go over. When I set up my company, I estimated that I would make $5,000 my first year, and was required to pay a $30 fee for my business license.

You should receive your business license in a little over a week, in most cases, and you are asked to display your business license in a visible space at your business. Your business license is usually good for a year. You will have to renew it every year if you wish to continue to do business in your community.

Checklist

- ☐ Choose a name for your business and make sure it's available. Check to make sure that your business name will be well received.
- ☐ Secure an easy-to-remember domain name and purchase it. A Web hosting plan is optional at this point.
- ☐ Talk with a CPA and fill out your paperwork to establish an LLC business.
- ☐ Apply for a free Federal Employer Identification Number (EIN) by going to the www.irs.gov website and obtain a business license *(if necessary)*.
- ☐ Open a business checking account with a bank.

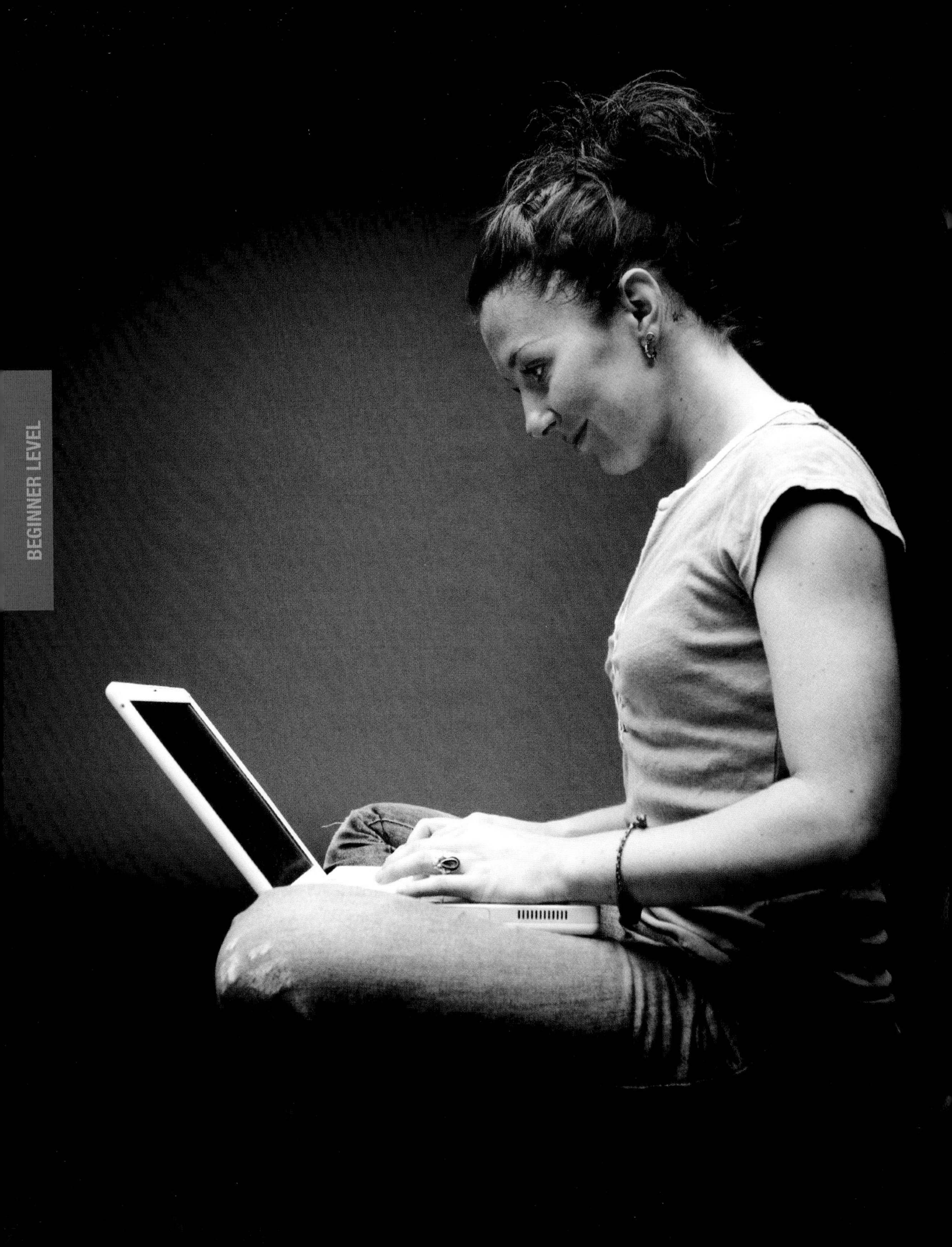

There's a First Time for Everything 5

Goals for Beginning Freelancers

College is all about gaining experience, and there's no better time than now to work with your first client. You might find yourself living away from home for the first time, opening yourself to personal discovery, and learning the skills you need to improve your quality of life. This is an exciting time because change is in the air. You might feel that starting a company is a tall order on top of everything else on your plate, but try to think about it as laying a foundation that you will build upon. Don't try to do everything all at once, or try and hit a home run every time you step up to the plate. All you have to do is take the first few steps and see how things go. Here are some initial goals for you to help you get started.

- Successfully set up your Sole Proprietor LLC (described in previous chapters).
- Purchase the equipment you will need to use for school and your business.
- Familiarize yourself with how to use a contract (and other forms).
- Work for a paying client.

You can probably accomplish the tasks on the list above with one hand tied behind your back, but it's important to not take shortcuts. We're going to add a little more complexity as you get comfortable. When you reach the advanced level, you'll be more selective about the clients you choose to work with, become more comfortable more complex projects, and probably make more money in the process.

The bulk of your expenses will come from purchasing a computer and software. It is important to take care of your equipment, so that it will last you a long time. I hope you're beginning to feel excited about the idea of working with clients because enthusiasm is going to be an important part of your success. Not everyone can say they own their own business, and even fewer can say they did it while they were in college! It's perfectly normal to feel excited about using the skills you've been honing in school and to feel a bit nervous, also.

Equipment to Purchase

Try not to go too deeply into debt when you purchase your equipment. Look for good deals and loan rates *(if necessary)*. I took out a computer loan during college to purchase my first Macintosh computer, and being a poor college student, I paid the minimum balance each month. Three years later, I still owed more on my Mac than it cost to buy a brand new one! I quickly paid off my computer and vowed not to purchase a computer through a line of credit again. If you cannot afford to purchase your computer outright, you might have no choice in the matter. But if you can afford to purchase your equipment outright, it may be smart to do so. Technology changes rapidly, and I think it's a good idea to pay for your equipment in cash as you go along.

Do your best to scour the Internet for good deals, and use your status as a student to your advantage. There are a variety of retailers out there who provide special pricing and financing options that only students can take advantage of, by providing a copy of a student identification card. In addition, look for seasonal deals, tax-advantage days, and bundled deals as you prepare to make your purchase. Buying refurbished equipment can save you a lot of money, but make sure that you understand the warranty and exchange policy before you make your purchase.

Many schools have a computer requirement, so it's good policy to check with your school to see if they require you to purchase a specific computer. Even if your school provides you with access to a computer lab, I still recommend that you purchase your own computer. Many schools prohibit students from using the school's equipment to work on freelance or other for-profit activities. In addition, most computer labs ask that you do not change the computer settings, request that you save all your work to external storage devices, refrain from loading any outside software onto their computers, and wipe all data from their computers routinely. Having your own computer dramatically increases your productivity and allows you to pursue opportunities that would otherwise be unavailable. Without a doubt purchasing a laptop is a big expense, but it is an expense that is well worth your investment.

APPLE LAPTOP

Almost everyone in the graphic design industry uses Apple Macintosh computers, and I recommend that you purchase an Apple laptop as well. Not only has Apple become a standard in the graphic design industry, but their operating system has proven to be stable and resistant to computer viruses and spyware.

While it's true that laptops generally lack some of the processing power of a desktop computer (specifically in regards to video performance), their overall utility and portability offers a huge advantage. Most Macs can also run Mac OS X and Microsoft Windows, which makes them extremely versatile computers that should meet all your academic needs.

To get the most bang for your buck, look for a mid-level Apple laptop instead of the most powerful (and expensive) model. Your laptop is going to take a beating while you're in school, so it's better to save a little money while you can. Keep an eye out for perks when you're shopping for your laptop, like getting a free iPod or inkjet printer with the purchase of a new computer.

If your college bookstore sells laptops, you might be able to save some money, because they sometimes have the ability to sell laptops at a discounted rate to students. If your college bookstore doesn't sell laptops, check the Apple website (www.apple.com/education). You may find educational discounts that are available to you if you fax in a copy of your college identification card.

While you're on Apple's website, take a look at their refurbished computer selection under the "Special Deals" section of the website. These are computers that have been returned to Apple, repaired to manufacturer standards, tested, and are being sold as "like-new" computers. These computers generally have a one-year warranty and offer significant discounts of between 15 and 30 percent off the retail price of a new computer. Whether you purchase a new or refurbished computer, I highly recommend you purchase the Apple Care Protection Plan. Apple Care provides you access to technical support, repair coverage on parts and labor for three years, which virtually guarantees that your laptop will remain in good working condition throughout your entire college career. Personally, I won't buy an Apple computer without simultaneously purchasing the Apple Care plan.

SOFTWARE

Before you begin purchasing software for your computer, check with your school and verify that they haven't included any software license fees in your tuition. All incoming undergraduate students at Virginia Tech are required to purchase Micro-

BEGINNER LEVEL

soft Office, and the college offers this software to our students at a discounted rate. You might try directing your question to your school's bookstore, software distribution center, or the chair of your program if you are unable to find the answer to this question on your school's website.

You also need to find out what software your program requires. It's perfectly normal for your program to require specific software. Don't make an expensive software purchase only to find out that you purchased the wrong software.

Often the software deals offered by your school can beat the price of many online competitors, but it's always a good idea to shop around to find the best deal you can. If you look online for software packages, be sure to ask if you are going to receive a limited or full license for the price being quoted. While a limited license will look cheaper at first glance, the license will eventually expire and force you to purchase another license after a certain amount of time has passed. You goal should be to find a full license at the best price you can find.

Most likely you're going to need to purchase the latest version of the Adobe Creative Suite, which includes Dreamweaver, Flash, Photoshop, Illustrator, Fireworks, Acrobat Pro, Soundbooth, Contribute, and Bridge. You'll also probably need to buy Microsoft Office, which includes Entourage, Excel, Messenger, PowerPoint, and Microsoft Word.

There are plenty of other software applications that may be helpful, but the Adobe Creative Suite and Microsoft Office are arguably the two biggest software packages you will need to purchase up front.

If you plan on specializing in a particular area like 3-D animation, Web design or video, you may need to purchase additional software. Check with your department to make sure the software you purchase is the same version of the software you'll be using in your classes, so you will be able to follow along when your teachers instruct you on using the software.

PHOTO-QUALITY INKJET PRINTER

Having the ability to print out proofs of your work is extremely helpful for school and an absolute necessity when you freelance. We (designers) make many of our decisions while looking at a computer screen, but how something looks on screen can be radically different from how it appears when printed. The size of type often looks different, colors can shift, and you will need printed mock-ups your work for client approval. An inkjet printer allows you to easily print proofs and will help you make better design decisions.

Color laser printers have a lower cost per print than inkjet printers, but they cost a lot more than inkjet printers and generally cannot handle as many paper sizes, weights, and textures as inkjet printers. For this reason, I recommend that you start by purchasing a photo-quality inkjet printer and eventually switch to a color laser printer once your freelance business has begun to turn a profit and you've paid off any debt you've accumulated along the way.

While a multifunction inkjet printer sounds as if it would be a smart investment, I don't recommend purchasing an all-in-one (inkjet printer, copier, scanner, fax machine) because they tend to do an average job at printing and usually aren't able to handle larger paper sizes or a very wide variety of paper weights.

Having the ability to print at an affordable price is your primary concern at this point. There are many brands and models of photo-quality inkjet printers, and you might be asking yourself, "How do I know which printer to buy?" Here are a couple of points for you to consider before making your purchase.

• **Paper size:** I recommend that you buy a printer that prints at least 12" x 18", so that you can trim out a full-bleed tabloid print. Tabloid-size paper is an industry standard, and not having to glue and tile together smaller pieces of paper can save you time and make your work look much better. The problem with purchasing a tabloid-size printer is that it often leaves a ¼" white border around the printout. Look for a borderless printer or one that can print 12" x 18" or larger.

• **Picoliter:** A picoliter is a unit of fluid volume, and a lower number results in a smaller dot size and allows more dots to be in the same area, which typically results in a better-looking image. Photo-quality inkjet printers usually have a smaller picoliter number than their non-photo-quality inkjet printers counterparts, and their prints usually look much better.

• **Ink:** Some of the best photo-quality inkjet printers use four to eight individual color ink cartridges. These ink cartridges can be expensive to purchase, so do a little research before you buy your printer and find out how much the ink cartridges cost. You should be aware that some inkjet printers will not print if any of the individual ink cartridges are empty. I have heard horror stories from people who have tried to refill their empty color ink cartridges, only to have disappointing results and in some cases printer damage. Others swear their experience was problem free and cheap! Because of these mixed reviews, you should assume that you will have to purchase color cartridges from the manufacturer until you find out otherwise.

• **Reviews:** Make sure you read reviews about the inkjet printer you are considering and talk to people who own (or have owned) the model you are considering. Ask if the printer prints quietly, or is it loud? Are there features that other people have found particularly helpful? How long do the ink cartridges usually last? Do you have to use a special kind of paper to get the best results? How quickly does the printer print? Do the prints come out looking vibrant and bright or do they look gray and washed out?

As always, shop around to find the best prices you can, but make sure to read the fine print. You might find an inkjet printer being sold for $15 less than the competition, but the cheaper price might not include the $20 cable you need to hook the printer up to your computer. Exercise good common sense, and you should end up with a printer that will last you throughout your college career and meet your freelance and academic needs.

EXTERNAL STORAGE DEVICE

Even if your laptop has a huge hard drive, you're going to need to purchase an inexpensive external storage device like a flash drive or a small USB drive to transport your files. These devices can be found in almost any local office supply store.

I prefer a 500GB USB drive ($60) over an 8GB flash drive ($20). I've accidently left small flash drives in my pants pockets only to stick my pants in the washing machine and realize my mistake later. For this reason, I prefer a physically larger USB drive because its deck-of-playing-cards size keeps me from unintentionally laundering it. It's silly I know, but choose whatever external drive works best for you. Some external storage devices may require you to reformat the drive before it will work on your Macintosh. The directions for reformatting an external drive can usually be found in the device's instruction manual.

How Do You Find Your First Client?

One of your goals is to work with a paying client. How do you find a client to work with? I recommend that you work with somebody you already know.

The reason your goal is to work with one client at first is to help you minimize your anxiety, give yourself enough time to find your client, have ample time to work on your client's project, and learn what's behind the scenes in running your own business. This is why I highly recommend that your first client be someone you know like a relative, a church or social organization, a friend of the family, or a

> *"Do not obligate yourself to a project that you cannot successfully complete."*

former employer. You want to work for someone who will be understanding about any mistakes you might make and who will give you constructive criticism about their experience working with you. Your goal isn't to make a lot of money (the money will come later). The goal is to familiarize yourself with the expectations and realities of working with a client. You want to find a client with a project that you feel confident that you can complete. Herein lies a very important lesson. Do not obligate yourself to a project that you cannot successfully complete. Sometimes this requires you to say, "No, I'm sorry. I don't think I will be able to help you." Then look for work that is more in line with your abilities.

I've taught Introduction to Graphic Design numerous times, and I require my freshman students to work with a client. They typically choose to work with a family member or a church. The last two times I've taught this class, my students averaged around $100 per job. I don't dictate my students' rates, and sometimes they work on a project for as little as $5. On other occasions I have had students make as much as $500.

The point to working with a client for the first time is to learn what kind of issues other than "design issues" are involved with freelancing. Sometimes you have to deal with strong personalities, picky clients, or clients that don't have a clue what they want! So the first step is to find someone you know and successfully navigate the uncharted waters of freelance unscathed.

Working on one freelance job isn't going to help you break any sales records, but it will help you establish a foundation that you will build upon over the next few years. Even though you may know your client, (in fact, your client might be your dad), you should practice being a professional by showing up to appointments on time, wearing the appropriate types of clothing, and trying to exceed your client's expectations.

What Type of Work Should You Do?

The most important thing at this stage is to work on projects that you will be able to successfully complete. This means carefully choosing the type of job that you can "knock out of the ballpark" and feel good about. I want your first freelance job to be a huge ego boost. Here are a few ideas for relatively simple graphic design projects that you might be able to complete easily:

• Custom Artwork	• T-shirt Design	• Company Logo
• Business Card	• Postcard	• Advertisement
• Poster	• Flyer	• Twitter background

On the following pages are several examples of projects that other Beginner freelancers in your shoes have completed. You will also be able to get an idea what they are charging for their services, problems they might have encountered and some of the lessons they learned along the way.

Sometimes hearing about someone else's experience can help you improve your likelihood for success because it helps you to demystify the designer/client relationship and helps you to understand your role more clearly. Each client you work with will have different needs and tastes, so your own experience is likely to be very different from the examples shown. That said, you will probably also find some similarities between the stories you read and your own experiences.

Many young designers don't charge very much for their first job because they are still getting their feet underneath them and learning the ropes. If you feel the need to reduce your rate for your first job, you might say something like:

> *I'm really excited to work with you on this project. You are my first official freelance client, and I'm going to do an amazing job for you. I'm still getting my bearings, so I'm not going to charge you as much as I should to complete your project. I just wanted to let you know that if you'd like to work with me again in the future my rates are likely to increase. I just want to be up-front with you about this so that you won't be caught off guard later. Thank you for the opportunity to work with you. I look forward to delivering a solution that we can both be proud of.*

I believe it's okay to work at a reduced rate for your first freelance job, but you need to bring your rates up as you continue to freelance. If you work too cheaply, you risk devaluing your work, as well as the work of other designers in your area. This is an excellent topic to discuss with your teachers and classmates and a topic that has both moral and ethical implications. As you gain experience freelancing, your rates will need to come into alignment with other freelance designers in your geographical area.

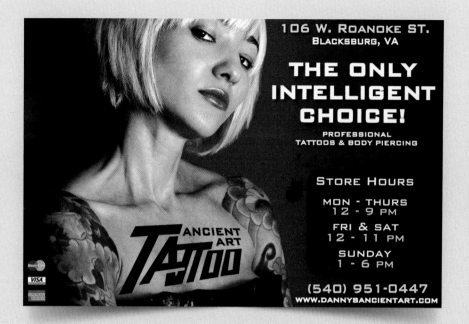

The ad shown contains the following text:

106 W. ROANOKE ST.
BLACKSBURG, VA

THE ONLY INTELLIGENT CHOICE!

PROFESSIONAL
TATTOOS & BODY PIERCING

STORE HOURS

MON - THURS
12 - 9 PM

FRI & SAT
12 - 11 PM

SUNDAY
1 - 6 PM

ANCIENT ART TATTOO

(540) 951-0447
WWW.DANNYSANCIENTART.COM

Ancient Art Tattoo Ad
Designed by Kyle Waldrop
Received $50.00

Ancient Art Tattoo tracked Kyle down when they found out that he was the designer responsible for creating an advertisement for them that ran in the *Collegiate Times* newspaper earlier that year. Kyle had been working part time as a graphic designer creating advertisements for local clients, but he had decided to quit his part-time job with the college newspaper and freelance instead.

When Kyle met with Vicki Rose for the first time said, "Vicki wanted to barter with me and trade a tattoo or piercing for my graphic design work. I thought long and hard about it, but I decided that my mom might kill me if I came home with a tattoo, so we settled on $50 to design the ad for her instead."

I asked Kyle what it was like having a tattoo shop for a client, and he said, "It was a cool experience, and Vicki was very laid back and easy to work with. Working with a client like Ancient Art really made me appreciate the creative freedom they gave me because so many other companies want their logo to be huge, and try to art direct you throughout the entire process. Vicki gave me a lot of creative freedom, and I really appreciated that she let me explore several ideas before we decided to use the solution you see here."

Twitter Page Background
Designed by Sarah Tanner
Received $99.00

Sarah told her sorority sisters that she was interested in picking up some freelance work, and she was put in touch with the father of one of her sorority sisters. After a little research on how much other designers were charging to create Twitter backgrounds, Sarah felt that charging a flat rate of $99 was appropriate.

Sarah said, "One of the unique things about this project was that I never met my client face to face. I contacted my client through e-mail, and he put me in contact with his colleague, who manages their Twitter page. I was e-mailed a logo and a description of what they wanted. I had the client sign a contract and send me a $50 deposit—everything ran very smoothly."

When I asked Sarah what she had learned from working on this project, she replied, "It's good to try and work on different types of projects. I never would have never done a Twitter page background if the client hadn't requested it. There are limitations and standards you have to deal with when working for a social media website such as Twitter. But through my research I learned what's involved with designing a good solution for this medium, and it made me think a lot about my design and how it would look when their content was added."

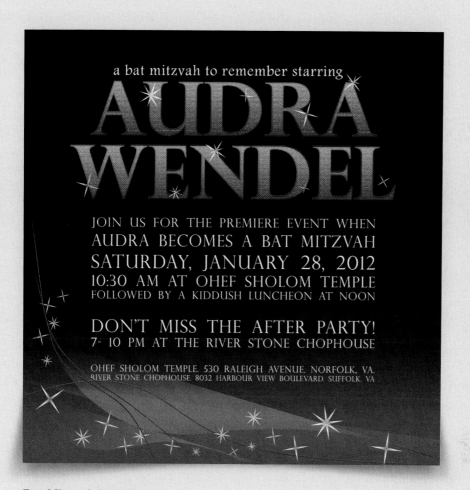

a bat mitzvah to remember starring

AUDRA WENDEL

JOIN US FOR THE PREMIERE EVENT WHEN
AUDRA BECOMES A BAT MITZVAH
SATURDAY, JANUARY 28, 2012
10:30 AM AT OHEF SHOLOM TEMPLE
FOLLOWED BY A KIDDUSH LUNCHEON AT NOON

DON'T MISS THE AFTER PARTY!
7- 10 PM AT THE RIVER STONE CHOPHOUSE

OHEF SHOLOM TEMPLE, 530 RALEIGH AVENUE, NORFOLK, VA.
RIVER STONE CHOPHOUSE, 8032 HARBOUR VIEW BOULEVARD, SUFFOLK, VA

BEGINNER LEVEL

Bat Mitzvah Invitation
Designed by Stephanie Livingston
Received $155.00

Stephanie worked as a babysitter, and when one of the mothers saw the wedding invitations that Stephanie designed for her sister, she asked Stephanie to design Bat Mitzvah invitations for her daughter, Audra. Stephanie agreed and met with Audra and her mother about the type of invitation they wanted. Stephanie says, "Audra said she wanted red carpeting and something glamorous!"

   Stephanie sent sketches to her client, who gave her feedback about what they liked best. Stephanie refined her design from their comments. Stephanie advises, "Be persistent. Clients may not call you back, so be polite but persistent in following up with your clients in order to get the job finished on time."

D2 Dining Services Flyer
Designed by Sarah Vernon
Received $200.00

D2, a campus dining services center, wanted to create a flyer for incoming freshman students, so they asked Sarah Vernon to come up with something to promote their culinary event. Recipes for favorite meals were collected from students so that they could get a "taste of home" throughout the semester.

D2 was one of Sarah's first freelance clients, and she says, "I was nervous to work with a client for the first time, but I learned a lot in the process. Particularly about editing photos using Photoshop to bump up colors to make them more vibrant." Sarah quickly added, "Working with clients gets easier over time, and everyone is nervous the first time—I certainly was. I didn't know what they were going to ask me to do, but once I got to know their preferences a bit better things just fell into place. For example, I learned that this client liked photography more than illustrations, and many of my initial concepts were illustrative. Things went a lot more smoothly after I figured that out."

I asked Sarah how she felt after working with her first client, and she replied, "It's rewarding to get some practical experience before I graduate. Now I know what type of tasks I may be asked to complete once I graduate, and knowing that I can accomplish them makes me feel better."

CHICKEN CUTLET

1. Parkside* $6.50
Breaded chicken cutlet with melted muenster cheese, bacon, tomato and Russian dressing on a kaiser roll

2. Sicilian Supreme* $6.50
Breaded chicken cutlet with melted mozzarella, sliced pepperoni and roasted red peppers on toasted garlic Italian bread

3. Bourbon Street* $6.50
Cajun chicken cutlet with melted cheddar, romaine lettuce, tomato, red onion and chunky bleu cheese dressing on an onion roll

4. Popeye's Favorite* $6.50
Breaded chicken cutlet, melted American cheese and spinach with herbed ranch dressing on a kaiser roll

5. Chicken Cordon Bleu* $6.50
A great combination of chicken cutlet, lean ham and melted swiss lorraine with a country bistro spread served on a french baguette

6. Chicken Grille* $6.50
Grilled chicken with roasted red peppers, crisp romaine, sliced tomatoes and creamy caesar on toasted garlic Italian bread

7. Carolina Crunch Wrap* $6.50
Grilled chicken with cheddar jack cheese, shredded lettuce, crunchy tri-colored tortilla strips and barbeque ranch dressing wrapped in a spinach tortilla

ROAST BEEF

8. Balboa* $6.50
Tender roast beef with melted havarti cheese on toasted garlic Rustic bread topped with horseradish sauce

9. Roast Beef Special* $6.50
Homemade horseradish spread tops this hearty sandwich of roast beef, tomato and cucumber slices on garlic toasted rye bread

10. Vermont Peddler* $6.50
Rare roast beef, sharp Vermont cheddar, our own Russian dressing and cole slaw on pumpernickel bread

11. Steakhouse Cobb* $6.50
Londonport roast beef, chopped iceberg lettuce and tomato with chunky bleu cheese dressing in a flour tortilla

12. The Wrangler* $6.50
Hot roast beef topped with monterey jack cheese, sliced red onion, shredded lettuce and barbecue sauce on an onion roll

13. Roast Beef Italiano* $6.50
Roast beef with melted picante provolone, roasted red peppers and pesto mayonnaise on toasted garlic Italian bread

TURKEY

14. Black Forest* $6.50
Smoked turkey, melted muenster cheese, Russian dressing and tomato served on pumpernickel bread

15. Turkey Supreme $6.50
Mesquite turkey, alpine swiss chee... bread and topped with Russian dr...

16. Taste of Honey
Oven roasted turkey breast, cream... greens and cucumbers drizzled w... served on 8 grain bread

17. The Gobbler
Roasted rotisserie turkey breast... cranberry sauce and topped wit... and mayonnaise

18. California Club
Rotisserie turkey breast, crumbled ba... monterey jack cheese, sprouts... all wrapped in a flour tortilla

19. Healthy Choice
Honey maple turkey and dip... layered with spinach leaves... mustard

20. The Virginian*
Smoked turkey, baked Virg... melted muenster cheese a... pumpernickel bread

21. Cajun Club
Cajun turkey, smoked bac... tomato on rye bread dres...

22. Egg-cellent Egg
Homemade egg sala... mustard on whole w...

23. Tongal Time
White albacore tuna... tortilla

24. Chicken Pump...
Chunky chicken sa... pumpernickel brea...

THE SANDWICH CLUB

Odell
525 North Tryon Street
P · 704.334.0133
F · 704.334.3803

The Green
435 South Tryon Street
P · 704.344.1975
F · 704.344.9957

Interstate Tower
121 West Trade Street
P · 980.219.7140
F · 980.219.7141

Order online at
www.sandwichclub2go.com

The Sandwich Club Menu
Designed by Alyssa Morrison
Received $300.00

Alyssa's parents own a chain of sandwich shops in Charlotte, North Carolina, and needed to redesign their menu. Alyssa told them that she could help them out and accepted the job. "I was both excited and nervous" Alyssa said. "It was the first time they saw my graphic design work, and I really wanted them to like the menu I designed for them. The hardest part of the job was waiting to see their reaction."

Alyssa took the photos of the sandwiches herself. "There were eight sandwiches and by the time I finished taking pictures of them, I had well over one hundred pictures." Alyssa advises, "Always take way more pictures than you think you'll need. It's a lot easier to drop in the perfect shot when you have options to choose from. If you need eight pictures and you only take a dozen, you'll probably have to reshoot a few pieces again to capture a shot that works perfectly with your design. You can experiment with your f-stops and shutter speeds while you shoot."

Writing a Contract

A contract protects both you and your client. It spells out the details of what needs to be done, when it needs to be completed, and how much it is likely cost. Signed contracts are legally binding documents, which means it's a good idea to make sure that you understand what's in your contract before asking one of your clients to sign it.

A contract is an agreement between two or more parties to do something (or in some cases to not do something). You should write a contract for every job that you agree to work on, but you should be aware that contracts can be amended to meet the constraints of the job. It isn't unusual for a client to submit a counter-proposal or ask for something in the contract to be amended, so it's a good idea to familiarize yourself with the process of writing and using a contract from the beginning.

It's easy to think of a contract as a chore instead of a life preserver—until the day comes that it saves your life. Well maybe not literally save your life. But there will eventually come a time when you'll either be really glad you had a contract or kicking yourself for not having one. Inevitably, you will have a dispute, and you'll need to go back to your signed contract to review your commitments before deciding how to proceed. Sometimes all it takes is a single business dispute to ruin your profit margin for the year. So try and think about the time it takes to write a contract as a necessary component of your company's overall success. If you ever have a question about your contract, you should talk to a lawyer.

Benjamin Franklin said that an ounce of prevention is worth a pound of cure. It might be better to pay lawyer fees to avoid a potential mess than it would to be found guilty of breaching your contract. For this reason, it's important to be honest when you write your contracts. If there's no way you can deliver a job by the time a client needs it, you need to communicate this to your client before entering into an agreement. Similarly, you expect your clients to pay you in a timely manner once the job has been completed. You should not have to chase your clients down and nag them about paying you for your services. Contracts are there to protect every-one's best interest, so don't think of your contract as a document that only protects you—it protects your clients' interests also.

I've included some descriptions of the components of a contract and how these items might protect you as you prepare to work with your first client. Using a contract isn't rocket science. Familiarizing yourself with your contract is a good idea in order to protect yourself legally and to communicate project goals clearly.

YOUR LOGO

Job Proposal

Today's Date

Client's Name
Client's Address
City, State Zip Code

Shipping Address (if different)
Client's Phone: (540) 555-5555

PROJECT: The name of the project ie.) T-shirt Design

SCOPE OF THE PROJECT: Describe the project in detail. <Insert your company name> will create two-color vector artwork that TriAdventure can take to get screen printed on a light gray T-shirt. The artwork will be created with Adobe Illustrator and the file will be saved as an Illustrator 5.5 EPS file and burned on a CD.

DETAILS: Describe what the client is getting for their money. Proofs will be delivered within seven days after all supporting material has been supplied by the client. This estimate includes the initial client meeting, research, sketching, concepts, design and production, and one round of revisions.

This estimate is based on the Scope of the Project defined above. Changes to the Scope of Work may result in changes to delivery time and price. Additional expenses (for example, illustation, photography, shipping expenses, etc.) will be itemized on the final invoice. This estimate is valid for 30 days from the date listed above. The fees for the project may vary as much as 15% from this estimate.

DESCRIPTION	TIME	BUDGET
Concept Development	X Hours	$ XX.XX
Design Development	X Hours	$ XX.XX
Production	X Hour	$ XX.XX
Project Implementation	X Hour	$ XX.XX
TOTAL	**X Hours**	**$ XX.XX**

TERMS & CONDITIONS:
• Sketches: The fee above includes XX preliminary sketches; additional sketches are $ XX.XX.

• Final artwork: The fee quoted includes one set of final artwork. Any changes to the final artwork once approved will incur an additional cost based on the extent of complexity.

• Rights: Upon full payment of all fees and costs, the rights to use this design transfer to the client listed above.

• Credit: The Designer shall be accorded a credit line on all material, to read as follows: "Design by <Insert your company name>" or be given permission to display this work in their portfolio.

• Overtime: Fees quoted are based upon work performed during the course of regular working hours. Overtime, rush, holiday and weekend work necessitated by the Client's directive is billed in addition to the fees quoted at $ XX.XX per hour or a mutually agreed upon fee.

YOUR COMPANY
123 Anywhere Street
City, State ZIP Code
(555) 555-5555

JOB PROPOSAL *(See page VIII for download instructions)*
Job Proposals or Contracts help protect both you and your client by ensuring that the goals for the project, expectations, and deadlines are clearly defined and understood by the designer and client. It's a good idea to use a contract for every job you work on in order to protect yourself legally and to avoid misunderstandings.

Understanding What's in Your Contract

Date: A date may seem like an insignificant detail, but it establishes a time frame for when you and your client entered into an agreement and when your quote will expire. Generally speaking, a quote is good for thirty days. Having a date on your contract allows you to revisit your price after a certain amount of time has passed. This can be helpful when you move from a slow season to a busy season.

For example, you might not be very busy in the month of May, so you might lower your prices to generate momentum. Let's say that several clients like your lower rates, and suddenly you have a full month of work ahead of you. Now that you're busy and working again, you'll want your rates to return to your normal amount instead of continuing at a discounted rate. This is one reason why it's a good idea to have your quotes expire after a certain amount of time has passed, and why including a date on your contract is a good idea.

Client name and information: This information establishes who the contract is with and how they can be reached. Having your client's name on the contract is necessary for your document to be considered legally binding.

Project title and scope of work: You may be working on several jobs for a client, so including a project title on your contract lets you know which job this contract is in reference to. It is extremely important for the designer to include as many specifics as possible in the Scope of Work description. For example, if you were to state something vaguely—like "I will create a website for my client"—chances are good that you will end up regretting that you didn't take the time to clarify your obligation down the road. When you deliver the website to your client and he says the website looks good, but asks you to add a shopping cart to the site, you'll wish you had not used the term "website" so generically.

When I write my scope of work descriptions, I try to write them in a way that uses as little technical jargon as possible, and in a way that makes it clear to the client and me when the job should be considered complete. It can be very difficult to say to a client, "That's not something that I agreed to do in our contract." I try to put myself in the client's shoes when I'm writing my scope of work description and try to include periods of feedback, a period for revisions, how the job will be delivered, who retains the rights, and when final payment is expected. Without these milestones, it's easy for your client to think that there's no rush to finish the job and that you'll work on his job for as long as he wants.

Let's say that you finish designing and programming a website for your client and upload it online. You send the client an e-mail saying the website is complete, and they reply back, "We love the new website, but when are you going to get around to setting up the e-mail accounts?"

You didn't say anything about e-mail accounts in your contract, so do you tell your client that you'd be happy to set up their e-mail accounts if they pay you a little extra money or do you set up the e-mail accounts for free because it is easier to just suck it up than risk letting your client down?

Pretend for a minute that you decide to set up your client's e-mail accounts for free because you don't want to risk damaging your business relationship. Even though you never really agreed to do this work in your contract, you try to be helpful. But you soon discover a problem that will take you an additional day or two to fix. What do you do now? Do you still perform the service at no cost to your client?

This is why a contract is so important when it comes to "misunderstandings"— like who is responsible for what and when does that responsibility end? Neither party in the example above was trying to take advantage of the other, but clearly some responsibilities were unclear. When these issues occur (and they will), the best policy is to have a polite and direct conversation with your client—clear and direct communication is key. Pick up the phone and talk to your client to save time if the situation would require you to write a lengthy e-mail.

Plan and budget: This allows your client to see how long you estimate it will take to accomplish the various phases of the project; however, this is not an à la carte menu that your client can "pick and choose" from. Your client may offer suggestions about how to reduce your time (e.g. they see you have two hours accounted for photography, but tell you it's okay for your to purchase stock photography instead). But your client should not expect you to eliminate time spent on researching the problem, ideating, or sketching potential solutions.

Your costs to do the specified job are also included at the bottom of this section, but any additional expenses you incur will be added to this amount. For example, if you had to purchase a typeface, this amount would be added to their bill.

If expenses are beginning to add up, it might be a good idea to inform your client so that he or she will not be caught off guard when your invoice arrives. I prefer contacting my clients by e-mail and letting them know about expenses periodically because it gives me a written record of my attempts to keep the client in the loop and eliminates the element of surprise.

Sketches: This determines the number of sketches that are included in your price, and the price you will charge if the client exceeds this number. Having this in your contract will help reduce the frustration of working with a client who doesn't know what they want, but will "know a good solution when they see it." Putting a limit on the number of sketches that you're willing to complete let's your clients know that they need to look at your sketches with a critical eye and make constructive comments that are likely to lead you to a solution.

Final artwork: Once you're at a point where the job is complete, you will give the client a mock-up or final artwork to approve. Usually the client will sign the mock-up and a Proof Approval form that states that any changes or revisions from this point forward will be at their expense (not yours). Before signing the Proof Approval form the client will need to carefully proofread and review the mock-up. The form states that the client acknowledges that the designer's job has been fulfilled.

Rights: This is a topic that usually generates questions from my students. This section of your contract basically states that once clients have paid you, they have the right to use your design. This does not mean, that your client has the rights to the digital files that you created, unless you agree to turn these files over when the project is completed.

For example, you may create a print advertisement for a client and give him a PDF file. Let's say down the road your client changes his business location and asks you to send him the InDesign document you used to create the advertisement. You could give him your file out of the kindness of your heart, ask him to pay your for the files because the files belong to you, or offer to make the changes he needs for a small fee. Your client may not be happy to hear that he will have to pay you more money to update his advertisement, but unless the rights to the source files were specified in your contract, you are legally in the clear. I generally try to work out a fair arrangement with clients, but I will not go out of my way to help them if they aren't current with their accounts.

It's a good idea to discuss rights and ownership with your client prior to this situation coming up because your client may feel that he paid you to create these files; therefore, the files belong to him. Rather than potentially straining a business relationship, explain this section to your client up front, and if they want your digital files along with the rights to use these files then charge him a bit more for this convenience.

Typically, once the you turn these files over to the client, the client has little need to use you again for that project. If the you retain the files, then you may get residual work from time to time to update the files or make a small changes. This is usually quick work for the you because you are already familiar with the project and can usually make changes quickly and easily.

While you might make careful and intentional design decisions, once your clients get your files, they may make last-minute decisions without your input, and these decisions may reflect poor design judgment (like choosing an inappropriate typeface). For this reason, if your client negotiates the rights to use the work and keep your digital files, your fee for completing the project should increase. Knowing that your client could potentially make poor design decisions and ruin your design, you may have to mentally prepare yourself to walk away from the project after completing it.

Credit: It's a courtesy when your client allows you to put a credit line on his job because it may help you generate business. Depending on the size of the project you're working on, there may not be enough room to add in a credit line, while other times space is not an issue. Placing a credit line on a job is a small detail in the grand scheme of things, and not one that I usually spend much time thinking about unless I'm doing the job pro bono (free). When I work pro bono, I want to be recognized for my contribution because I won't get compensated financially for my services.

Unless the job has incredible exposure, like a very large print run for a large audience or a high-traffic website, I won't reduce my prices to add in a credit line. My sentiment is that, while I appreciate the client allowing me to promote my business, I can promote my business on my own, and I'd rather have the money in the bank than a credit line at the bottom of my client's job. Unless you sign a nondisclosure agreement with your client or agree to a privacy statement, you can put examples of the work you did for your client in your portfolio and generate your own publicity while still getting paid full price for your services.

Overtime: When you are required to work more than forty hours a week to complete a job at your client's request, you should be compensated for your efforts. The overtime section addresses what kind of work is considered "overtime" and how much you will be compensated for going above and beyond.

Billable items: This section of the contract states that you will be compensated for the money you spend on items like shipping expenses and other incidental charges that are necessary to complete the project. If you need to hire a photographer or illustrator, you would itemize this expense on your invoice and your client would reimburse you. Keeping clients in the loop when it comes to additional expenses prevents them from trying to bargain with you when they receive your invoice because the amount of your invoice may be higher than what you originally quoted.

Purchasing: Occasionally, you will have to spend money to complete a job for your client. Legitimate purchasing expenses should be paid for by your client and not come out of your profits. Obviously, you should not charge your client for items that are not directly related to their project (like office supplies for your company), but if you have to purchase stock photography or a font, your client should reimburse you for these items. Once you are reimbursed for these items, your client owns them, so do not reuse the photograph that you purchased for your client—this would be unethical.

When I need to make a large purchase on my client's behalf, I look for the best product at the lowest price. I try to obtain several quotes to choose from, and then ask the client which option he prefers. If I need to purchase a piece of stock photography, I might look for an image on a few stock photography websites and let the client weigh in on which company to use. Usually the client will defer to me, but sometimes the client will surprise me and offer a suggestion or opinion that I hadn't considered.

I like asking my clients to get involved with decisions like these because they become invested in seeing the project succeed, and they begin to learn a little bit in the process. You certainly don't want to appear as if you can't make a decision on your own by asking your clients a million questions, but asking them a few strategic questions here and there lets them know that you value their input, that their project has your full attention, and that you are conscious of their budgetary limitations.

Scheduling of payment: When you finish a job and deliver it to your client, there usually isn't a check waiting for you. Most businesses normally take between thirty and ninety days to pay their bills, which can really hurt a young business if you really need the money to stay afloat. Waiting up to three months to get paid can seem like an eternity, but you can help speed the process up by specifying how long your client has to settle his account after you've finished the project in your contract. I typically allow my clients thirty to forty-five days to settle their balance and then add a small amount of interest to the unpaid balance after this date. This way the client feels a small sense of urgency to settle the account in a timely manner.

It's a good strategy to avoid going into debt as much as possible, so I require my clients to pay 50 percent of my estimate up front before I begin working on a job. I sometimes have to hire a copywriter or purchase items to complete the job for the client, and I do not want to carry around this debt until the client pays me. A 50 percent deposit when a project is launched helps offset many of my expenses.

Collecting 50 percent of the estimate up front also helps cut down on clients who want to hire you to work on a project, but then drag their feet because they don't have the money to pay you when you finish the project. It also helps reduce the number of projects that get "killed" before they ever see the light of day, which is discussed in more detail below.

Termination policy: If both you and your client agree to walk away from a project and terminate the contract, you will need a written document specifying the details, and both parties will need to sign the document. This releases you from performing the service and the client for paying for these services.

On occasion, a project may be "killed," or eliminated, because of a budget reduction, time constraint, or other external factors, which can be problematic if you already have already invested time or money working on a particular project.

Having a termination policy in your contract keeps you from not being paid for the time you spent working on the client's project and allows you to recover any expenses you incurred. If I were hired to do a booklet for the local theater company and began the project while unbeknownst to me some of their expensive stage lights malfunctioned and needed to be replaced, the theater director may choose to "kill" the booklet project he had planned on hiring me to create in order to divert this money to purchasing a new set of stage lights. Having a kill fee in my contract allows me to collect money for the time I spent on the project even though the booklet was never completed, and it keeps me from walking away from the deal empty-handed. Your client may not realize that you may have turned down other clients in order to work on his job and that you shouldn't feel the pinch financially because of his malfunctioning lights. A kill fee is designed to cover you in case your client's priorities shift.

Terms of proposal: Specify the length of time your client has to sign the contract and how long your quote is good for. Your client should have a specific length of time to accept your proposal before the contract becomes invalid.

Signature: Without the designer and client signatures on your contract, it isn't a legally binding document. If you started an LLC, you need to write your business's name where the designer would normally sign and then print your name on the line below this one. This insures that the contract is between your business and client, and not you personally. It's a good idea to make a copy of the entire contract and give one to your client and keep one yourself in case you need to refer back to it later. Make sure that you store your contract and other documents in a safe place in case you need to refer to them again in the future.

Meeting Your Client

It's exciting to work with a client for the first time. I remember feeling very nervous when I saw my client pull up outside the coffee shop where we were meeting. There's really nothing to be anxious about, and as you get more comfortable meeting new clients, the feelings of butterflies in your stomach will eventually go away.

Since your first client is someone you know or are already familiar with, you probably won't feel terribly nervous, but this is a great opportunity to practice being professional. Below are a few tips for you to consider when you meet your clients for the first time.

Where to meet: I love meeting clients at coffee shops, especially at a time when they aren't crowded. I'll happily buy a client a cup of coffee and let him sip it as I go over the contract and ask questions about the project. I like coffee houses because they smell good, they usually have free wifi, and they are usually decorated artistically and help to put the client in a creative mind-set. I try to schedule my meetings at a time other than peak business times, and I try and meet at places that will not make my client smell like a french fry when they leave.

I try and avoid lunch meetings because I don't want my client to have to eat and talk at the same time. To be honest, I'm also a little cheap and don't want to have to pay for a client's lunch, which will eat into my profits! A cup of coffee or tea is considerably less expensive than a meal and is still appreciated.

Arrive at your meeting place a few minutes early to reserve a table that is out of the way and quiet, but do not place your order until your client arrives. Ideally, you will want to choose a table where your client can find you quickly and easily and yet is quiet enough to have a normal conversation without having to yell. If your client prefers to meet you at his office or a location that is more convenient for him, make sure you get directions as well as your client's cell phone number in case something causes you to run late. In many cases, it's small things like letting your client know if you're unavoidably late that can help you save face with a client if you run into problems.

How to dress: You should dress comfortably but not too casual. Make sure your clothes aren't worn out, frayed, or too revealing (even if it's the latest style). You need to instill feelings of competence and show that you pay attention to details, so dress in a way that makes you look capable, competent, and trustworthy.

You may be in your late teens or early twenties, so you'll want to dress in a way that reinforces your creativity (maybe wear a unique piece of jewelry), your intellect (a blouse or button up shirt), and attention to detail (well manicured, haircut, clean shaven, ironed clothes, etc.). You want to make your client feel comfortable around you, so don't wear a suit and tie—this is too formal! Shoot for the middle ground and aim for a business casual look.

What to bring: The first time that you meet with your client, you should bring two copies of your contract (with as much of the information as possible already filled in), a note pad, and two pens. If your client has forgotten to bring a pen to sign your contract or to take notes, offer him one of your pens to use.

Sometimes a quick sketch or brainstorming session can open up a conversation and help you identify a direction to begin exploring. Since you have your client right in front of you, jot down a few ideas, but make sure you listen to what your client says and try to determine what a successful solution might look like. While your client is talking about the project, jot down keywords, phrases, and details. I have a horrible memory and often forget details, so I always take notes and refer back to them later to refresh my memory.

What to say: When your client arrives, give him a big smile and a firm handshake. Thank him for taking the time to meet with you and tell him that you're looking forward to working with him on his project. Ask how his day is going and offer to buy him a cup of coffee or tea.

Once you're seated and have transitioned into business mode, ask your client to explain his project to you—especially the goals of the project. Take notes as he describes the work he needs you to do, and if you need him to explain something in greater detail, be sure to ask. Make sure you ask your client to explain who the audience is, what the project goal is, and when the project is due. It's easier for your client to explain something to you now (while you have his full attention) than it will be for him to explain it again over the phone or in an e-mail later. Make sure you take advantage of your client's time by getting all the information you can to complete the project.

Once you've finished your conversation and had your questions answered, thank your client for his time again and tell the client when he can expect to hear back from you to look at some sketches. This will be your first deadline, so make sure you give yourself enough time to do a great job.

When the meeting has concluded, shake your client's hand again and tell him that you'll work up some sketches for him to look over. You will probably need your client's input, so prepare him for this now by saying something like, "I'll sketch out some ideas for you to look over with me next week in order to confirm that you like my direction. Do you want me to call you on Monday to set up a time that's convenient for you to meet with me?"

Creating Your Sketches and Concepts

When you first sit down to sketch, your goal should be to generate as many ideas as possible. You should refrain from self-editing and sketch out your good ideas, okay ideas, and bad ideas. Your sketches don't have to be done on the computer or even particularly well drawn or shaded, but they should be able to communicate your approach to solving your client's need. In these early sketches you're trying to attack the problem from various angles and looking at possible solutions through a variety of lenses.

Once you've finished brainstorming and sketching, pick three of the sketches that meet your client's need the best and sketch them again. Put each sketch own its own piece of paper. While you are redrawing your sketch, clean it up and add

SKETCHES AND CONCEPTS FOR PEACH STONE

Anne Jordan and Meaghan Dee combined forces to create this cover for "The Peach Stone," a short story by Paul Horgan. Anne comments, "We chose leaves as a visual metaphor for life and death, the changing of seasons, and the precious nature of human life. We laser cut typography into leaves we collected, using the element of fire itself to form the title so the words emerge organically."

Ideation and exploration allows designers to test the communicative value of a particular direction, adopt design principles to achieve project goals, and provide an opportunity to make new discoveries. Your sketches don't necessarily have to be done with a pen or pencil, but it's important to choose a medium that allows you to be loose and gestural. The point of the sketching phase is to generate as many ideas as possible and then identify the best ideas—the key to

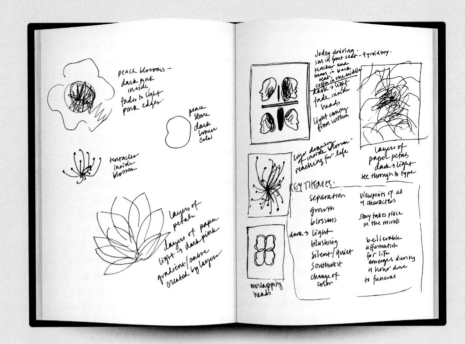

sketching and brainstorming is to not self-edit. Editing and refining your ideas comes during the next phase. Just keep generating options for now. Continue to ideate as long as your time constraints allow. After you have spent a reasonable amount of time on the exploration, begin refining your ideas by taking all of your sketches that show promise and developing a series of more refined sketches. You can continue to experiment, but start folding more of your project constraints and design considerations into the mix as you go.

At periodic intervals, test the value of your direction, and notice if a trajectory towards a solution begins to emerge. If so, this will be a key point for you to discuss with your client during your next meeting.

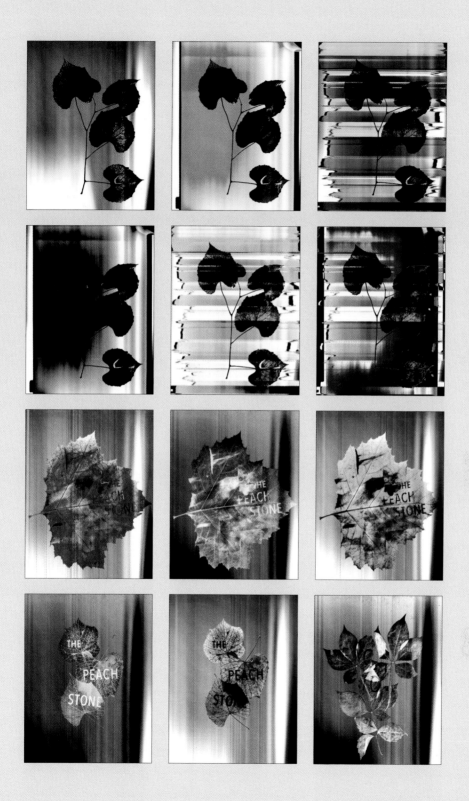

a bit more detail and information about your concept. You might begin to think about your color palette, typefaces, and other design considerations as you are finishing up the sketches that you will show the client.

After you're finished, put the three best concepts in a large envelope or folder along with all your other sketches (do not fold your sketches) and call your client to make an appointment to discuss your initial concepts and get his feedback.

Showing Your Client Your Concepts

Similar to when you first met your client, greet him warmly and then tell him that you have some sketches to show him and you'd like his feedback. Once you're settled and have your client's attention, remove your sketches from the large envelop or folder (one sketch at a time) and talk about that particular concept. Let your client look at each sketch for a minute and take it in before sharing your next sketch with him. After you've shown a sketch, leave it on the table face up, so he can continue to look at the work and see all your sketches at the same time.

Hopefully, your client will like one of your sketches and suggest that you go in a particular direction. Be ready with your pad of paper and pen to take any notes, suggestions, or criticism that your client offers. Talk to your client about the potential pros and cons of each concept and how you think the audience might react to the piece. If the client criticizes something about your work, try not to get defensive. Ask him to explain his point of view and try to address or defuse these issues if you need to rework your sketches.

Typically, one sketch will emerge as the most successful concept, so try to pick up on this quickly and focus the conversation on getting more feedback about this particular concept. If for some reason you client doesn't like your three sketches, pull out all of your other thumbnail sketches and let your client take a look through them.

I advise that you only let your clients look at your other sketches if they are disappointed with your top three sketches. Sometimes, too many options can overwhelm the client and make it extremely difficult for them to make a decision. Sometimes, when clients see many thumbnail sketches, they want you to "Frankenstein" a sketch instead of picking a direction. What I'm referring to here is grabbing parts of several sketches and trying to stitch them together to make an entirely new concept. Similar to how Frankenstein was the equivalent to a human abomination in the movie, graphic design solutions made this way are often visually confusing and don't do a great job of communicating a message clearly to an audience. To avoid this, ask your client to pick two or three of their favorite thumbnail sketches and explain what he liked about these sketches in particular. Then use this information to create an entirely new series of sketches and meet with your client again to discuss your concepts again.

If your client liked one of your three sketches (which hopefully is the case), then it's time to begin finalizing your solution. Ask your client how soon he needs to see a first proof and what form he'd like to see it in? Does he want you to bring a color print, a full- or half-sized mock-up, or a PDF file on a USB drive? Try to avoid sending a digital file of your proof in lieu of delivering it in person if possible. You will want to be present when your client sees the proof so that you can gauge his reaction to your work, take notes on any comments or suggestions your client might have, and make sure you understand what you need to do from this point forward.

Delivering Your Proof

Similar to the last several times you've met your client, you need to dress appropriately, give your client a warm greeting when you meet, bring a mock-up of your solution, and fill out and print a Proof Approval Form with you—but keep this form hidden for now. After you've gained your client's attention and are free from distractions, remove your proof from its envelope or folder and hand it to the client. Be prepared to write down your client's feedback on a sheet of paper (or directly on the proof) so that you will be able to remember his requests.

If your client doesn't like your solution or has major changes, your immediate goal is to understand what he doesn't like about your solution and assure him that you will make the appropriate changes. The worst thing you can do is to not know what the client wants and have to guess at what needs to be done next. Perhaps your client has an image in his head that he is having a difficult time communicating to you, or perhaps you misunderstood the goals of the project or made more errors than you care to admit. You may feel a bit frustrated, but it's important to have a good attitude. Reassure your client that this is all part of the design process, and work hard to deliver a product that will meet his needs.

If the client wants you to make major changes or revisions, take good notes to make the changes requested. Tell your client that you will bring a Proof Approval Form with you for him to sign the next time you meet. This way you will have a chance to address your client's major concerns first, and the client will be asked to articulate any additional changes in writing when you meet again. You and your client both want the same thing, to finish the job and feel good about the work. Your Proof Approval Form is a good tool to help you to accomplish this goal. It's important to balance being helpful against trying to match an obscure picture in your client's head. By making the changes he requested and bringing this form with you the next time you meet, you are likely to expedite the revision process and finish the project to your client's satisfaction.

If your client likes your solution, but has a few small suggestions or changes, pull out your Proof Approval Form from your large envelope or folder and pass it to your client and explain the purpose of the form. Tell your client that it's very important that he look over your work and make note of any changes or revisions he wants done. If he has revisions, then he needs to check "Option 01" on the Proof Approval Form and write out the changes he would like to make in the space provided on the form or on the mock-up you brought with you. If he needs additional room to list the changes, he can flip the form over and use the back side or use an additional piece of paper.

Once your client gives you this form, you will need to make all the changes requested and give him a final proof to review. I usually try to do this within the next twenty-four to forty-eight hours whenever possible. When the work is complete, I make a new proof and bring a fresh Proof Approval Form for the client to sign. This time there hopefully won't be any changes or revisions, so show him that you've made all the corrections he requested and that he needs to carefully read and check "Option 02" on the form, sign and date the document, and return it to you.

If your client likes your solution and has no changes, then job well done! This is the best possible scenario. Even though your client doesn't have any changes, you still need him to sign the Proof Approval Form that you brought with you. Take out this document and ask your client to read and check "Option 02" to verify that he doesn't require any changes and have him sign and date the form at the bottom of the page.

By checking and signing Option 02, your client is stating that he releases you from design and content mistakes and that if any additional work is required, it may be subject to additional charges. When your client signs this document, he is stating that the job is finished to his satisfaction and ready to complete.

Proof Approval Form

Today's Date

Client's Name
Client's Address
City, State Zip Code

PROJECT: The name of the project ie.) T-shirt Design
This proof is provided as a way for you, the client, to check the design and accuracy of your project before it is put into production. Please check all aspects of the project including layout, design, spelling, colors, and your contact information. When you are finished reviewing the project, please fill out one of the options below and return this form to <insert your company name> with the proof by <insert the date you need the proof returned> in order to make a final round of changes or begin production.

OPTION 01:
I verify that I, as an authorized representative of the client named above, have reviewed and approved this project. I understand that any changes requested after this project is put into production, whether due to mistakes or preferences, may incur an additional charge. I also acknowledge that mistakes or preferences that are not discovered and specified at this time are not the responsibility of <insert your company name>. I accept full responsibility and authorize <insert your company name> to put this project into production.

_____   _____
Signature of Authorized Representative   Date

OPTION 02:
I would like the following items to be changed and would like <insert your company name> to submit a new proof. Please write directly on the mockup or describe your changes below.

_____
_____
_____
_____
_____
_____
_____
_____
_____
_____
_____
_____

YOUR COMPANY
123 Anywhere Street
City, State ZIP Code
(555) 555-5555

PROOF APPROVAL FORM *(See page VIII for download instructions)*
The Proof Approval Form is an extremely valuable document to the designer because it gives your client a chance to list any changes that are required to the job, and it also releases you from mistakes or changes in preference. It's important that your clients look over this form and read it carefully before signing it because it basically acknowledges that the design is complete.

Delivering the Final Product

Once your client has signed off on the Proof Approval Form, you'll need to make arrangements to output and/or deliver the job. While the design part of your job is over as soon as your client signs the Proof Approval Form, you're not finished completely just yet; you have to get the job into the right person's hands now.

Internal work: If you agreed to produce the piece yourself, for example printing one hundred flyers for your client, then you need to make sure that the product you deliver looks exactly like the proof your client signed off on. Be sure to check that your colors haven't shifted and that everything matches the proof that your client signed. Once you've finished producing the work, package up everything neatly and promptly deliver the job to your client, along with your invoice.

External work: If you agreed to send the job to print or deliver it to someone else, then it's important that you call and talk with this person or company and ask how the files should be prepared. You may receive a bill from the vendor if they have to go back and fix or edit your files. Usually a quick phone call or Internet search is all you'll need to find out how the vendor wants the files prepared. Prepare your files in a way that is compatible with the vendor's specifications.

If the files you prepared are going to be printed, you would normally convert any images you used to CMYK color mode and make sure they are at least 300dpi to avoid their being pixilated or blurry. Some printers will ask for your native files and all the fonts, images, and artwork that you used. Other printers want you to send them an Adobe PDF file, which automatically packages the images and fonts that you used to create the file. If this is the case, then ask them if they want you to use a bleed and/or include crop marks or color information in your PDF document.

I'm happy to make all the printing arrangements on my clients behalf, but I charge them a 15 percent fee to do so. It takes time to get printing quotes, prepare files to the printer's specifications, and check their work. This fee also includes making sure that the job has been printed correctly and working with the printer if any errors occur. Most of the time a job gets printed successfully, but sometimes I might have to spend extra time on a job if something doesn't go as planned.

If you're creating files for the Web, then you would normally convert any images you used to RGB color mode and save the images at 72dpi. You will also need to make sure that none of your file names contain spaces or odd characters that are not Web compliant.

TriAdventure: Postcard Campaign

DESCRIPTION	08:00 - 08:15	08:15 - 08:30	08:30 - 08:45	08:45 - 09:00	09:00 - 09:15	09:15 - 09:30	09:30 - 09:45	09:45 - 10
Analysis	X	X	X	X				
Research						X	X	X
Development	X	X	X	X	X	X	X	X
Implementation						X	X	X
Testing			X	X	X			
tion								

TIME SHEET *(See page VIII for download instructions)*

Keeping track of where you spend your time is necessary in order to make sure you get compensated for the time you spend working on a project, but it's also a way to help you be more profitable in the long run. When someone asks, "How much do you charge to design a business card?" you can look back through the time sheets of similar jobs and come up with a number that is likely to reflect the length of time it will take you to complete. Keeping track of this data gives you a more accurate way of estimating your prices and will help you maintain profitability. Of course, each project will probably have unique constraints for you to consider, but having a average to work with can be extremely helpful.

I keep my time sheets as an internal document; meaning I don't give them to my client when I finish a project. However, I use a lot of the information I collect on my time sheets in the invoice that I give to my client when the job is complete.

If you write a clear and succinct description of what you were working on and for how long, then writing an invoice will be a snap. Being accurate when quoting jobs is an important tool of maintaining business profitability, and it is a quality that all companies try to become more proficient at over time. Keep track of your hours as you freelance because this data is important.

Sending an Invoice

Once you have successfully delivered the job, it's time to send your client the bill and get paid! Filling out the Invoice Form is relatively straightforward, and you can get a lot of information right from your time sheet. Simply fill out the client and job information, write a description of your services, and include an itemized list of any purchases or expenses you made on your client's behalf.

The money you collect should go into the Business Checking Account you opened (described in an earlier chapter), and you need to set aside around 30 percent of this money for taxes. The remaining 70 percent can be used to pay yourself for your work, pay off any debt or bills you've accumulated, or accrue in your account until you need to use it. Just make sure not to withdraw cash (you will need a paper trail to show where the money goes). If you want to pay yourself for your time and effort, write yourself a check—do not withdraw cash!

Lather, Rinse, Repeat

Congratulations on completing your first official freelance project! Hopefully, you have a better idea about how the system works. If you decide to work with other clients, we'll look for ways to improve your efficiency and reduce your costs to improve your profitability.

Don't forget to save examples of your graphic design work, so that you can put them in your portfolio and use them to find more clients and promote yourself. I usually try to keep between five and ten samples from all my freelance jobs (and it's always a good idea to save your sketches). Tuck this work away in a safe spot and keep it nice and safe because you may need them again someday. Sometimes I look back through my collection of samples and they stir memories of bad clients, great colleagues, tough breaks, outstanding successes, and expensive lessons that were learned the hard way. Your samples can also help you when you go to put your portfolio together in your senior year. So save your work and sketches along the way.

Beginner Checklist
- ☐ Purchase the equipment you will need for school and your business.
- ☐ Familiarize yourself with how to use a Job Proposal, Time sheet, Proof Approval and Invoice forms.
- ☐ Successfully work with a paying client.

Invoice of Services

Today's Date

Client's Name
Client's Address
City, State Zip Code

Shipping Address (if different)
Client's Phone: (540) 555-5555
Invoice Number: XXXXX-XXX

Thank you for choosing <insert your business name>. Your business is appreciated, and it is a
pleasure serving you. Feel free to call us if you have any questions or concerns about the <insert
project name> that was recently completed.

Please make checks payable to <insert your business name>.

DESCRIPTION		AMOUNT
Concept Development		$ XX.XX
Design Development		$ XX.XX
Production		$ XX.XX
Project Implementation		$ XX.XX
	INITIAL DEPOSIT:	$ XX.XX
	REMAINING BALANCE:	$ XX.XX
	SHIPPING:	$ XX.XX
	TAX:	$ XX.XX
	TOTAL	$ XX.XX

TERMS
Invoices are payable within 30 days of receipt. Design documents including, but not limited to,
sketches, proofs, designs, illustrations, photography, models, and all other design documents
are the exclusive property of the <insert your business name>. Upon full payment of all fees and
costs, <insert your client's name> is granted the right to use the designs as specified. Rights
transferred are limited to: <insert your client's name>.

All other rights remain the exclusive property of <insert your business name>.

YOUR COMPANY
123 Anywhere Street
City, State ZIP Code
(555) 555-5555

INVOICE OF SERVICES *(See page VIII for download instructions)*
Creating an invoice for your services is quick to fill out and easy to complete.
You'll need to gather a few bits of information about the project and describe
what you spent your time and energy on. If you collected 50 percent of your estimated cost up front, don't forget to deduct this amount from the balance due,
and don't forget to add in any expenses or purchases you made.

Gaining Momentum

6

Goals for Intermediate Level Freelancers

Now that you have your freelance company going, purchased your basic computer equipment, and successfully worked with your first client, it's time to build upon your successes. None of your Intermediate freelance goals should be too hard for you to accomplish, so pace yourself. Don't spread yourself too thin by trying to do too much at once. Your schooling should still take priority over your freelance endeavors, but you can continue to fold your academic lessons in with your freelance experiences by using good time management techniques.

As you gain more confidence in school and freelancing, you'll begin to see trends in how you attack problems and your visual voice (or style) will become more pronounced. Having a unique style is a good thing because it will help your work stand out from your classmates' efforts.

The Intermediate level is about gaining momentum with your confidence and experiences, so don't be shy about working on freelance projects as long as you don't let them interfere with your academic work. You can't fake experience, and you're going to begin working on projects that have the potential to make it into your portfolio. So grab a Red Bull and get pumped up. It's time for you to eat, breathe, and sleep graphic design! The work you produce is likely to be some of your best work to date, and you will need to produce enough work to help you fill your portfolio.

The biggest expenses at the Intermediate level is purchasing a digital camera and expanding your font collection. Make sure that you take, or have taken, a photography class in order to learn to use your equipment properly and take full advantage of your investment. Not only will good photography skills help you in your classes, but they will be helpful in your freelance career as well.

Here are a few goals that you should try to complete at the Intermediate level.

- Work with five clients, including a nonprofit organization, a small-business owner, and a client who will barter services or goods with you
- Create an online presence and business card for your company
- Improve the work flow of your business
- Document your process work
- Land an internship

Equipment to Purchase

DIGITAL SLR CAMERA

Your digital camera is going to be the largest investment at the Intermediate level, and it will help you begin to integrate more photography into your graphic design work. The ability to work with images is particularly important, and learning to master your Digital Single Lens Reflex (DSLR) camera will take some time.

I recommend that you purchase a mid-level DSLR camera instead of a compact digital camera. A DSLR camera will allow you to change the lenses so you can add micro, macro, telephoto, wide angle, and other lenses. Knowing which lenses work best in a given set of conditions is important in producing a specific photographic effect.

A DSLR camera allows you to see what the lens sees when you look through the viewfinder. DSLR cameras have large image sensors that produce high-quality photos and don't take as long between pressing the shutter release button and capturing the data as compact digital cameras do. A DSLR camera will give you more control, a faster framer rate, and more flexibility when taking pictures continuously. Even though the initial cost is higher than a compact digital camera, your up-front costs will be money well spent because DSLR cameras can continue to be upgraded as your photography skills improve.

When you begin your search for the perfect DSLR camera, talk to faculty at your school to see if there is a particular brand or model that is required for your program. In many cases your instructor can recommend a particular brand or a local merchant who can help you find the best camera for your money.

It's easy to get confused by technical jargon when shopping for a DSLR camera, so here are a few aspects of DSLR cameras that you might consider before picking the one that's right for you.

INTERMEDIATE LEVEL

• **Megapixels:** Cameras with more megapixels allow you to make large prints, but just because a camera has a lot of megapixels it doesn't mean it's better than other cameras. Often, cameras with high megapixels cost more, but the most notable difference is file size. If you purchase a 14-megapixel camera, but only print 5"x 7" images, then you've wasted a lot of money because you didn't need to purchase such a high-end camera. You need to find a balance between finding an affordable camera and a camera that will suit your needs. It's fine to use to scale down your images when you need to, but scaling your images up doesn't work very well. If you shoot with a 4-megapixel camera, a 4" x 6" photo will be perfectly clear, but when it's printed at 11" x 14" it will lose its image quality. I recommend you purchase a 10- to 12-megapixel camera unless you find a really great deal on a higher megapixel camera. For most situations that you'll find yourself in, a 10- to 12-megapixel camera will be able to do everything you need your camera to do.

• **Match the camera to how you plan to use it:** If you're planning to shoot in low light situations, look for a camera with the best possible ISO performance to eliminate noise in your photographs. Perhaps also look for a camera that offers some kind of internal image stabilization feature. Conversely, if you plan on shooting in a studio, portrait, or macro work, a camera with a "live view" function might be a good feature for you to consider. Having an LCD screen on the back of the camera really helps when you're working in a studio. It allows you to stand upright rather than having to bend over and look through your camera's viewfinder to compose your shots. This will save you from a backache from having to bend over for long periods of time to look through your camera's viewfinder.

• **Do you already own a camera?** If so, you may want to stick to the same brand because sometimes you can use SLR lenses on a DSLR camera. This is something worth checking out before you buy a different brand of camera. Make sure that you buy a full-frame digital camera or your lenses may produce very different results on your digital camera.

• **Size, weight, durability, and menus:** It might seem obvious, but if you can't use your camera's features, then you aren't using it to its full potential. Make sure to take some time to play with the camera's interface, and make sure you understand the camera's interface. If you plan to shoot in harsh conditions, look for a camera with some kind of weatherproofing. If you prefer to travel light, look for a lightweight camera so that you won't have to lug a heavy camera around with you all the time. In a nutshell, you should choose a camera that has an easy to understand interface and is a good match for the environment you will be taking pictures in.

• **File formats:** There are two file formats that are helpful to shoot in: Your DSLR camera should be able to shoot in both JPG and RAW formats. JPG files are usually smaller in size and can be viewed, shared, and edited easily. JPGs are files that are processed and compressed in the camera, while RAW images are unprocessed and must be edited on a computer. RAW files are basically the equivalent of a digital negative that is unprocessed. You can make adjustments before you finalize your image.

PANTONE COLOR BRIDGE

As you get more comfortable designing, matching colors will become increasingly important to you and your clients. Pantone is a company that developed a color matching system that is used by printers and designers. The Pantone color guides allow designers to select, specify, and match colors closely. As you will learn, some colors translate well into four-color process work (CMYK) and others do not. The Pantone Color Bridge Book helps take the guesswork out of what to expect when you specify certain colors on your print jobs. I recommend shopping around on the Internet to find the best price on the Pantone Color Bridge Book because it's unlikely that you'll find a better deal in your local art supply store or campus bookstore.

FONTS

Purchasing fonts individually can get expensive quickly. I advise you to purchase a font collection at first, and then add fonts to your collection over time. In the book, *Typographic Specimens: The Great Typefaces,* authored by Philip Meggs and Rob Carter, the authors surveyed over one hundred prominent designers to see what typefaces were timeless. When the results came back the following typefaces were identified.

• Baskerville	• Franklin Gothic	• Goudy Old Style	• Sabon
• Bembo	• Frutiger	• Helvetica	• Times New Roman
• Bodoni	• Futura	• News Gothic	• Univers
• Caslon	• Garamond	• Palatino	
• Centaur	• Gill Sans	• Perpetua	

When you look for a font collection, you may want to look for one that includes some of the typefaces listed above. Type collections can range in price from $59 to $3,000 or be purchased individually for $25 to $50 for each type style. While you're shopping for typefaces don't just look for expressive typefaces. Keep in mind that you'll need options for body copy in both serifs and sans serifs. Sometimes, a typeface that is well drawn and readable is all that's needed to complete the job, while other occasions call for a more expressive typeface. You should look for a collection that includes both types of fonts to start your collection.

You can look for package deals from type foundries like Adobe, Bitstream, Linotype, P22, T26, Agfa, ITC, and Emigre. In addition, there are a variety of websites online where you can download free fonts. However, use caution! Sometimes these fonts have been poorly drawn, missing key glyphs, or can sometimes cause Post Script errors that may cause your document to crash or print incorrectly. Be sure to test any free fonts you download well in advance of any deadlines you might have, so that you will have time to troubleshoot if something doesn't work as planned.

PHOTO SCANNER

Depending on your needs, you might consider picking up an inexpensive scanner. There are a variety of good scanners to choose from for less than $100. If you decide to purchase a scanner, look for one with a scanning resolution of at least 600 dpi by 1200dpi, the ability to scan in 24-bit color, and a scanning bed size of 8.5" x 11" or larger. Some scanners come bundled with Optical Character Recognition (OCR) software that allows you to scan the image of a page of text and convert the image into actual text. Other scanners have transparency and film-scanning capabilities that allow you to scan slides, transparencies, and film negatives, which can be useful at times. But I don't use find myself using these features very often, so don't get sucked into paying for scanner options that you are unlikely to use.

For the most part, you'll use your scanner to scan in sketches and textures, old photographs, and documents you want to archive. Wait until you find a good deal on a photo scanner before making your purchase.

GRAPHICS TABLET

Depending on how you prefer to work, you might consider purchasing a graphics tablet. This device allows you to use a stylus to draw in certain software programs. Wacom is one of the best-known graphics tablet manufacturers, but there are other companies around that make high-quality products also. One nice feature of a graphic tablet is the ability to lay a photograph over the tablet surface and trace an image directly into Photoshop, Illustrator, or other software program, as well as varying your line weight when you press one the graphics tablet surface.

• **Size:** Size is one of the first factors to consider when choosing a graphics tablet. The most common dimensions are 4"x 5"and 6"x 8" tablets, but there are also larger tablets available. Of course, the larger your tablet, the more expensive it will be, so test out several sizes and see what works best for you before making a purchase. Contrary to what you might think, bigger isn't necessarily better when it comes to graphic tablets. Choose a size that fits how you plan to use your graphics tablet, as well as your budget, and don't just purchase the biggest tablet you can find.

• **Pen/stylus:** Your tablet should come with a pen that feels comfortable and natural in your hand. Check to find out if your stylus requires batteries or if it's tethered to the tablet with a cord. Many pens will have a switch or buttons built into the pen, and some have an eraser at the end. The button on your pen can usually be programmed for specific functions or automatically activate the eraser tool. You'll want to choose a pen/stylus that matches your ergonomic preference and is easy to program and use.

• **Pressure sensitivity:** Pressure sensitivity refers to the pressure on the surface of the tablet. Most tablets have either 256, 512, or 1,024 levels of pressure sensitivity. Pressure sensitivity can be set up to control variables like thickness, transparency, or color, and the tablet can be programmed to act very similarly to a variety of mediums like charcoal, ink, watercolors, airbrush, and so forth to get the type of effect you're looking for.

How Do You Find Clients?

One of your goals at the Intermediate level is to work with three completely different types of clients, including a nonprofit organization, a small-business owner, and a client that who will barter with you for your services.

Working with these different types of clients will help give you a better understanding about how clients function and how they make business decisions. You might find yourself talking to a committee rather than a manager or owner when you work for a nonprofit organization. Small-business owners are usually engaged with every facet of their business, and working with them can be challenging because they may be reluctant to give you control. However, a word-of-mouth reference from them can help you drum up more business quickly. Finally, you will barter with a client, and you must determine what your services are worth when you work for products and services instead of money. Bartering with a client will help you discover the value of your graphic design services, and you may have to do some good old-fashioned horse trading in order to negotiate a fair deal. Sometimes compensation doesn't come in dollars and cents, so knowing the value of your services will keep you from getting the short end of the stick. Working with each of these types of clients will challenge and stretch you in ways you can't yet imagine, but the lessons you learn will be priceless.

The best way to find these clients is through word of mouth. If you did a good job for your first client, perhaps they may be interested in using you again for a future project. But let's take a moment to identify other ways you can find additional clients. After you've gone back to your family, friends, teachers, and acquaintances and asked them if they know anybody who is in need of some graphic design services, you might begin your search by reading the local newspaper, talking with local trade groups, and paying attention to e-mail blasts that you've received. You might also consider talking with your city's Chamber of Commerce, Rotary Club, and local charities. You will have to introduce yourself, talk about the services you offer clients, and look for opportunities to make connections to organizations, local businesses, and charities.

Cold-calling a client can be a bit more tricky than having a friend or family member recommend you. Some people would rather spend a day at the dentist's office than spend the day cold-calling clients. However, it doesn't need to be such a painful experience. When you cold-call a client, your conversation should not sound like this:

You: *"Hello, my name is <insert your name here>, and I'm a graphic designer. I was wondering if you needed any graphic design work for your business?"*
Them: *"No, I don't think we need any help right now."*
You: *"Oh well, okay. Thanks.*

Instead of trying to make a sale out of the blue, you should focus on positioning yourself for the opportunity to make a sale. Pick a time to call the business that isn't during a peak business hours and when they might be able to talk to you for a couple of minutes. Instead of trying to make a sale right away, start your call by finding out some information. Remember being patient is key!

You: *"Hello, my name is <insert your name here>, and I am trying to find out what your store hours are?*
Them: *"We are open Monday through Saturday from 10 a.m. to 6 p.m."*

You haven't learned much by asking this question, but you're trying to establish a conversation by asking a question that has an easy answer.

You: *"Are you the owner or manager of <insert the business name here>?"*
Them: *"No, I just work here. The owner usually comes later in the day."*
You: *"Do you think she would be there tomorrow at 3 p.m.?"*
Them: *"Umm, most likely. Would you like to leave a message for her?"*
You: *"Well, I'd really like to speak with the owner for five to ten minutes. Do you think she'd have time to talk with me at 3 p.m. tomorrow?"*
Them: *"Probably. She usually gets in around two and then spends some time taking inventory, so you could probably meet with her around three."*
You: *"That sounds fantastic! What did you say your name was again?"*
Them: *"My name is Scott."*
You: *"And what is the owner's name?"*
Them: *"Her name is Linda."*
You: *"Scott, I really appreciate your time. Have a great day, and thanks for all your help."*

From this conversation we learned that Linda will be at her business tomorrow and can probably meet with you at 3 p.m. and that Scott said that he thought it would be okay to talk with her for five to ten minutes. This is a great start! Now it's time to do a little reconnaissance work about the company and think of a few ideas about how you could help Linda promote her business. Don't just look at Linda's business. Try to think about her competitors too.

If it's possible, then stop by the competition's business and have a look around. You're looking for things that you could use as talking points when you meet with Linda the following day. Does the competition have any literature that you could look at? Do they have business cards or brochures? Do they have a website? How were you greeted when you entered the business? Do they sell the same products or carry a different brand?

The following day you arrive at Linda's business at 3 p.m. looking friendly and dressed nicely. Take a quick look around the business, noting differences from and similarities with the competition's business you scouted out the day before. Then introduce yourself if she isn't extremely busy.

You: *"Hi, my name is <insert your name here>, and I was hoping to talk with Linda. Is she around today?"*

> *"It's estimated that 80 percent of new sales are made after the fifth contact, yet most sales people give up after the second attempt."*

Linda: *"I'm Linda. How may I help you?"*

You: *"I spoke with Scott yesterday and he said I might be able to talk with you for five to ten minutes today. Do you have a moment to spare?"*

Linda: *"Sure, what can I help you with?"*

You: *"I'm a graphic design student at <insert your college here>, and I do some freelance design work on the side. My rates are reasonable, I do great work, and I have a couple of ideas for your business that I'd like to share with your if that's okay?*

Linda: *"What kind of ideas do you have?"*

Here's your chance—this is your opportunity to pitch some of your ideas to Linda and to get her talking. You might mention that you took the time to stop by her competition's business and noticed a few differences between the two businesses. Ask Linda if she would like to hear more about how you might be able to help her if she were so inclined.

Resist the urge to talk the entire time and do a little listening to what Linda has to say—have a conversation. Don't act like a know-it-all, but try to be helpful and make the point that you would do a great job for her, be very pleasant and easy to work with, and that you're eager to add her as a client. If Linda isn't in a position to use your services now, ask her if she would mind if you checked back with her in three to six months. Chances are good that she won't mind if you check back with her, and next time your visit won't be a cold call.

When you return home, send Linda a thank you note and tell her how much you appreciated talking with her. Tell her that if she needs any help, she should feel free to contact you. Assure Linda that if you should meet anyone that is in need of her services, you will point them in her direction. Mark on your calendar when you talked with Linda and when you should check back with her again. If Linda's business has a busy season, then send her a card or small promotional item (with your contact information on it) a few weeks before her busy season begins.

It's estimated that 80 percent of new sales are made after the fifth contact, yet most sales people give up after the second attempt. Remember that patience is key! Don't pester your prospective client, but let them know in small ways that your services are only a phone call away if they are needed. You might think that all you need to do to find work is to announce that you are accepting clients, but it can take a fair amount of time to find the right kind of clients. This is just another reason why starting a freelance business while you're still in school is such a good idea. Some relationships simply need time to develop and for feelings of trust to be established. Starting these types of relationships now can pay off for you down the road. Don't wait until the last minute before you begin fostering these types of designer/client relationships.

Keep in mind that you're not just looking for any freelance work. You're looking for work that you can complete successfully, work that has the potential to become a portfolio piece and that will pay you for your time and effort. You will have to determine if your needs match your potential client's and determine if the project is a good fit—and be strong enough to walk away from opportunities that aren't.

Sometimes when clients hear the words "student" and "graphic designer" in the same sentence, a switch goes on in their brains, and they begin to think, "Maybe this person would be interested in working for free in order to use my job as a portfolio piece." This means they are hoping that you'll do their job for free or at a significantly reduced rate, which rarely benefits the designer as much as it benefits the client. Unless working pro bono helps you break into a market you wouldn't have been able to reach otherwise, or is a truly significant project to have your name attached to, I would avoid working for free.

I receive a few e-mails a week from local businesses who want to offer my design students a "unique internship experience" and from clients who "don't have much of a budget. "These are usually just code words for "I need a designer, but I don't want to pay for their services." I don't want anyone to take advantage of you. Your graphic design work has value, and even though you need to work with clients, you should realize that your clients need someone to help them craft and shape their message. There are many ways in which you can help each other out, but it may take a little time and negotiation in order to find a solution that benefits you both. Don't get so eager to work with a client that you aren't compensated fairly for your time and effort. Similarly, do not promise to deliver more than you are capable of delivering. Both of these scenarios are a recipe for disaster and should be avoided at all costs. You can quickly find yourself in over your head if you don't find a client who fits your constraints.

If a client doesn't have a very large design budget, then negotiate full artistic control over the project. Essentially, the client is agreeing to take the solution you provide and produce it as-is with limited input. This helps you get professionally printed work in your portfolio. Additionally, if the client wants you to lower your hourly rate, ask him to put you on a retainer to guarantee a certain amount of hours each month. This way you will receive a small amount of money each month, and the client will receive a certain number of hours of your time each month to work on his project.

There are many ways to work around a slim budget beyond simply agreeing to work for free. Working for free may be benign in some cases, but clients may eventually begin to expect you to work for little or no pay simply because you didn't stand up for yourself. If you're wishy-washy about the value of your work, it likely come back to bite you (or the next designer this client works with). Make sure to have an honest and direct conversation with your clients when the topic comes up and make sure they understand that the work you do for them is not free and that you need to be compensated.

Establishing boundaries is healthy; it helps both you and your client understand what is acceptable and what is not. Don't wimp out and avoid having a heart-to-heart talk when the situation presents itself. It's better to be a designer without a client than an unhappy designer who isn't getting paid for his work and resents his client. My advice is to lay some ground rules, remain flexible and open to finding alternative solutions, and be mature enough to walk away if necessary.

WORKING WITH A NONPROFIT ORGANIZATION

A nonprofit organization (NPO) is an organization that does not distribute its surplus funds to owners or shareholders, but uses these funds to help pursue its goals. While some NPOs may not have much money in their budget, working with a NPO does not necessarily mean that you have to work for free. The wealthiest NPO in the United States is the Bill and Melinda Gates Foundation, which has an endowment of approximately $38 billion dollars.

You can treat an NPO just as you would any client, but you may wish to contribute to the cause by reducing your rates or working for free—the client would certainly appreciate the offer. If you do decide to work at a reduced rate or for free, talk to the NPO about giving you a tax credit for the services you provide. If they accept your work as a donation, it may reduce the amount of money your business will be taxed at the end of the year because your time and efforts will be viewed as a charitable contribution. If you decide to work for free in order to receive a tax credit, you should request contribution documentation from the NPO.

Pros: Nonprofit organizations are generally receptive to highly creative solutions, and working with an NPO may help lead you to making other business connections. Often, printers and other vendors will donate their services because they want to support a worthy cause, and this will sometimes give you an opportunity to experiment with printing processes or techniques that may no be possible to use within a typical client's budget.

If you are working with an NPO on a project, talk to the printer sales representative about the possibility of using die cuts, embossing, varnishes, or any of their unique services to see if they will allow you to exercise a little creative flexibility. They might want to use your client's pro bono piece to show off some of the more expensive services they offer and use your piece as a sales tool to entice other designers to consider using these services as well.

Many companies receive tax breaks for their pro bono services, and there is a good chance that you will be able to write off some of your expenses as well. In addition to feeling good about your contribution, generating business leads, and becoming more connected to your community, working with an NPO can be rewarding because they are usually very grateful to receive your help.

Cons: Many nonprofit organizations use a committee to make their decisions. The idea is that "many hands make the work light," but working with a committee can slow the pace of a project down considerably. Additionally, you may be asked to work for free or at a significantly reduced rate in order to support their cause. In some cases, NPO projects may have slim budgets, and the committee may be unfamiliar about the process of working with a graphic designer. Members of the committee might not be aware of the value of your work or how to prepare their files, so plan on taking extra time to talk to them about the steps they need to take in order to make your job easier to complete.

Talk to your NPO early about your fee structure, needs, and deadlines because people there may not understand the significance of these things. In addition, you may want to write a project brief that covers your needs, deadlines, budget, and responsibilities. Decisions are often made by a committee, which can sometimes be difficult to work with because there are so many voices and opinions being offered.

The best way to avoid being sent into a tailspin by a committee is to ask the NPO to designate one person (instead of the entire committee) to communicate the NPO's needs to you and to represent the voice of the entire committee. This will help minimize receiving mixed messages. The representative should be

> *"When you are choosing an NPO to work with, begin the process by looking for an organization that you have a strong connection to and want to support."*

responsible for orchestrating and gathering information that you need to complete the job, such as e-mailing you logos, sending you supporting documents, and sharing the NPO's mission statement with you to name a few examples.

I volunteered to work with a local church on a cookbook they were going to sell to raise money to build a playground. I remember spending more than forty-five minutes with the committee trying to pick a shade of green that everyone liked. After leaving the meeting feeling frustrated that so little had been accomplished that day, I asked the church to appoint a leader to the committee who could help me expedite decisions like this by keeping the group focused and moving forward.

Nonprofit organizations are generally receptive to highly creative solutions, much more so in my opinion than small-businesses. This can be an opportunity to allow you to produce some really creative work for your portfolio, in addition to serving the needs of your client. Even though you may be working for a reduced rate, that doesn't mean that you can't get anything out of your relationship with your NPO. If it's appropriate, ask to put a credit line on the work that you design for them or send out a press release to announce how your business is helping the NPO achieve their goals. If your client has allowed you some creative flexibility, and the project has come out well, consider entering the piece in a few graphic design competitions to increase the exposure for both you and your client.

When you are choosing an NPO to work with, begin the process by looking for an organization that you have a strong connection to and want to support. You'll do better work if you can rally behind the NPO's cause. Try to think about ways you can support the organization beyond just helping it out with a single project. Ask the organization to give you a list of projects that it needs to complete, so you can work on a few projects when your business is slow. I prefer working with local organizations; however, there are some really great national and international nonprofit organizations you might consider working with. As you look into finding an NPO that you'd like to work with, don't forget to look on the local, state, national, and international levels to find organizations with graphic design needs.

WORKING WITH A SMALL-BUSINESS OWNER

Small-business owners are often fixated on the bottom line. When they look at a deal, they often approach it from a "What will this cost me and what will I get in return?" type of perspective. There is certainly nothing wrong with this, but you need to make sure that they are being realistic with their expectations. Graphic design isn't a hard science that makes clients appear out of thin air, and you certainly shouldn't sell your services to small-business owners this way. Good design can certainly have significant and positive effects for small-business owners, but it needs to be viewed as a component of a healthy business plan rather than a quick fix or magic bullet. Unfortunately, many small-business owners view design as "decoration" rather than as a vehicle to communicate with their clients, so you may have to spend some time educating them on the value of design and the type of outcomes they can expect to see.

For this reason my approach to working with small-business owners is to avoid selling them a "piece of design" like a business card or brochure. Rather, I talk with them and figure out what problems they are having and about how I can help solve these problems. Sometimes, the best solution is a business card or brochure, but other times a business card or brochure simply isn't the right tool for the job. My goal is to help their business succeed, not just to design and sell business cards and brochures. When you approach the problem this way, it helps the client to understand that one piece of graphic design isn't going to solve his problem entirely, but it begins to establish some momentum for branding his company, shaping its message, and reaching new clients.

Pros: Lots of small-business owners need graphic design work. The owners are usually able to make decisions quickly, and they are passionate about their business. One of the perks about working with small-business owners is that you have an opportunity to educate them about the value of design, and if you service a small-business owner well, he can be a very loyal client. Small-business owners are usually proactive in networking with each other, so if you do a great job for them they can be a great source for referrals.

Cons: One of the problems of working with small-business owners is that they are highly invested in seeing a tangible return on their investment. If they don't see a return on their investment quickly, they might feel their money was not well spent. Occasionally small-business owners may want to micromanage you because they

> *"When you see your client beginning to make a poor design decision, it is your job to inform him that you think he is making a mistake…"*

are so heavily invested in seeing their business succeed that they leave nothing to chance. Small-business owners tend to spend a lot of your negotiating with you to make sure that they'll get the most bang for their buck. Sometimes they get so spun around searching for a strategy to save money that it actually costs them more money in the long run! Occasionally, small-business owners may want to stretch out or delay payment for your services, so make sure the terms of payment and penalties for delayed payment are clearly spelled out in your contract. Some of the most successful small-business owners started their business from a hobby. Our hobbies come from our passions, and passion is a key ingredient to running a successful business. Small-business owners aren't particularly tricky to figure out, but you will need to take a few preventative measures to make sure that you and your client are both on the same page.

I try to be receptive to client feedback and keep an open mind, but small-business owners sometimes have a tendency to try to art direct me. I try to listen to my clients, but I also have to trust the lessons I've learned throughout my career and strike a balance between my client's wishes and my design sensibilities. I know that trying to advertise every item they sell on a 4″ x 6″ advertisement is going to end in disappointment. When you see your client beginning to make a poor design decision, it is your job to inform him that you think he is making a mistake and to try to convince him to go in a more intelligent direction. If he insists on trying a direction out to see if it will work, then inform him that you will do as he asks. But politely let him know that your hourly rate is still ticking away and that if this direction doesn't pan out as intended, he will still have to pay for the time you spend exploring this option. As long as he agrees that you will get paid for your efforts, you need to do the best job you can and protest silently if you disagree with his direction. If you feel very strongly that he has missed an opportunity, then perhaps you can work up an alternative idea and show him your idea also.

By working this way, you will gain your client's trust, and hopefully your client will be less combative with you in the future. If you dig in your heels and refuse to do the job your client asks, you will risk your business relationship. Your client may damage your reputation by telling others that you are stubborn and refused to do what was asked of you. Believe it or not, your client's recommendation is not something that you should take lightly! Small-business owners talk frequently and are involved with business associations and Chamber of Commerce groups. If you gain their trust, they can be extremely loyal clients and recommend your services to other small-business owners. But if you get a bad reputation, it may take you a while to shed your reputation. You don't want to be pushy and need to work with your clients rather than working against them. Working on projects with small-business owners may take more time to complete than working with other types of clients because you may have to spend some extra time explaining your design decisions and getting them to buy into your ideas.

Sometimes you'll run across a small-business owner who may be a bit too proactive and try to make your job easier, only to make it more complex in the long run. Usually this happens because the owner is trying to save money. Looking for ways to save money isn't a bad idea, but obsessing over a few dollars may affect the quality of your work. For example, if you're working on a brochure for your client, and he wants to have photos of his products, he might want to take pictures himself instead of hiring a photographer. Your client may think to himself that he's saving money, but if it takes him eight hours to photograph the work, and it takes you three hours to color correct his photos and clip them all out, then perhaps this wasn't such a good shortcut to take.

These are situations where you have to once again be proactive in your communication with your clients and be receptive to their ideas while also looking out for their best interests. Perhaps you might suggest that he takes a dozen test photographs to estimate how long it would take him to photograph the entire line of products. Then you'll take these photographs and color correct and clip them out from the background and estimate how long it will take you to complete the task. Once you know how long it takes to get the photographs he wants to use, you can estimate how long it will take you to photograph the entire product line. Now you have some real data to work with and can determine if hiring a photographer is worth the time and effort it will take you both to do the photography in-house. By taking the time to test the client's idea, it doesn't come across as your "telling" him that he is wrong, as much as it is "testing" to see if better options are available.

BARTERING YOUR SERVICES

Bartering your services can be a lot of fun, and you can get some really great deals by bartering services because clients may be short of cash, but have inventory or services that they are willing to trade with you instead. The biggest caveat in bartering services is that you must set up the terms of the agreement and have a contract drawn up to specify what each party is expected to contribute and receive. Bartering services has a long history in the United States and has often been relied upon in times of financial crisis.

I've bartered my graphic design services for hang gliding lessons, gym memberships, meals at local restaurants, a surfboard, and so much more. I've found that when I barter my services, my clients are generally very appreciative of the work I do for them. When they see that I've gone out of my way to deliver a project that exceeds their expectations, they've respond by going out of their way to exceed my expectations in return!

Pros: Bartering can be a lot of fun! You may be able to negotiate for more goods and services than you realize. Many businesses get their inventory at a lower rate than what you could purchase it for. So you may be able to negotiate for more bang for your buck. In some cases, designers and clients may strike a deal under the table and not report their trade as income, but be careful! The IRS states, "Barter dollars or trade dollars are identical to real dollars for tax reporting. If you conduct any direct barter or barter for another's products or services, then you will have to report the fair market value of the products or services you received on your tax return." Keep good records of all your transactions! In any case, if you're having trouble finding a client, then you might try suggesting that you're willing to barter for your services.

Cons: Bartering depends upon a mutual want or need, and each party must want what the other has to offer. If you want to barter for services or goods, you must find a client that wants or needs your design services or else the deal will most likely fall through.

Another pitfall of bartering is that if you don't know what the value of the items you are bartering for are worth, or what your graphic design services are worth, then you might wind up with the short end of the stick. In addition, you might find the long lost art of negotiation difficult to master if you have a timid or introverted personality.

It's a good idea to practice bartering for your graphic design services at least once at the Intermediate level because it forces you to put a value on the skills that you possess. Being able to negotiate is a skill that will serve you well as you transition from being a student to being a professional and will help you deal with potential employers later who are trying to get the best designer they can find for the best possible price.

What Type of Work Should You Do?

The type of work that you're going to be doing at the Intermediate level may be slightly more complex than what you did at the Beginner level. While many of the types of projects you work on will be similar to what you did at the Beginner level, the biggest change is the number of projects and types of clients you work with. Here are a few ideas for graphic design projects that you might be able to complete for your clients.

- Custom Artwork
- Business Card
- Poster
- Brochure
- Signage

- T-shirt Design
- Postcard
- Flyer
- Booklet
- E-mail Blasts

- Logos and Branding
- Advertisement
- Small Websites
- Letterhead
- Annual Reports

Soon you will begin putting your portfolio together, but if you work hard and stay focused at the Intermediate level, this task will be considerably easier for you to complete later. Now might be a good time for you to begin thinking about which aspect(s) of graphic design you might like to specialize in (like Web design, print design, package design, or other areas). Since you'll be looking for new clients to work with anyway, try to find clients who need the services you would like to specialize in. If you can begin to take advantage of a few opportunities like this at the Intermediate level, you'll be able to show potential employers later that you not just "thinking" about working in these areas—you'll have some experience to back it up.

It's easy to tell someone that you think you'd like to work in packaging design, but it's far more impressive to have some work to back up your statement. If you're interested in specializing in website design, try to find a client who needs a website. If you are unable to find a client who needs the types of services that you're interested in specializing in, don't get discouraged. There will be plenty of time in your senior year to create a few fictitious projects to round out your portfolio. But if the opportunity presents itself, and if you feel comfortable working on this type of project, then you should go for it!

In your Senior year you will most likely put between eight and twelve outstanding pieces in your portfolio, but I recommend having around twenty pieces total to choose from, for swapping in and out pieces as needed. The eight to twelve pieces you put in your portfolio need to be relevant to the requirements for the job description and showcase your talent as a designer. So having a variety of work to choose from is definitely a good strategy. The work you do for your clients at the Intermediate level can help give you options and make your senior year less chaotic.

As always, you are the only person who can gauge your stress level and who knows how much you can accomplish outside of your academic commitments. Be sure that you don't get in over your head and promise a client more than you can deliver. It's better to say, "I don't think I can do that," or "I would love to help you with this project, but I have exams coming up" than to overcommit yourself and then have to bail out halfway through the project. Keep a positive attitude, and don't be afraid to try something new. But don't commit to taking on more work than you will be able to complete. There's a balance to be struck between the opportunities that present themselves and the amount of work you can successfully complete.

Far too often I see students who overcommit themselves or who never commit to any outside graphic design activities. Finding a healthy balance between working hard and not working at all is important. The Intermediate level is a great time to pick up a few tricks on how to work smarter, not harder. Talk with your peers and compare how long it takes you to complete similar tasks. If you are consistently spending more time in a particular area than your peers, look for ways to improve your efficiency in this area.

When you're in school you might have three weeks to complete a project, but when you're working at an agency you might have three days. Teachers usually like to monitor their students process, concept development, execution, and presentations. Deadlines are longer in school than what you can expect to find in the working world so that teachers can accommodate a large number of students and provide ample feedback. One of the biggest surprises that graduates have when they enter the workforce is how tight the deadlines are, compared with the amount of time they had to work on a project when they were in school.

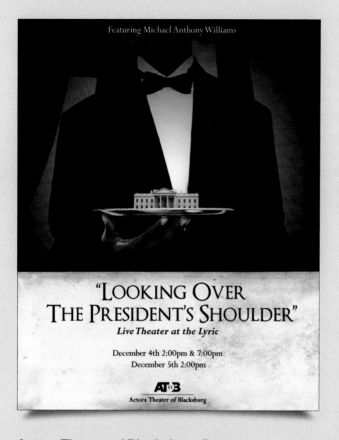

Featuring Michael Anthony Williams

"LOOKING OVER
THE PRESIDENT'S SHOULDER"
Live Theater at the Lyric

December 4th 2:00pm & 7:00pm
December 5th 2:00pm

AT·B
Actors Theater of Blacksburg

Actors Theater of Blacksburg Poster
Designed by Sauksata Vongsouthi
Bartered for VIP tickets to the opening night performance

Sauksata bartered with actor Michael Anthony Williams, pictured on the theater poster above, in exchange for tickets to his opening night performance. Sauksata asked one of her friends to dress up and model for the poster and then used Photoshop to composite the images and textures together. Sauksata says, "I didn't really want an illustrative feel for my poster, so I decided to use a photographic approach instead. I felt like live theater lent itself more towards photography than illustration, and I'm really happy with how the poster came out."

I asked Sauksata if there was anything she learned while working with her client. She said, "I think it's important for students to follow their instincts and trust their gut. I try to visualize solutions before I begin working on a project. If I get stuck, then I refer back to my notes and research."

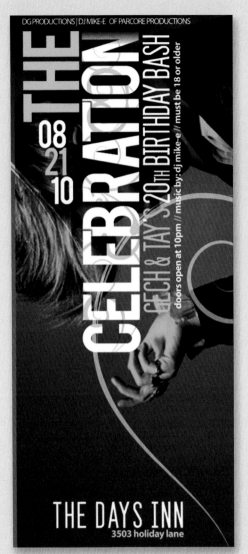

DG PRODUCTIONS | DJ MIKE-E OF PARCORE PRODUCTIONS

THE
CELEBRATION

08
21
10

GECH & TAY'S 20TH BIRTHDAY BASH

doors open at 10pm // music by: dj mike-e // must be 18 or older

THE DAYS INN
3503 holiday lane

INTERMEDIATE LEVEL

Celebration Flyer
Designed by Tim Austin
Received $50.00

Tim's client throws a lot of parties and wanted him to design a flyer with a classy feel. Tim decided to make the flyer vertical, like a ticket, and use cool colors to capture the feeling of the party.

Tim estimates that he works on thirty to forty freelance projects a year. I asked Tim what he charges to design a flyer, and he quickly replied, "I charge $50.00 for a one-sided flyer, $75 for two-sided flyer, and I usually have a three-day turnaround for most projects."

I asked Tim where he found his clients, and he said, "I don't even have to look for clients now. I'll just get an e-mail or a call from some-body saying I was recommended to them. I don't even have to look for my clients anymore."

I asked Tim what advice he thought might be helpful to share with other freelancers. He replied, "Well, sometimes clients try to push you in a particular direction. Sometimes they want everything on the page to be eye-catching, or try to get you to use a lot of typefaces. I've learned that I need to hold my ground and take the time to explain why this isn't a good idea. Everyone I've worked with so far has been pretty recep-tive to my suggestions, but there's always a client that wants something their way. For the most part, clients listen to my advice. I was really nervous the first time I told a client that their idea wasn't so hot, but I've become more comfortable talk-ing with clients over time."

Metal Resources Letterhead
Designed by Matthew Stay
Received $650.00

Matthew worked for his dad's company, and word quickly got out that he was a freelance graphic designer. Metal Resources saw some work he had done and was impressed with what they saw. Matthew says, "I believe it's important for a designer to get to know their client, their process, and their demographics before attempting to create an identity for them."

I asked Matthew what advice he has for other freelance designers. He replied, "Creating a relationship with your client is essential. Graphic designers don't just provide our clients a service, we build an experience. It's important for us to guide clients through a design and help them understand what makes good design decisions, so they will know how our choices reflect their business or organization. Developing this relationship is critically important to the success of a project. It's impossible to give clients a good solution without a mutual understanding of their needs and our design process."

Independent Engineering Services Website

Designed by Jon Newman

Received $2,000.00

Jon created a website for his uncle in Denver, and word quickly spread that Jon was doing some great freelance website work. Independent Engineer Services, LLC got in touch with Jon about designing their website and wanted Jon to build them a website that was created in Drupal, an open-source content management system. While Jon felt comfortable designing the website and writing some of the code, he solicited the help of a friend in the Computer Science program to help him program the website in order to turn the project around quickly and beat his deadlines.

Jon comments, "If I had it to do over again, I'd set firmer deadlines with the client. The client wanted the work done quickly, but getting information we needed from them was never as quick as what we'd like it to be. Having a list of deadlines written out would have helped a lot." I asked Jon if he had any words of wisdom after having finished this project. He said, "Work with a good programmer. Luckily, I worked with a great programmer, and he made my job a lot easier."

Terra Fit Sizzle Video
Designed by Charles Wood
Received $500.00

In high school Charles Wood worked for a company called Advanced Video Productions, which specialized in filming and editing wedding videos. One day they received a call from someone who needed video edited and computer graphics (CG) work. A few weeks later, Charles found himself freelancing for Terra Fit.

Terra Fit wanted a sizzle video to show to potential investors to raise money to bring their project to life. They asked Charles to create 3-D mountain bike trails that would be projected on a screen in front of a class using their fitness bikes. Later Charles was asked to work on print advertisements, instructional material, and promotional items, as well.

Charles freelanced for Terra Fit over the next few years and produced the video excerpts that you see on above. Charles submitted the video to the local American Advertising Federation ADDY competition, and before he knew it, he was on his way to Louisville to accept a national student ADDY award.

Charles estimates that he spent three weeks working on this video and says, "If you take the time it took me to produce this video and divide it by the amount I was paid, I probably made $1.50 an hour! At least the piece was well received."

I asked Charles if he could go back in time and give himself advice, what would he say? Charles replied, "Don't be afraid of failing, and don't compare yourself to your classmates—compare yourself to the rock stars in the design profession because if you shoot for the stars and miss, the worst that can happen is that you land on the moon."

Establish an Internal Work-Flow System

It's important to establish a thorough and concise system for managing jobs because there are times when it will be important for you to put your hands on information quickly and to track your current jobs. You'll need to create a system to record any expenses you incur, to keep track of your hours and client requests to make changes, and to record your e-mail correspondence, quotes, invoices, proof approval forms, and other documents. It is important for designers to keep this information filed away to protect themselves legally in case a dispute should arise.

Freelance designers have to act like business people and make smart, informed business decisions. On the flip side of the coin, a designer's success is often linked to his or her ability to maintain a high level of creativity and artistic vision. Your success as a designer requires you to balance practicality and creativity, so you'll need a work-flow system that is simple to use but easy to modify to meet your needs.

I'm going to walk you through the work-flow system that I use, but feel free to modify it to suit your needs. This is the system I implemented when I was hired as a business consultant by a graphic design agency to help improve their work flow. This system can be scaled up or down depending on your needs. Even if you don't have a client to work with, you can practice using this system with the projects you are assigned in school. I have my students keep track of their hours on each of their projects, and I collect their time sheets at the end of each project. This way my students can see the average amount of time they spent on a project and determine if they need to work on increasing their efficiency.

Creating a Master Client List

Step One in establishing an internal work-flow system is to create a master list of your clients. I usually create this document in Microsoft Word, but you can use whatever text editor you prefer. I keep my list in alphabetical order because it's the easiest way for me to quickly find a client I'm looking for. This document is a "living document," meaning that each time you begin working with a new client, you will add his or her name to your Master Client List and keep this file up to date.

The next step is to assign each client on your Master Client List a three or four-letter abbreviation that you will be able to remember. For example, one of my clients is TriAdventure: Multisport Coaching and Fitness. I use the abbreviation "TRIAD" when I am referring to this client. This abbreviation saves me time, and it also becomes part of a code I use to track the time it takes me to do work for this company. How you use this code will become more apparent as you read on, but for now the important thing to remember is to keep a list of clients, assign each client a three or four letter abbreviation, and always keep your Master Client List up to date.

Creating a Master Job Tracking List

Now that you have a Master Client List, it's time to start a document that you can use to track individual jobs that you do for these clients. You will need a unique number for every job you work on in order to track of your hours and recoup any expenses you incur while working on a particular job.

Your Master Job Tracking List is basically a large table that contains the following information: a job number, a job tracking code, the start date, the due date, the date the first proof was delivered to the client, the date an invoice was sent to the client, the date payment was received from the client, the number of hours quoted, the number of hours actually worked, and your profit margin for each job. This information is essential to track because it shows the areas you where you make and lose money—which is extremely important to know in order to keep your business profitable.

I use Microsoft Excel to manage my Master Job Tracking List because it's easy to use, and I can run a script to calculate my profit by dividing the number of hours I billed my client by the number of hours I worked. Similar to your Master Client List, you'll want to keep your Master Job Tracking List up to date. Every time you get a new job or finish a job, you should update your Master Job Tracking List.

On January 1 of each year you will retire your Master Job Tracking List and begin a new one. Each year you will start numbering your jobs with 001. After you fill out the Job Tracking List for a while, you will begin to see which jobs are the most profitable and how accurate the quotes are. If you see a trend emerge where you are making 87 precent profit, you might adjust your quotes to reflect 13 precent more time to complete these projects. Recording information like this is important because it becomes a tool for checking the health of your company and gives you data you can use to make informed decisions. You'll want each job's profit margin to equal or exceed 100 percent, but occasionally you'll do a job that comes in below 100 percent. This doesn't necessarily mean that you're losing money. It means that the hourly rate you set for this job has been reduced.

For example, let's say my hourly rate is $10 per hour. I worked for thirty hours on a job, but I gave my client a quote that it would only take twenty hours. My client is expecting a bill for around $200 ($10 x twenty quoted hours), but it took me thirty hours to complete. So I would like to charge him $300 ($10 x thirty actual hours). This means that if I stick to my original quote and charge my client the $200 we agreed upon, my profit margin is 66.67 percent. If I take my rate of $10 per hour and take 66.67 percent of this amount, I quickly realize that if I charge him for twenty hours, I will make $6.67 per hour on this job, instead of the $10 per hour rate I was hoping to receive. Clearly, it's important that your quotes are accurate and reflect the actual time it will take you to complete the project. We'll talk about filling out the Request for Quotation Form a little later, but there is a clause on this form that states, "The actual fees for the project may vary as much as 15 percent from this estimate." This means that I retain the right to bill for up to three additional hours (15 percent of my estimated twenty hours), making my bill $230 instead of the $200 and raise my hourly rate to $7.67 per hour. The danger here is that most people get a little upset when they expect one thing and are given another. Your chances to work with this client again has to be weighed against the extra $1 per hour that you'll make by increasing your bill.

I recommend completing half a dozen freelance jobs or so before going back to review the accuracy of your quotations in order to see if a trend emerges. Over time you will get a better sense about the amount of time it will take you to complete a job and what constitutes a fair rate for your efforts. For now, be careful about overcorrecting and reacting too quickly. Aim for making small adjustments over time and try to gauge how your clients might react to these changes before setting them in stone.

TRIAD12-023

Client Abbreviation **+ Last two digits of the year - Job Tracking number**

Tracking Your Jobs

You need to assign each job a unique number to record the hours you worked, the expenses you incur (like stock photography, copywriting, or programming), and the invoice sent for the job once it's been completed. We'll get to how you should record your hours and expenses later, but for now let's focus on how to generate

Enology Society Banquet

April 3rd 7–10pm
Super Wine Hall

Come Get Shitfaced in the Classiest Way Possible

Members $5 · Non-members · $10

NAME YOUR FILES CAREFULLY: A CAUTIONARY TALE

Graphic design student Brendan O'Connor learned the hard way that naming your files can be very important. Brendan worked on a poster for the Enology Society at Fresno State University. Enology is the science and study of wine and winemaking, and his client hired him to create a poster to promote a banquet they were planning. After Brendan finished making the poster for his client, he created a spoof of the poster that said "Come Get Shitfaced in the Classiest Way Possible" and sent the spoof to one of his friends, who shared a laugh with Brendan.

A few weeks later Brendan was offered a job to make a brochure for the Valley Interfaith Child Care Center, and his client asked to see a few examples of his work in order to make sure it was up to par. Brendan put together some samples of his work and sent them off. When Brendan's contact received his e-mail, she forwarded it to the executive director of the Interfaith Child Care Center. It wasn't until later that Brendan realized that he sent the spoof of the Enology poster instead of the real thing. Needless to say Brendan had to offer a few quick apologies and felt terrible about the mistake. Luckily, everything worked out. But it was a lesson he learned the hard way—always name your files carefully!

a job tracking number. The first thing you need to understand is how this number is created. While it might seem like a random string of numbers and letters, the sequence contains some very easy to decipher information. The naming convention is broken down into three parts: a three- or four-letter client abbreviation (the same one you assigned to your client on your Master Client List), the last two numbers of the current year, and the job number (from your Master Job Tracking List). When you combine these three elements together you create a unique string of letters and numbers to use to track the details of a job.

Print master file

Name ▲
▶ 📁 ** Final Version **
▶ 📁 Artwork
▶ 📁 Fonts
▶ 📁 Images
▼ 📁 Supporting files
▶ 📁 Correspondence
▶ 📁 PSD files
▶ 📁 Research
▶ 📁 Sketches
▶ 📁 Text files
▶ 📁 Work in progress

Digital master file

Name ▲
▶ 📁 ** Final Version **
▶ 📁 Images
📄 index.html
▼ 📁 Supporting files
▶ 📁 Animations
▶ 📁 Artwork
▶ 📁 Code resources
▶ 📁 Correspondence
▶ 📁 Fonts
▶ 📁 Movie files
▶ 📁 PSD files
▶ 📁 Research
▶ 📁 Sound files
▶ 📁 Storyboards
▶ 📁 Text files
▶ 📁 Wireframes
▶ 📁 Work in progress

Archiving Your Work

Archiving your work is a relatively simple procedure, but if you don't do it, then you will wind up wasting time trying to find your missing fonts and files. The best way to archive your work is to develop a simple archiving system. Then get into the habit of always using it. I find it helpful to make a master folder on my desktop, duplicate it, and change the name of the copied folder. This way all the folders and subfolders are instantly created and you don't have to create them individually. If you don't have any material in a folder, you can leave the folder empty or delete it.

I keep two versions of my master file structure on my desktop because I use one for clients who need print work and the other for the digital work. These folders are similarly structured, but the digital folder structure has a few more subfolders in it. You can see how the folders are structured differently in the two graphics above.

ARCHIVING YOUR PRINT JOBS

- **Final version:** This is where the most recent or final version of your document is kept. The asterisks in front of "Final Version" make this folder appear first when your files are sorted alphabetically, making this folder easy to find.

- **Artwork:** This folder contains any Illustrator or vector files you used in your document. If you downloaded or created any vector files, they should be kept in this folder.

- **Fonts:** This folder is where you keep the fonts you used in your files. Just because you may have used a font like Garamond, don't assume everyone has the same version of this font that you do. There are many varieties of Garamond. If you send your file to a printer without also sending the correct font, it may quickly become a problem for you.

- **Images:** This folder contains all of the images you used in your document. The files here will most likely be .tif, .eps, .jpg, .png, and .gif files. The exception to this rule is Photoshop files, which will be stored inside a different folder that has been designated for native PSD files. I prefer using .tif and .eps files whenever possible when I'm working on a job that will be printed.

SUPPORTING FILES

- **Correspondence:** This folder is where you would keep copies of any relevant correspondence from the client. Hang on to e-mails with job-specific details, changes to the scope of the project, and feedback from proofs that you sent to your client to review in particular.

- **PSD files:** This is the folder where you keep all of your Photoshop (.psd) files. You'll want to keep all your photographic documents in layers and then save a copy of your flattened image in your "Images" folder.

- **Research:** This folder contains any research or information you may have found or created while working on your client's project. This folder may contain bookmarks and links to websites, paper prototyping, and any other kind of research that aids you in making your design decisions.

- **Sketches:** If sketches need to be saved, scan them or take a photo of them with your digital camera and keep a copy of them in this folder. If you're still building your portfolio, sketches and other process work can be a helpful to keep and show a potential employer.

- **Text files:** This folder contains text files you created, received from your client, or received from a copywriter.

- **Work in progress:** This folder contains older versions of your final version or concepts that have been initially rejected by your client. As the project develops, you'll want to stop and save a copy of your progress in this folder. Occasionally, these documents may need to be referred back to later to show how client input affected the direction of the project or decisions that were made. These files can be helpful to have on hand in case your client has a dispute about the way a job progressed.

ARCHIVING YOUR DIGITAL JOBS

When you archive your digital and online jobs, you'll need to add a few more folders. I won't repeat the descriptions of folders that are common to both print and digital files, but below are some folders that are unique in archiving your digital and online files.

- **HTML/CSS/PHP files:** When you are working on a website that uses HTML, CSS, or PHP files, these files should be stored in the "Final Version" folder, which will also serve as your root directory.
- **Animations:** This folder is where you would keep your Adobe Flash, Moto, and Maya animation files.
- **Code/Javascript:** This folder is where you would keep a copy of resources, bookmarks, and links to tutorials you referenced or used. It's a good idea to keep an original copy of code you used in case you need to refer back to it later. You can copy and paste most code into a TextEdit document in order to archive it.
- **Movie files:** This folder is where you would keep your Adobe After Effects, iMovie, Final Cut Pro, Quicktime, or other video files.
- **Sound files:** This folder contains any audio files that you used on your project. These can be sound files you purchased from a vendor, music or sound effects you created with Garage Band, or other sound editing software.
- **Storyboards:** If you needed to create a storyboard for a project, scan in your storyboard and keep a copy of it in this folder.
- **Wireframes:** If you created wireframes for a website or mapped out a website, or created a user-experience chart, keep these files in this folder.

If you save and file your work as you go along, you'll always be able to find it and make changes later. This will be especially important as you work on putting your portfolio together in your senior year. I guarantee that you will want to go back and fix or tweak some of your earlier work. Being able to find your fonts and images will be much easier if you've archived your projects correctly.

Archiving your work is also important when you're working on projects for your clients. You might design a business card for a client, and as time passes his information may change, or he may add new employees and require new business cards. Hopefully, your client will come to you first to fix his business cards, since you created them originally, and you will not want to have to recreate the files again from scratch because you didn't archive them properly. Working on follow-up jobs like these are an easy way to make a few extra dollars for minimal effort on your part.

Creating a Business Card

A business card is a simple way to let the world know who you are and what you do. Having a professionally printed business card helps you establish that you are serious about your business, and it may help you land new clients.

The typical dimensions of a business card are 3.5" x 2", and the cards are usually printed on 80 lb. to 100 lb. card stock so that the cards won't feel flimsy. Getting your business cards printed is relatively inexpensive; there are many online deals for one hundred to five hundred business cards costing between $10 and $20. If you begin to add in extras like die cuts, UV varnishes, thermography, and custom paper choices, your costs will rise.

Many online printers "gang-print" their clients' business cards. Gang printing means that the printer runs a number of jobs out on one big sheet of paper, and after the job is printed, the business cards are cut apart and delivered to the respective clients. By grouping a large number of business cards together on one sheet of paper, the printer saves time and money. This allows them to sell cheaper business cards. The more unique your business card becomes (custom paper, unique inks, die cuts, etc.), the less likely the printer will be able to gang print your card. This is why the cost of printing business cards can rise quickly when you break out of standard business card formats.

GETTING MORE BANG FOR YOUR BUCK

Before you get too far into designing your business card, I suggest that you go online and do a little detective work. I like to check printers out and make sure their work looks good before I send them my files. Most online printers allow you to request samples of their work, free of charge, so that you can see the quality of their printing and products. This is helpful because you can see firsthand what different weights and styles of paper feel like and look at different printing techniques, such as thermography, gloss varnishes, foil stamps, and so on. Seeing how these printing techniques and materials look in real life might just send you back to the drawing board to see how you might integrate some of these materials and techniques into your own business card.

Once you get your business cards back from the printer, don't be afraid to make alterations on your own. On Ashley Shoemaker's business card on the top right, she bought a corner punch at an art and craft store and rounded the corners on her card, saving a considerable amount of money in the process. Ashley could

have paid the printer to round the edges of her business cards for her, but her solution cost around $10. It's a good idea to look for ways in which you can show off your creativity and pinch a penny when possible. You might consider custom rubber stamps, hand-held embossing equipment, dry transfer letters, and letter-press printing for sources of inspiration. One of the biggest advantages of being able to print your business cards yourself is that you can choose custom papers to print on. If you use an online printer, you may have to use their house paper and not have a choice in the matter.

Great deals on a four-color business card and a gloss varnish are sometimes available. It may be worth your time to ask your print representative how much it would cost to add a varnish to your business card. Some online printers run seasonal promotions where you can get an UV varnish either for free or at a signifi-cantly reduced price.

No matter how you print your business card or what technique you use, your contact information should be easy to read. If you end up with a business card that looks cool, but doesn't function as a business card, then you need to go back to the drawing board and try again.

Take the time to shop around for printers who specialize in printing business cards. You can search for "business cards" online and quickly find a long list of printers, or thumb through magazines like *Print, How, Graphis, CMYK,* and *Communication Arts* to find a number of good deals.

One of the biggest dilemmas students face is deciding what information to include on their business cards. Many students live in dorm rooms or move residences frequently, so including their address on their business card is difficult. When you are designing your business card, include your name, title, phone number, and e-mail address, and if you have a website or Tumblr account, you should include this information also.

I recommend that you get a small quantity of business cards because you are probably likely to move around during college or change your contact information at some point. Around fifty to two hundred business cards should be more than enough, and by the time you pass them out, you'll probably want to tweak your design and update your contact information again anyway.

So what do you do with a hundred business cards? Try to make it a habit of carrying a few business cards with you in your wallet. If you run into someone at the post office or grocery store, you can give them one of your cards. When someone gives you his business card, don't just stuff it in your pocket. It's considered polite to take a few seconds to look at the business card. It makes the person feel important, and you might find some information on the business card that sparks a conversation.

It's easy to think of passing out your business card as an act of vanity or shameless self-promotion. I prefer to think of it as a way to invest in a potential relationship rather than as a way to pat myself on the back. In many cases, I hand out multiple cards at a time. For example, if I run into someone, and in our conversation I discover that they know someone who needs some graphic design work, I might hand them four or five cards and let them know that I would really appreciate the referral. You'd be surprised how effective these referrals can be and how a good attitude can help you get your foot in the door when you might have struggled for weeks cold-calling this same individual.

You never know who or when someone is going to refer you to the "right" people, so don't be stingy with your business cards. Pass them out liberally and make sure to enlist the help of your friends and family to help you distribute a few business cards on your behalf. Before long you'll have all kinds of business contacts and referrals. This is a great position to find yourself in because now you

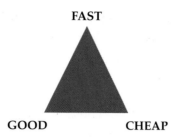

FAST

GOOD CHEAP

In many cases, working with a vendor is like only being allowed to pick two options from the graphic above. You can have fast and cheap work, but it won't be good; or cheap and good work, but it won't be fast; or fast and good work, but it won't be cheap. Sadly, it's difficult to find a vendor who offers all three options.

have a team of people who can recommend you and are helping you promote your business. Get your business cards out of the box they were shipped in and start passing them out to anybody and everybody. As they say in Hollywood, there's no such thing as bad publicity, so don't be afraid to pass out your business cards rather than keeping them stored away in a box on your shelf.

Working with Vendors

There will be times when you will need to work with a vendor who has goods or a service that you need. You might consider using a vendor if you realize he or she can perform a service cheaper or better than you can. For example, if you have a client who needs an iPhone application and you don't feel confident programming the application yourself, you might consider subcontracting this portion of the job out to a vendor. Using a vendor at strategic times can help you stay on budget, work efficiently, and make sure the job gets done correctly. However, you need to choose the people you work with very carefully. After all, it's your reputation that is at stake. If the vendor does a poor job, you may be the one who feels the pinch!

You can find vendors from trade magazines, the Yellow Pages, referrals, and other sources. You will want to talk to multiple vendors because it will help you determine who has the best quality, price, and turnaround time. Once you're ready to get a quote from your list of vendors, you'll need to prepare a Request for Proposals (RFP) document and send it to your top candidates.

When you are writing your Request For Proposals document, you'll need to be as detailed as possible when describing your needs. You'll need to communicate your needs to vendors by using works like "will," "shall," and "must" in your proposal, as well as your criteria for selection, deadlines, and constraints.

When I write my Request for Proposal, I do not give out specifics about my client—only the job I need done. For example, if I'm working on a website for Bravo Signs, I never mention the Bravo Signs name. I don't want to give any dishonest vendors the chance to contact Bravo Signs directly and underbid my job. Instead, I'll describe the job as "needing HTML/CSS for a sign company's website" and wait until I have the vendor sign a contract with me before I disclose the client's name. This way the vendor can't steal my client away from me without breaking their contractual agreement.

It's important to realize that just like your company, each vendor you contact will have strengths and weaknesses. Some vendors will try to be the lowest bid, while other vendors take pride on doing the best job. It's a good idea to determine what type of results you're looking for before sending out your Request for Proposal form. When I send out my Request for Proposals to vendors, I make sure that I specify how long the vendor has to send me a quote and how I will choose the winning bid. I generally include a statement that says, "Bids are due on the date specified above, and all bids will be reviewed to make sure they meet all of the requirements specified. Negotiations with the winning bidder are expected to result in a contract that will be awarded within two weeks."

I typically try to give vendors five business days to put their bids together and ask them to submit their bids by a certain date and time. If the Request for Proposal is particularly complex, vendors may need additional time to put their quote together. Putting a due date on your request can be helpful because it helps you gather all the bids at once rather than waiting for them to trickle in over days or weeks. It will also help you calculate your expenses and talk to your client in order to double-check and make sure that you fully understand the project goals.

Each proposal you receive back in response to your Request for Proposal will be different, so be prepared to read each bid thoroughly to make sure you're comparing apples to apples before determining which vendor to use. If a vendor will be supplying a key service to your operation, you might consider asking him to attend strategic meetings with the client that involve their part of the job.

I think it's a good strategy to find a vendor who fits your needs and develop a long-term relationship with him. While you might save a little money shopping around for each job, you never know how hopping from one vendor to another will affect quality. When I find a vendor that I like working with, I keep it a closely guarded secret. If I tell other designers about my vendor, then there is a good chance he may become too busy to work on my projects in the future.

Request for Proposal

Insert Date

This is a Request for a Proposal (RFP) for <Insert your company name> and the vendor will be chosen by the best offer received by <Insert date that proposals will stop being collected. Usually around 10-15 business days>.

OBJECTIVES & DELIVERABLES
Insert details about the type of work or services you need. Be as specific about what you need the vendor to do as possible. Inform the vendor if they will be expected to work from scratch or if they have any resources at their disposal.

ASSUMPTIONS & AGREEMENTS
• This project must be completed by <Insert completion date>.
• A preliminary budget for this project has been approved. Your fees should include cost, plus any estimated expenses.
• There will be no significant changes to the task/job/policy during the project.
• At the conclusion of the project, all materials developed by the project team will become the exclusive property of <Insert your company name>.

ABOUT YOUR WORK
• Please provide 3-4 references for that is similar to our project.
• Please provide a brief company profile and your core competencies.
• Discuss any vendor relationships you are proposing as part of this proposal.

BUDGET
It is a good idea to provide vendors a budget framework to work within and list what you expect the budget will cover such as all programming, licensing fees, etc.

HOW TO SUBMIT YOUR BID
Bids should be sent to <Insert your email address> or mailed to <Insert your mailing address> by <Insert date that proposals will stop being collected>.

JOB AWARD & NOTIFICATION DATE
The winning bid will be selected on <Insert date that the winning vendor will be notified>, and the results will be kept confidential.

YOUR COMPANY
123 Anywhere Street
City, State ZIP Code
(555) 555-5555

REQUEST FOR PROPOSAL *(See page VIII for download instructions)*

The Request for Proposal Form will help you get quotes from vendors by giving them the information they need to give you an estimate. When you fill out this form, you should describe the kind of work you need done as specifically as possible. But you should avoid mentioning your client's name until the vendor has agreed to the terms of your contract.

Managing Your Time

Managing your time continues to become increasingly important as you begin to work with multiple clients and projects. Make sure you keep track of your deadlines by writing them down on the calendar. Give yourself as much time as possible to work on your client's project by starting projects as early as possible. Murphy's Law has a way of ruining last minute plans. If you wait until the last minute, I guarantee that your printer will run out of ink, your electricity will go out, or something else will go wrong!

I write down a plan to accomplish a few necessary tasks each day when I'm under a deadline, putting my most important tasks at the top of my list. This helps me plan my day and keeps me from having to rush around at the last minute. In addition, I try to break down larger, more complex tasks, into smaller parts so that I feel a sense of achievement as cross them off of my to-do list.

I try to avoid time-wasting activities like checking Facebook, e-mail, or doing other nonessential tasks whenever possible. Small diversions such as these can really add up over the course of a day and eat into your productivity. If you can delegate some of your tasks and lighten your load, consider doing so in order to give yourself as much time as possible to work on your biggest priorities. I'm a big fan of doing the job right the first time. Even if it takes me a bit more time up front, I'd rather spend a bit more time to do something the right way the first time than to have to go back and fix errors after the fact.

If you have a task that you're dreading, try breaking the task up into ten minute increments and spreading it over a day or two. It'll keep you from getting project fatigue. If you mix some of your more fun duties in with your less fun tasks, it makes the job less tedious. It's important not to forget to take breaks from time to time. Go for a walk, do some stretches, or simply get out for a few minutes. Since much of the work graphic designers do is on the computer, your body needs relief from time to time from sitting in the same position and staring at a computer screen.

Don't forget to give yourself plenty of time at the end of a project to finish strong. This means leaving yourself enough time to prepare your files correctly, eliminating any unused swatches from your art boards, checking your spelling, and labeling your files in way that can be easily understood. Basically, you want to leave yourself enough time for every aspect of this project (including how you built your files) to look professional. It may sound silly to budget time in order to finish strong, but your clients will appreciate the extra effort.

Documenting Your Process Work

Documenting your process work helps show potential employers how you solve problems and how the research you gathered influences your design solutions. Looking at process work can be incredibly revealing about how you think and can be insightful for potential employers to see during an interview.

Many designers use various methodologies, or processes, for problem-solving, brainstorming, and finding creative solutions. At other times they skip using a methodology altogether and try a more intuitive approach to design. Showing your process work helps a potential employer understand how you prefer working and may provide a sense of how good a fit you would be with their company.

You don't need to show process work for every piece in your portfolio, but it might be smart to include at least one such project in your portfolio. You might want to pick one of the clients you will work with at the Intermediate level and document your process work as you complete their project. Make sure you document your research and sources, save and scan in your sketches, take periodic screen shots as you work on the project, and record any other information that might reveal your decision-making process. After the project is complete, be sure to collect post-project information, such as quotes from your client and the project's audience, any changes in sales or profits, and reactions to your solution. This type of information will help you demonstrate your effectiveness in achieving your goals and will give your design decisions some credibility.

Collecting information about your clients and design solutions now will help you in your senior year, when you're putting your portfolio together. When you decide to record data on a project, pick the project that is most likely to have the greatest degree of positive change for your client. It's far easier to collect more data than you need while the project is still fresh in everyone's mind than it is to try and collect the data after a few weeks or months have passed.

INTERMEDIATE LEVEL

A SKETCHING METHODOLOGY: *Based on Lisa Fontaine, Associate Professor of Graphic Design at Iowa State sketching methodology.*

When Professor Troy Abel, Assistant Professor at Virginia Tech announced that his students needed to develop a personal mark or brand, he provided his students with a methodology to assist them in this task. Dr. Abel comments, "I wanted to teach students to sketch. I started the project to introduce the students to the difference between an idea family and iteration within those families. Students used design principles to assist in family generation, which they then iterated. This process continued until the final refinement phase. Then they began a series of systematic form recisions, which included analyzing the internal geometry and ratios within their mark."

Allison Bhatta, a senior graphic design student, started her visual exploration by generating a list of words and phrases to describe herself.

· Sleek	· Photographic	· Tweakable	· Handmade
· Detailed	· Crafted	· Organized	· Poised
· Sans serif	· Resourceful	· Reliable	· Dedicated
· Bright	· Meaningful	· Efficient	· Thorough
· White space	· Vibrant	· Dexterity	· Compulsive
· Meticulous	· Timely	· Simple	· Clean

Phrases that Allison used to describe herself included: a very thorough and detail-oriented designer with dexterity in handmade craft; make a difference in someone's life; positive outlook; hates stock photography, but loves candid photos; original imagery; driven for perfection; inspired by simple details that are normally overlooked; likes to know how and why; sucker for a good deal; organization queen; crafting addict; loves a good grid and layout; thinks outside the box; and multiperspective thinker. After putting together a list of words and phrases, Allison went back and highlighted the qualities she felt were most important and relevant.

Allison's next challenge was to build a matrix to generate idea families that she could use to influence her mark. She combined her highlighted terms to describe herself with some design principles to create idea families that she could use to develop further. This methodology helped demystify the sketching process and allowed each student in the class to develop a mark based on the qualities they felt were important and unique to them.

A matrix is basically a framework for creating iterations of a visual mark or form. Allison was asked to take the seven words that she used to describe herself and combine these words with seven design principles, lay them out on a grid, and explore what the intersection of these two ideas might look like.

Once Allison completed her matrix, she was asked to take some of the more visually interesting marks that she created and explore them even further. In the matrix below, the marks that Allison chose to explore further have had their backgrounds darkened, so that you can identify them more clearly.

	ORGANIZED	VIBRANT	DETAILED	DEXTERITY	TIMELY	SIMPLE	CLEAN
RADIATION							
ANOMALY							
SHAPE							
REPETITION							
ALIGNMENT							
PERSPECTIVE							
HIERARCHY							

INTERMEDIATE LEVEL

Creating a mark or identity to brand yourself can be a difficult task because it's hard to know where to start. The matrix is a methodology to help you get your mind in gear and to help you outflank this difficult task. It is also a way to get past the "paralysis by analysis" mind-set and takes the pressure off of you to constantly be working at a high aesthetic level. You are basically beginning to visually brainstorm and "doodle with intent" in order to generate directions that you can explore more fully later. Resist the urge to tighten up your sketches because this phase is about casting a wide net and opening yourself up to new ideas. Once you've finished your initial round of sketches, go back and mark the ones with the potential to be developed more fully.

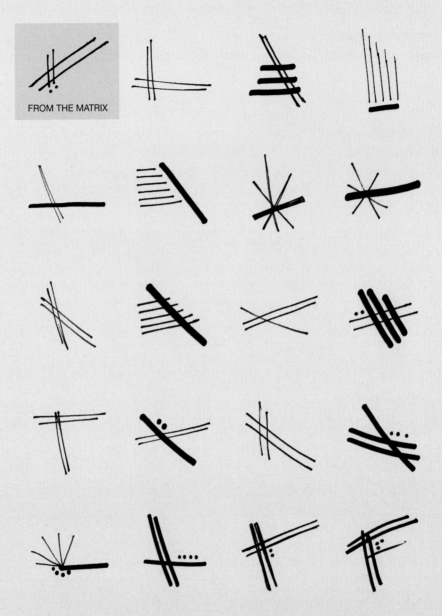

You can see how Allison does not draw the same mark over and over, but tweaks her sketches slightly each time while she experiments with line weight, composition, direction, emphasis, and other design principles. This variation of form is important because the meaning and interpretation of the mark will continue to change and evolve as the process continues. But there is an obvious relationship among all of the marks in this series (or family) of sketches.

INTERMEDIATE LEVEL

ORIGINAL

If the methodology doesn't yield a solution that you're happy with, you may need to go back to the beginning and repeat the entire process again. After Allison explored the seven marks that she identified in her matrix, she continued to sketch because she wasn't satisfied with the outcome. By the end of her sketching phase Allison produced over 680 sketches and permutations. Once Allison identified a sketch that she liked, she began to refine her mark and

improve it. Her professor, Dr. Troy Abel, helped her identify areas in her mark that she could improve. This involved taking a closer look at the construction of the mark, its proportions, and its relationships to a grid, as well as testing how changes in scale and proportion affect the mark. Throughout this entire project, the students in this class met with Dr. Abel on a regular basis to show him their progress and to receive feedback.

Finding an Internship

The Intermediate level is about rolling up your sleeves and doing as much graphic design work as possible. You've learned about the history of graphic design, the principles and elements of design, and what's involved in working with clients. Now it's time for you to really shine by polishing your graphic design skills through practice. You should work on as many projects with the potential to become portfolio pieces as you can. In addition to picking up freelance work, internships are a great way to add work and experience to your portfolio and résumé.

Many companies welcome a little extra help around the office, and you should look for ways to contribute to the company's success. When you begin searching for an internship, resist the temptation to e-mail a company about internship positions. Opt for a phone call instead. While you're on the phone be sure to ask how many internship positions are available, how you should apply for the internship, whether the internship position is paid or not, how long it will last, and what type of work you are likely to be asked to do if you are offered an internship.

Generally speaking, internships aren't very difficult to land and have been known to occasionally lead to a job offer. When you intern for a company, pay close attention to the way the employees interact with each other and their clients and how a project moves through the company from start to finish. Identify who is responsible for making certain decisions.

When you're at your internship, don't make the mistake of texting friends, checking your e-mail repeatedly, wasting time on Facebook, or casually surfing the Internet. There is always something productive you can do to help the company out and to keep yourself busy. People will notice if you're always around to lend a hand, so look for opportunities to volunteer to help out. If you finish your assigned job early, then take the trash out, clean up the kitchen area, wash dirty dishes, make coffee, or sweep the office floor. Take initiatives rather than hovering around your boss and repeatedly asking him what you should be working on. If the office is tidy and there is nothing that you can find to do, look for ways to expand your skills—like watching software tutorials—or begin working on a promotional piece for the company.

When I worked as a creative director, I hated it when the interns asked me fifty times a day what they should be doing. I'm sure that at some point, I yelled, "Look around and find something to do! I don't care what it is, but leave me alone!" I wasn't trying to be rude, but I had work that I needed to complete, and I didn't have time to find put a to-do list together for an overanxious intern.

When you intern for a company, you want to be a problem solver, rather than someone who needs constant attention and is unable to make a decision on his or her own. It's important that you act like a member of the company rather than a student who requires constant attention. If you have a question, by all means ask someone, but do not make your supervisor repeat himself again and again. Take notes when you need to and anticipate questions you may have when you're getting briefed about the tasks your company wants you to complete.

Every internship has a transition period as you get to know the company and its system. It will take some time before the employees get to know you and the skills that you bring to the table. There is always something that you can learn from every employee, so make sure to be pleasant and friendly to everyone.

If you get the opportunity to work on a project, ask if it's okay to document your part in the project and add this work to your portfolio. Don't assume that you can put this work in your portfolio—get permission first! Sometimes clients require companies to sign a nondisclosure agreement, or an agency may have a reason to keep information out of the public eye. Even if you completed the job entirely by yourself, you can still get into a lot of trouble if you put that work in your portfolio without permission. Ask rather than making assumptions.

Once you've finished your internship, ask to meet with your supervisor and talk to him or her about areas that you can improve and areas in which you shine. You can use this information to make yourself a stronger candidate for the next job or try to address some of the issues that have been brought to your attention. You never know if an internship will lead you to an opportunity to get your foot in the door. So approach your internship with focus and commitment.

Ethical Considerations

In 1998 I worked at a graphic design agency located in a small town in North Carolina. I had graduated from college two years earlier and had accepted a position at a local graphic design firm. I enjoyed the work I was doing at the time and worked with some really fun personalities. I was learning a lot about the publishing industry and having a good time putting my college education to use.

One day my boss asked me to design a magazine advertisement for a local sports bar, and I remember being excited about the opportunity. The sports bar had purchased a full-page color ad in a local magazine and wanted me to design an advertisement to increase its visibility.

I decided to take the sports bar's logo, place it in the center of the page, and create a composition where all types of athletic images (football, basketball, golf, hockey, and so on) burst out from behind the restaurant's logo. I worked on the advertisement until I was happy with the results. Then I showed the advertisement to my boss. He made a few suggestions, gave me a thumbs up, and told me to contact the client to arrange a meeting and show him the ad.

The next day the client and I met and I showed him the advertisement I had designed. The client responded, "I like the concept a lot, but there are too many black people in the ad."

I didn't understand what the client meant—there were thirteen athletes in my ad, and nine of them were black. Perplexed by his response I wondered silently what he meant. Surely he didn't mean what I thought he meant. Some of the athletes in the ad were well-known, and I didn't understand why my client wouldn't want these athletes in an advertisement for a sports bar. I sat in silence, perplexed, and trying to wrap my head around the client's unusual request. "Give it another go around and get back to me when you're done," he said. I nodded. The client stood up and shook my hand and left.

After the client was gone from the building, I went in to talk to my boss about the meeting. "How did it go?" he asked. "I'm not sure," I replied. "The client liked the concept, but he told me there were too many black athletes in the ad."

"Let me see the ad again," my boss said. I pulled out the ad and handed it to him. My boss scratched his beard and said, "Do what he asked you to do. Take off a few of the black athletes and replace them with other athletes, okay?" I nodded and went back to work to make the changes.

I worked on "fixing" the ad by replacing four of the black athletes with other athletes, and I printed out a fresh copy of the advertisement. Now there were thirteen athletes in the advertisement. Five were black, and the rest were Caucasian and Latino. I showed my boss how I had changed the advertisement, and he told me to drive down to the client's establishment and show him the revisions.

I called the client to ask if he had a few minutes to spare and then left to meet him with the updated ad. When I walked into his establishment I shook his hand, and he directed me to the bar. We sat down so he could take a look at the revisions. I pulled out my fresh copy of the ad and handed it to him while he pulled out his reading glasses and put them on to get a better look. Within ten seconds the client sighed rather loudly and removed his glasses. "Ben, I don't think you understand. There are still too many black people in this ad," he said.

I countered, "Clearly, I don't understand what you want—there were nine black athletes and now there are five. How many do you want?" The client looked at me and exclaimed, "None. These aren't the type of people we want to attract to our bar!"

I didn't know what to say. I had never encountered such blatant racism before. Dumbfounded at his ignorance, I replied, "It's Barry Bonds and Michael Jordan—two of the best professional athletes on the planet!" I don't remember what the client said to me after that or the drive back to work, but my next memory was bursting into my boss' office. Obviously upset, I remember yelling, "Our client's a racist! He wants me to get rid of all the black athletes in the ad!"

My boss tried to calm me down. "Look, I need you to focus. If the client doesn't want any black people in his ad, then take them out." I didn't know what to say. I told my boss that I wasn't going to work for this client anymore, and if he wanted to keep this account, he was going to have to finish the job himself. I expected my boss, whom I respected greatly, to be on my side, but it seemed clear to me at the time that we had different priorities.

This job became a point of contention between my boss and me. He resented that I removed myself from this project and dumped it in his lap, and I resented that it felt like he was asking me to abandon my ethical principles and to do what our racist client wanted. A few months later I gave my boss my notice and decided it was time for me to move on to greener pastures.

A good graphic design job had gone south because I stuck to my principles and refused to work on an advertisement. Over the next few years, when I found myself back in this town, I stopped by to said hello to my former employer. But our relationship would never be the same again. I realized that even though I felt I made the right decision, I had burned a bridge with him.

Graphic designers make choices every day that affect our clients, ourselves, and our audience. Some of our choices might involve doing the right thing and can have a huge impact on our profit margins and on the people whom our work is intended to reach. The Graphic Artist's Guild (GAG) publishes *The Graphic Artists Guild Handbook: Pricing & Ethical Guidelines,* which provides great information about some of the ethical issues that are common in the graphic design profession. The American Institute of Graphic Arts (AIGA) has a variety of helpful articles on design business and ethics on their website that you can view and download for free. These resources can help you make informed ethical decisions and are resources worth having in your bookcase and bookmarked in your Web browser.

Ethical decisions are different than feelings, and ethics go deeper than doing what you have to do. They are about doing what you should do. Feelings certainly influence our ethical choices, but sometimes people feel good when they are making bad choices—ethics often transcend our feelings. Doing the right thing isn't easy and sometimes takes a great deal of self-control. When you find yourself in an ethical dilemma, stop and think about your situation in the following ways:

- Before you do anything, determine who will be helped and who will be harmed by your decision.
- Think about the six pillars of character: trustworthiness, respect, responsibility, fairness, caring, and citizenship. Ask yourself whether or not this decision would be likely to undermine your integrity if it were made public?
- Use the Golden Rule as a guide. Ask yourself, "Would I want someone to treat, me this way if the situation was suddenly reversed?"
- Ask yourself, "If everyone did this, would it be a good thing?"

After you've thought about your situation from various angles, clarify your goals and prioritize them. In the process, try to separate your wants from your needs. I could not in good conscience continue to work for a racist client, but I shouldn't have given my boss an ultimatum either. I should have worked with him to determine the facts, develop some options we could both agree upon, weigh the consequences of our actions, and chose the best option together as a team.

Perhaps the results may have been the same, but more than likely we would have found a solution to our dilemma—one that wouldn't have strained our business relationship. Looking back now, I realize that I never gave my boss a chance to react. I was thrown off balance by the sheer ignorance of our client, and when my boss told me to do what the client wanted, I felt that my boss was siding with the client instead of with me. In reality, my boss probably wanted to get through the project and end the business relationship, but I never gave him the opportunity to do so.

Even though I made an ethical choice, I realize now that I could have handled the situation better. When you find yourself caught up in the heat of the moment, take some time to stop, refocus, and put together a strategy to get you through your ethical dilemma. You might feel like an emotional wreck on the inside, but it's important to approach your ethical dilemma with focus and control—and to do as little damage to yourself and others as possible.

RESOURCES FOR GRAPHIC DESIGN ETHICS

There are many great resources available for purchase and online on the topic of graphic design ethics. Two major contributors to this important topic are the AIGA Design Business and Ethics series and the *Graphic Artists Guild Handbook: Pricing & Ethical Guidelines*, but there are certainly other resources available for you to consider as well like Lucienne Roberts' book *Good: An Introduction to Ethics in Graphic Design*. Don't forget that you can search for "business ethics," as well as "graphic design ethics," when you are searching for information online.

AIGA

The AIGA Design Business and Ethics series outlines many of the critical ethical and professional issues commonly encountered by designers and their clients. This document is mailed to all new professional and associate-level members when they join the AIGA.

The AIGA website states, "New topics in the AIGA Design Business and Ethics series will be published periodically to build a basic library for designers and their clients. The intent of this series is to develop content that is useful to designers, as well as being a resource to educate clients on standard practices and legal requirements faced by design firms."

GAG

On the flip side of the coin, the *Graphic Artists Guild Handbook: Pricing & Ethical Guidelines* is available when you join the Graphic Artists Guild or can be purchased at bookstores and online.

The Graphic Artists Guild website states, "For years, the *Graphic Artists Guild Handbook: Pricing & Ethical Guidelines* has been the industry bible for graphic designers and illustrators. The 13th edition continues the tradition with new information, listings and pricing information based on surveys of working designers. It addresses legal rights and issues such as how copyright laws affect the income and work of graphic artists. It also provides tips on how to negotiate the best deals and how and what to charge for work, and includes sample contracts. For design and illustration professionals, there is no more comprehensive and informative resource."

More than likely you won't encounter an ethical issue like the example I just described. The ethical dilemmas that you encounter are likely to challenge you in other ways. For example, what will you do when you give your client a quote and finish the job using far fewer resources than you expected? Will you pass these savings along to your client or pocket the extra income?

Would you help market a product or service that deceives customers into believing that they will get more value than they actually receive? Deception can take the form of misrepresentations, omissions, or misleading the consumer and are not ethical. Everyone is looking for an angle to promote their business, service, or product, but you must be sure that you are representing both yourself and your client honestly and with integrity at all times. If you do not, your clients and their audience will seek other sources for the services you provide.

We've all been burned by not reading the fine print, so avoid deceptive practices like using false comparisons, using misleading suggested selling prices, omitting important sales conditions, or employing a bait-and-switch technique. It's far easier to run your business ethically than it is to cheat people out of their hard-earned money and constantly be watching your back. People remember when they get burned, and you can damage your reputation irreparably by not acting ethically and responsibly. You can spend years building a good reputation and destroy it in less than a day with a bad decision. Make sure that your actions and your words are ethically and morally aligned.

Intermediate Level Checklist

- ☐ Purchase the hardware and software you need for school and freelance.
- ☐ Work with a nonprofit organization, a small-business owner, and a client who will barter with you.
- ☐ Establish an internal work flow system and begin tracking your jobs.
- ☐ Archive your jobs, and document your process work.
- ☐ Create a business card for your company.
- ☐ Manage your time more efficiently.
- ☐ Find an internship.

Stretching Your Wings

7

Goals for Advanced Level Freelancers

The Advanced Level is when you're going to begin the transition from student and freelance designer to young professional ready to enter the workforce or graduate school. The bulk of your efforts at the Advanced level will go toward working on jobs that are likely to become portfolio pieces and support your post-college plans. You will also create a print and digital version of your portfolio, write your résumé and cover letter, research the jobs or graduate schools you are going to apply to or for, and create a monthly budget.

It's perfectly normal to feel some anxiety because you will soon be out on your own—without the support of your classmates and teachers. One of the most important things you can do before you graduate and leave school is to network like crazy. Hopefully, you've become involved with some graphic design organizations, taken advantage of design workshops, entered your work into competitions, and taken advantage of many of the opportunities your school provides. If you haven't gotten involved, it's time for you to catch up by making a focused effort to connect with the professionals in your geographic area. Look for opportunities to tour local graphic design agencies, get to know the companies in your area, apply for internships, and join at least one graphic design organization.

The American Institute of Graphic Arts (AIGA) and the Graphic Artist's Guild (GAG) are two great graphic design organizations that you might consider joining. Not only do affiliations with these types of professional organizations look good on your résumé, but they also allow you to network with local designers and help you stay up to date on graphic-design-related issues in your area. In addition, these organizations usually offer portfolio reviews that you should take advantage of if you have the opportunity to do so.

Any professional contacts that you can make now may be beneficial for you in the future, so don't be shy about getting involved and meeting new people. Here are a few goals you should try to complete the Advanced level.

- Create a monthly budget spreadsheet and keep records of your incoming and outgoing expenses.
- Produce a minimum of twenty high-quality pieces for your portfolio.
- Create a print and a PDF version of your portfolio.
- Decide what you want to do after college.

Equipment to Purchase

PROFESSIONAL ORGANIZATION MEMBERSHIP

Full-time students can get a one-year membership in the American Institute of Graphic Arts (AIGA) for $95, compared to the $315 membership fee that you will pay once you graduate. With your AIGA membership, you can receive numerous discounts from vendors like Lynda.com, Apple Computers, Adobe Systems, and FedEx. You'll also receive a copy of *Design Business and Ethics* and the *AIGA Survey of Design Salaries* book, space to upload your portfolio online, job postings on their website, and discounted rates for conferences, seminars, and workshops.

Full-time students can get a one-year membership to the Graphic Artists Guild (GAG) for $105, compared to a $230 membership fee that you will pay once you graduate. With your GAG membership you help advocate for fair pay, appropriate working conditions, and ownership of your work. Your membership also comes with a copy of the *Graphic Artists Guild Handbook: Pricing & Ethical Guidelines*, access to group health insurance and disability plans, a newsletter, and access to job referrals, trade shows, and other activities. Similar to AIGA, the Graphic Artists Guild offers discounts on many frequently used products and services, including art supplies, car rentals, and advertising in many illustration and graphic design directories.

In order to pick the organization that would benefit you most, go to the AIGA and GAG websites. Look for active chapters in your area and review the advantages of membership. Regardless of whether you choose AIGA, GAG, or another option, you should take advantage of many of the free services that these organizations routinely offer—portfolio reviews, job postings, and opportunities to meet other professionals in your area.

If you can't afford to purchase a new lens, you might consider renting one. An online search will reveal a number of companies that rent camera lenses and tripods that can be delivered right to your door.

CAMERA LENSES AND TRIPOD

Now that you're at the Advanced level and beginning to develop a strategy about putting your professional portfolio together, you're going to need to borrow or buy more photography equipment to help document your work. The first piece of equipment you'll need to get your hands on is a tripod. While you might have steady hands, you can't hold your camera as steady as a tripod can. Not only will you eliminate unintentional motion blur from your photographs, but you will also give yourself more photographic options when you use a tripod. Using a tripod allows you to set your camera's position and then adjust your lighting, composition, and camera settings without having to reposition your camera. If you need more light, you can drop your shutter speed, change your camera's exposure modes, and essentially test different lighting and camera settings while your photographic composition remains unchanged. Your photos will be look different because of the camera adjustments you made, but your composition will be the same because your camera's position on the tripod has been constant.

Why are images with a fixed composition helpful? Well, it gives you the opportunity to edit and collage images together in Photoshop very easily. For example, if an area in your photograph is too light, you can copy an area from a darker image and paste it into place, using blend modes and shifts in your layer opacity to darken or add information back into your image.

Camera lenses collect light for the camera, and built-in flashes rarely produce good product shots. A built-in flash is likely to cause hot spots in your image, create dark shadows, or make your images look flat. For this reason you're going to want to use additional lights, a soft box, photography tent, or infinity table to capture the most flattering images of your work. If your compositions aren't well lit, you will find that a tripod will come in very handy. The camera will be stabilized as the shutter stays open for longer periods of time. If you were to hold your camera in your hands, the image would most likely appear blurry, grainy, or have artifacts in the image.

When you shop for camera lenses, be sure to take your DSLR camera with you. Some people like using a wide-angle lens with a macro feature to shoot their product shots, while others prefer using a macro lens. As you try different lenses, keep an eye out for rectilinear distortion, which is a lens effect that makes straight lines show up as curved, especially towards the outer edges of your image. It's acceptable to have some small amounts of rectilinear distortion. This can be corrected with Photoshop. But it's far easier to choose a lens that minimizes this effect than to edit each individual image. It's important to remember that you're not just looking for a lens that will allow you to zoom in closely, but are trying to find a lens that minimizes distortion in your image, while maximizing the amount of light that gets into the camera. Your local camera salesman should be able to provide you with a few tips and also offer you suggestions about which lenses will work best with your digital camera for the types of shots you are going to take.

PORTFOLIO

You're going to need to purchase a portfolio to display and present your work. Every designer has a personal preference when it comes to deciding the number of pages, size, and construction of their portfolio. Each has its merits and drawbacks, so spend a little time thinking about your needs and what will serve you best before committing to a particular type of portfolio.

Most art directors will want to see eight to twelve samples of work, so you will want a portfolio that can comfortably hold that amount without having extra blank pages in the back. Choosing a format that allows you to swap pages in and out of the portfolio can be very helpful. Occasionally, you will run across a job description that will ask the candidate to demonstrate specific skills or portfolio pieces. If your portfolio allows you to swap projects in and out easily, it makes modifying your portfolio quick and painless.

An example of a nontraditional portfolio from the graphic design firm QUANGO in Portland, Oregon.

Choosing a portfolio is a very personal decision, but you don't have to use an off-the-shelf portfolio. I've seen old suitcases that had been converted into portfolios, custom-made cases, and many other nontraditional portfolios. The goal of your portfolio is to capture the attention of the creative director or person interviewing you and to display your work in a flattering way.

If the investment in your portfolio helps you to land a good job, it could be argued that your investment was money that was well spent. Catching the eye of an art director can prove to be a difficult task, so take advantage of every opportunity to do so. While a portfolio shot on ViewMaster reels is likely to be more expensive to produce, its nontraditional format has a certain "Wow!" factor that makes people stop and take notice.

I've seen a lot of students present their portfolio on an Apple iPad, and I have to admit that some of these presentations have been quite nice. One of the features I like most about presenting a portfolio in this format is that when you want to point out a specific detail, you can use Apple's pinch-to-zoom interface to zoom into the area that you're talking about. The iPad is an expensive purchase, but it has several unique features, like the one mentioned previously, that would be impossible to do with a print portfolio. Another perk of using an iPad is that if you wish, you can e-mail a PDF version of your portfolio from your iPad to an art director immediately after a successful interview. The art director will have a copy in his inbox before he even makes it back to his desk.

If you decide to drop the money and present your portfolio on an iPad, you need to familiarize yourself with the iPad OS and its applications before you present your work. You will need to be conscious of any reflections or glare on the screen that might distract your viewer. Make sure to hold the iPad still, so your work can be viewed easily, and avoid making your viewer strain to see your presentation.

There is some debate as to whether it's better to hand your iPad over to the person interviewing you or to keep possession of the iPad and walk the interviewer through your presentation. I believe it's best to ask your interviewer what he or she prefers and adapt your presentation to that preference. If your interviewer chooses to hold the iPad so that he can see the work clearly, then you may need to get up and change position in order to see what he is looking at and to talk about your work. Don't sit there silently across the table while your interviewer looks at your work, because the chance for your interviewer to get to know you better will slip silently away.

SMALL LEATHER PORTFOLIO

A small 9"x 12" leather folder can help you get organized, provide a place to store a clean copy of your résumé, and give you a space for you to take notes during a job interview. Don't purchase a fake leather or plastic folder, but look for a leather one with a pad of paper inside where you can take notes. Many graduates choose a leather folder with their college or university's emblem on it, which is perfectly acceptable—in fact, this may even become a talking point in an interview if your interviewer notices your the emblem.

The note pad inside allows you to take notes throughout your interview, which you can use to refer back to later—for instance remembering everyone's name when it's time to write your Thank You letters after an interview has concluded. The note pad also allows you to buy yourself some time to collect your thoughts if you are asked a tough question during an interview and need a second to collect your thoughts. Simply appear to be writing down a note to yourself while you collect your thoughts and decide how to respond to the question that you have been asked.

Types of Clients You Should Work With

Unfortunately, this isn't an easy question to answer, and part of the answer depends on what you're interested in doing after you graduate. One of your big goals at the Advanced level is to become more selective about the types of projects you work on. If you're interested in working at an Interactive Design firm after you graduate, you should try to include a few projects like website design, desktop and mobile applications, usability testing, Search Engine Optimization strategies, and other pertinent work.

If you know of any clients needing these types of services, you might benefit from working with these clients. If you can't find a client who needs the type of work you're most interested in doing, try to work with clients that give you a high degree of creative freedom. Your goal this year is to continue to make money, while generating work that has the potential to become a portfolio piece.

As always, your education should take priority over your freelance pursuits, but as long as you know your limits and can manage your time well, you should be able to successfully complete both. However, if you are nervous about being able to manage your academic and freelance commitments, it's probably a good idea to reduce the amount of freelance work that you commit to until you feel more comfortable.

If for some reason you feel that you may be spread too thin to continue freelancing and feel that you need to focus on school instead, talk to your clients and let them know how you feel. Tell them that you're happy to help them transition to working with another graphic designer and that you hope they understand your reasons for excusing yourself.

It's important to understand that you shouldn't bail out on a job that you agreed to complete, but you aren't obligated to take on new projects either. If you feel that you need to reduce the amount of freelance work you accept, perhaps you can recommend one of your classmates or another designer that you believe will do a good job for your client. The goal of stepping out of a relationship with a client is to not make your clients feel like you've left them stranded. Offer useful suggestions and help your client out as best you can while you lighten your extra curricular commitments. If you take the time to help your clients find a graphic designer to work with, your client will continue to hold you in high regard. If you leave a client stranded, chances are good that it may come back to haunt you later.

General Motors Billboard Promotion
Designed by Carter Reed
Received $200.00

Carter was contacted by a General Motors Promotional Company about creating a billboard to promote several Richmond, Virginia, Chevy Dealerships. He was told by his client that they were looking for a patriotic sign featuring a Camaro and Aveo, along with a list of dealerships, and was given access to the General Motors photo library.

Carter had forty-eight hours to present his concept and another twenty-four hours to finalize the work once it had been approved. Carter commented, "Payment wasn't spelled out completely, which was partly my fault. I was just excited for the opportunity. In the end I billed the client for my hours, but was paid a flat $200 in American Express gift cards (kind of like cash, I guess), but I wasn't compensated nearly enough for the time and energy I invested."

When I asked Carter what he learned from this project, he replied, "Getting freelance clients, especially big name clients is a great way to boost your résumé and portfolio. Make sure, regardless of your connection to the client, you have a contract for your security. It's a sign of professionalism, and it covers your butt. Get all the information up front, not a half-baked brief like I received."

Iowa Hospice Book
Designed by Becky Murphy
Received $1,000.00

Becky was hired to tell the story of Iowa Hospice in a book. Each page was to contain biographies of employees at various hospice locations. The book was designed to be warm and inviting to those considering hospice care. Becky comments, "The topic itself can be dismal, so I wanted to make sure that it communicated hope instead of despair. I didn't expect to be so moved by the text. By the end of the project, I was calling local hospices to see if they needed volunteers."

"This venture worked out swimmingly. I had a good relationship with my client and we were clear about payment and deadlines. I was paid $25 per hour and the project totaled $1,000. I'm glad I negotiated a price that was a little higher than I was comfortable with at the time. It doesn't hurt to ask and it shows that you are assertive and can vouch for your work with a dollar sign."

Becky advises, "Be tenacious when it comes to networking. Freelance work was scarce at first, but I soon became involved all kinds of projects. Don't ever disregard what seems to be a 'no.' The future is going to come whether you are prepared or not, and when it does it helps to have a lot of friends. One of my goals is to always try and do things right the first time."

River City Rhapsody Project
Designed by Ryan Musselman
Received $2,500.00

River City Rhapsody is a Drum and Bugle Corps competition hosted by the Blue Stars Drum and Bugle Corps. Ryan had been involved in the organization in the past and noticed that they desperately needed graphic design help. Ryan did a few small projects for them for free at first, which eventually led to paying project.

Ryan did a wide variety of work for River City Rhapsody and was paid a lump sum of $2,500 for his work. Ryan says, "It took the entire summer and fall to complete my work for them. Of all the work I did for this group, the project shown above probably represents 15 to 20 percent of it."

Ryan added, "This client was borderline freelance/pro bono because they are a nonprofit organization, and I already had connections with them. My advice for other freelancers might seem obvious, but make sure you and your client agree on how much you are getting paid, and how you get paid, before you start working. I've run into various issues relating to compensation in the past. I found a great video from Mike Monteiro, cofounder of Mule Design Studio, called 'F*ck You. Pay Me,' that talks about the importance of always using a contract." This video can be found online at http://vimeo.com/22053820.

The Center for Excellence in the Arts and Humanity Poster
Designed by Laura Weible
Received $1,500.00

The Center for Excellence in the Arts and Humanity (CEAH) supports distinction in faculty research and scholarship in the arts and humanities at Iowa State University. Annually, they host a poster competition to advertise their featured conference. One student's work is chosen, and that student works with the center to design the poster and coordinates print and production with the university printer.

Laura worked with the center two years in a row and was paid $1,500 for the poster above. The job was advertised to pay $500, but by the second year Laura had established such a great relationship with the center that they tripled her earnings. Laura states, "My experience with this freelance project was one of the best I've ever had. I learned how to grow a relationship and see the long term benefits. It pays to go the extra mile, literally."

ADVANCED LEVEL

Creating a Web Presence for Your Company

Apart from the business card you completed the Intermediate level, a website is one of the most economical means of promoting your business. If you've never built a website before, this project can be a great way to learn what the process entails and give yourself an idea about how long it might take you to complete a similarly sized website for a client.

Your goal is to build a website of one to three pages in order to promote your freelance business. Think of a "web presence" as an online brochure, and you'll get a rough idea about how much information about your company to include. Building a full-blown website might be a bit overkill, so keep your investment of time and money to a minimum for now.

Building a website doesn't have to be an overwhelming process, and there are many tools available to help you complete this task. You can design and code the website yourself from scratch or modify an existing template to meet your needs.

DOMAIN NAME

Hopefully, you purchased your domain name when you registered your company as an LLC. But in case you didn't, you'll need to go to a website like godaddy.com and purchase a domain name.

WEB HOSTING

If you don't have a Web hosting plan already, it's time to choose a hosting plan to host your website files. For a simple Web presence website, you don't need lots of bells and whistles, just a simple hosting plan. I decided to use godaddy.com because I also used them to purchase and manage my domain name. Godaddy is relatively inexpensive, around $5 per month for their hosting services, but there are many Web hosting options out there that you might consider also.

If you decide to use godaddy.com, they will try to sell you additional features; however, you probably won't need these options. The most basic plan will probably be more than sufficient for your needs. You can find Web hosting plans that will give you Web hosting space for free, but they usually put ads at the top of all your pages. You won't be able to control which ads appear on your page, and I think it makes the page look a little cheap. I think it's worth spending between $5 and $7 per month to not have someone else's advertisements at the top of your page. To put this in perspective, you can host your website for a month for the price of a Starbucks coffee—an easy decision for me to make.

If you decide to use a service like www.squarespace.com, you might want to hold off on purchasing a Web hosting plan because this is a feature that is included in their monthly rate. For around $12 per month, you can build and update your website easily—and this price includes Web hosting. While Squarespace is a little more expensive, it's relatively easy to set up a professional-looking website within a matter of minutes. Squarespace has a number of video tutorials available that you can follow that will teach you how to set up and modify your website using their online tools.

Companies like Squarespace allow designers who aren't familiar with HTML or CSS or who do not have software like Adobe Dreamweaver to put together a website quickly and easily. Squarespace even allows you to try their services free for a week so you aren't out any money if you decide that Squarespace isn't the right direction for you.

Squarespace's fees are a little more expensive, but it's incredibly easy to set up, manage, and modify your website from any computer that has an Internet connection. If I have a client who is simply looking for a Web presence and wants the ability to change the information on his website himself, I might suggest that he consider using an option like Squarespace.

Personally, I prefer to build my websites myself since my content probably won't change a great deal. But you should pick the option that works best for you. In the end all that matters is that you have an online presence so that clients can find you easily. You'll have an additional sales tool online that you can use to promote your services.

ADVANCED LEVEL

Planning for What Comes after School

It's a good idea to do a little research before making any life-changing decisions—like deciding what you are going to do after you graduate. Most of my students seem to go in one of three directions after they graduate from college. They enter the workforce, freelance, or apply to graduate schools. While there are certainly other options available to choose from, it seems that most of my students fall into one of these three categories. Deciding on your next major goal can be tough, and if you haven't done so already you should do a little soul-searching and think about what comes next in your life.

How do you decide which direction is the right direction for you? Well, the best way is to research your options and account for as many variables as you can. You should consider variables like relationships, financial constraints, obligations to friends and family, and any religious or civic duties. When I teach seniors, I require them to write a paper about their postgraduation plans. Students are asked to interview at least three people who hold the position that the student would like to occupy. Having students write a paper helps them ground their goals in reality. In fact, almost every year I've had students do a 180-degree turn with their postcollege plans after completing their interviews for this assignment.

It's easy to assume things will just "work out" once you graduate, and I hope everything works out for you. But having a plan in place is always a good strategy. The research you gather as you soul-search will either confirm your trajectory and make you even more excited about your future or leave you feeling anxious and unsure about your options. John Lennon once said "Life is what happens to you while you're busy making other plans." So even if your plan doesn't work out as well as you hope, rest assured that you're probably not alone, and you're never out of options.

You may be asking yourself, "Why is it so important that I decide right now?" The answer is simple. You need time to prepare, and this is probably close to your last year in school. If you've decided on a particular direction, you can prepare in advance to make sure that you not only land on your feet but have many great options to choose from.

Speaking from experience, I believe it's easy to fall into a situation where you are working incredibly hard, but making very little progress. This is what you want to try to avoid. The biggest reason to identify your goals early is to ensure that you can be efficient with your finances, resources, and time. You'll realize how important it was for you to be prepared later, after you've started making the transition

When you're putting together your portfolio, you should consider including pieces that can fit into many categories. Kyle Waldrop's Sneaker Fresh project can easily be seen as a branding, packaging, or product redesign project and can become a topic of conversation in an interview.

from student to professional. Front-loading work now while you're still in school will save you an unbelievable amount of stress later—don't wait until the last minute to get serious about identifying your goals and working towards them.

Choosing the Right Portfolio for The Job

Your portfolio is a highly personalized object, but its function is just as important as its form. Before you begin putting together your portfolio, identify what your goals are after you graduate college. In fact, the more specific you can be in answering this question, the better your chances are in putting together a portfolio that will help you meet your goals.

AGENCY PORTFOLIO

If you're interested in working at a graphic design agency after you graduate, you will need to create a portfolio that contains eight to twelve examples of your best work. I think it's a better strategy to show fewer "awesome" portfolio pieces than to spread yourself thin by watering your portfolio down with more "okay" pieces. Employers look for many things in a portfolio, and art directors weigh different

> *"Even though you will only show a potential employer eight to twelve pieces in your portfolio, you should have twenty portfolio pieces to choose from."*

assets more than others from agency to agency. In most cases, the person interviewing you has his agency's clients and needs in the back of his mind as he looks through your portfolio. More than likely, he is trying to determine if your work is marketable to his clients, so putting the right type of work in your portfolio is a crucial component in the hiring process.

When you're putting together your portfolio, you'll want to try to include pieces that can fall into multiple categories. For example, you might try to include a project like Kyle Waldrop's Sneaker Fresh project, shown on the previous page. An art director might look at Kyle's piece and get a good idea about his design sensibilities, as well as his branding and packaging abilities. A good portfolio piece will attempt to answer questions about your design skills, while a poor portfolio piece may raise questions about your skills as a designer.

If Kyle simply showed a logo he designed for Sneaker Fresh, it would be hard for an art director to see how he would implement it in a system. By going beyond simply creating a logo, Kyle has attempted to identify and address some of the questions an art director would have and has created a portfolio piece that is likely to capture an art director's attention. Kyle's piece is likely to start a conversation with the art director and create an opportunity for Kyle to take advantage of. The more an employer feels that he knows you, the easier it is for him to hire you.

Even though you will only show a potential employer eight to twelve pieces in your portfolio, you should have twenty portfolio pieces to choose from. Why the extra work? You have to think like an employer instead of a graphic designer. Employers want employees with specific skills, and they want to see work that reflects the attributes they are looking for in a candidate. If you have exactly eight to twelve pieces to show, what are the chances that these pieces will reflect the exact attributes they want their candidates to possess? When you have twenty pieces to choose from, even though you are only going to show eight to twelve pieces, you are far more likely to be able to put together a selection of work that will impress.

Read through the job description on the next page and try to think about what kind of work might be good to include in your portfolio if you were applying for this position.

Job Type: Graphic Design and Marketing position

Description: Best known as the publisher of *Nursing Monthly* and *Cutting Edge Medical*, Johnson & Hapner is a leader in the health-care industry. We provide an award-winning nursing library, seminars, webinars, and certification test reviews. We have a thirty-plus-year reputation for quality and expertise in health care that gives us a competitive advantage in the market. We are seeking a talented graphic designer to join our office. You will be part of a skilled and dedicated team supporting our online education retail operations.

Requirements:
• Develop creative solutions to accommodate client needs.
• Collaborate with development team to build user interfaces.
• Research and analyze audience characteristics and trending.
• Analyze, develop, and refine user processes.
• Organize Web content and test functionality.

Desired qualifications:
• Experience in publishing, e-commerce, or education systems
• Experience building print advertising campaigns
• Creativity, intelligence, and focus

Let's decode this job announcement a bit more and come up with a strategy for applying to this job. Clearly, Johnson & Hapner provides support for the health-care industry, and it looks as if it produces print and online material. This means that in order to be a good fit you will want to include some print pieces along with any websites or apps that you've designed with the following characteristics:

• An example of website architecture and navigation system
• An example of education and e-commerce components
• An awareness of user processes and functionality
• An analysis of audience research and data

Fitting all these components into a portfolio that is between eight and twelve pieces in size is a tall order. A good strategy is to show several examples of work that exhibits some of these characteristics, as well as a few additional pieces that

> *"While your work represents your skill as a designer, it's important to build a freelance portfolio for your audience instead of yourself."*

you feel might be relevant. Perhaps you should include a portfolio piece showing your process work, audience research, website architecture or website analytics. This may help give the impression that your design solutions are grounded in reality. Or better yet, it may help you strategically position yourself as a candidate who might be able to bring unique skills and design methodologies to the company.

From the job description, it's clear that you'll also need to show that you're proficient in print design. Include portfolio pieces like magazine or newsletter tear sheets, or an advertising campaign, since the company mentioned that this was a qualification that it was looking for. This means that four to six portfolio pieces have already been chosen for you by the Johnson & Harper job description. All that's left is to include a few select pieces to show off your creativity, intelligence, and graphic design skills. You can see from this example how you need to match the work in your portfolio with the job description of the position you're applying for.

When you hear of a job opening, respond to the announcement quickly! Having a body of work ready to pick from gives you two advantages—having a variety of options to choose from and the ability to throw your name into the hat for a job posting quickly and getting your application reviewed immediately.

FREELANCE PORTFOLIO

If you're interested in freelancing full time, then you will need to build a portfolio that acts as a sales tool and includes the type of work that will appeal to potential clients. While your work represents your skills as a designer, it's important to build a freelance portfolio for your audience instead of for yourself. The work you include in your portfolio should be the work your audience wants to see. If you have a client that needs a monthly newsletter to send out to his customers, he will be particularly interested in seeing other newsletters that you have designed in the past. For this reason, if you're going to continue freelancing after you graduate, you need to clearly identify the type of work your company will support, and you'll have to reverse-engineer your portfolio to include examples of this type of work and other related projects. Once you've built up a client base, you can begin to branch out and add more variety to your portfolio.

You certainly don't want your work to appear monochromatic, so look for ways to integrate tangential projects as well. For instance, if you're going to specialize in creating newsletters, perhaps you should also consider including logo designs, postcard campaigns, and other projects that are likely appeal to this type of client in your portfolio. Address the client's most immediate need first, but look for an opportunity to assist him with other projects in the future. While you're delivering a solution to the client's most urgent need, plant the seed that you'd like to discuss some of your other ideas with him in the near future.

I believe the best way to get work isn't by selling one business card at a time, but by helping your clients develop a plan to solve the problems that keep them up at night. This approach involves talking with them and clearly identifying their needs, researching and discovering the best means of creating a solution to help them achieve their goals, working within time and budget restraints, and discovering solutions that exceed their expectations. Now that's a formula for success, and if you can repeat this process and deliver good results, clients will continue to come back to you again and again.

Projects that have statistical information attached to them are great to include in a your portfolio. For example, when I worked with Fütprint, a small marketing and design agency, we talked to an owner of a local restaurant and found that he wanted to increase bar sales. Fütprint's owner, John Wallace, asked how much money bar sales had brought in over the previous two months to establish a baseline for the effectiveness of the marketing plan that he was about to implement.

John developed a strategy, and the team created a series of tabletop menus that could be used at specific times throughout the year, advertisements strategically hung below all the televisions in the restaurant, and a series of posters that were hung in a reception area and could be viewed by customers as they waited to be seated.

After all the table-toppers, advertisements, and posters were displayed, our client reported that his bar sales increased 37 percent over the following two months. Fütprint's success at increasing their client's bar sales led to an opportunity to redesign the restaurant's gift certificates and menus, and eventually led to a retainer contract to handle the restaurant's graphic design and marketing needs. Fütprint got its foot in the door and knocked the ball out of the park with the first job it was given—increasing bar sales. It did such a great job with the jobs it was given that it made itself indispensable to the restaurant and gathered some impressive data in the process.

ADVANCED LEVEL

If you collect data on the projects you work on, you can use this information as a sales tool to help convince clients who are on the fence that they should work with you. While you can't promise to increase sales 37 percent for every client you work with, you can point out that you've been success at helping your clients fix the problems that keep them up at night in the past.

GRADUATE SCHOOL PORTFOLIO

There are many types of graduate schools across the country, and there isn't a standard format for preparing your application, but I can give you some tips to help you improve your portfolio. Typically, graduate schools put together a committee to review applications and rank the quality of the applicant's work. It's hard to know what each of these committee members is looking for, so there isn't a specific thing that you should to increase the chances of being accepted. However, here are some points that you may want to consider.

- Graduate programs want to work with students who are likely to succeed and ultimately make their graduate program look good.
- Graduate programs want to work with students who have a body of work that supports the topic they say they are interested in exploring.
- Graduate programs want to work with students who might be able to help secure grant money, teach undergraduate classes, or help make connections to industry.
- Graduate programs want students who have good grade point averages, GRE scores (if required), and a history of academic success.
- Graduate faculty want to work with students who have research interests that are similar to their own research interests.
- Graduate faculty want to work with students who have defined an area to explore, but are receptive to different points of view.

Most graduate schools require a portfolio of twenty pieces—no more, no less. If you're considering going to graduate school, then you will want to include examples of work that will help answer how a degree will help you achieve your goals. You'll want to show the committee how your work has begun to explore a particular topic and how it might connect to further investigations.

Every graduate school posts what format your portfolio work should take. Make sure you do not deviate from their requested formats. Graduate committees are usually made up of faculty members who are very busy and have limited time.

Committee members do not have the time to devote to portfolios that have been prepared in an incorrect format, and you risk not having your work seen if you deviate from the requested format.

Putting together a graduate school application takes a lot of time. I recommend that you identify the date the application is due and begin working on your application at least three months before this date—especially if you are applying to more than one graduate school. Candidates are often asked to supply a statement of intent, letters of reference, and other materials, and it takes time to create these documents and prepare all your materials in the requested format. Your application is not complete until all your materials have been received, so leave yourself plenty of time and check with the graduate school to make sure they have received the items you sent before the deadline has passed—especially your letters of reference.

Choosing the Right Portfolio Pieces

Imagine a scale from one to ten, where ten represents a solution that embodies an extraordinary level of research, creativity, and craftsmanship, while one represents a not-so-good solution. With this scale in mind, you should only include pieces in your portfolio that are an eight or higher. I've found that most seniors become so invested in particular project that they have a difficult time seeing their work objectively. Herein lies a dilemma.

Perhaps you might have won an award for a project, worked incredibly hard on a project, received an A+, or worked on a project that was printed or recognized professionally. Unfortunately, this doesn't automatically mean this piece should go into your portfolio. The thing that matters most is the quality of the work in your portfolio. Don't get me wrong, having awards and good grades are great, but most employers want to hire designers based on the quality of work in their portfolio.

Employers don't want to hire graphic designers who are just okay; they want to hire designers with creative, fresh, and have exciting work in their portfolio. Employers want designers who bring something to the table, have the potential to expand the range of services the company can offer, and make the clients happy.

It's incredibly hard to look at your work with fresh eyes, but that's exactly what you have to do when you're putting together your portfolio. You have to look at your work, forgetting all the hard work you poured into your projects, and only keep your best pieces. There are no rules when it comes to putting together your portfolio, so feel free to rework projects. Shed project and client constraints that

ADVANCED LEVEL

you previously had to adhere to and put your best foot forward. I've found that most of my senior students have two to six projects that they completed during school that are close to being ready to put into their portfolio. They have an additional three to five projects that need some further revisions, but have the potential to be portfolio pieces, and need nine to fifteen new pieces.

A good way to relieve some of the pressure of having to produce nine to fifteen new portfolio pieces is to set some goals for yourself. If your give yourself a goal of producing five portfolio pieces every four weeks, as long as you are disciplined and keep working, you won't have a problem gathering the twenty pieces you need for your portfolio in a semester.

This is where working with a freelance client who gives you a large degree of creative control can be very helpful. These types of clients allow you to continue to generate creative work for your portfolio while simultaneously collecting a paycheck for your efforts. This scenario is win-win for designer and client and is the type of relationship you should seek out at the Advanced level.

As you continue to freelance and generate new work for your portfolio, I recommend that you show your work to your peers and get as much feedback as you can along the way. Here are some ideas about where you can start to get feedback on which of your projects are working the best.

- Talk to professionals in your area and ask them if they would be willing to meet with you to look at your portfolio work and give you feedback.
- Look for portfolio review opportunities with your school or professional design organizations and participate in these reviews.
- Make appointments with your professors and talk to them about your work. Ask them to give you feedback.
- Talk to your classmates and peers and critique each other.

CREATING A SYSTEM
Your portfolio needs to be designed as well as the projects inside it are designed. The work in your portfolio needs to be photographed or attached in a flattering way. One thing you may consider when you're putting your portfolio together is to take note of how many of your projects fall into a particular area. If you decide to divide your portfolio up into categories like "Websites" or "Annual Reports," you should be conscious of how many pieces you include in these categories. Try to evenly distribute the number of pieces in each category or eliminate the categories

Rachel Ritchie chose to display her poster hanging on a post at the farmer's market in her portfolio. This gives the piece context and shows that she's thinking about where it will be displayed as she's designing the piece. Sometimes showing a two-dimensional piece in a photograph with depth adds interest and helps the viewer understand why the designer made the decisions she did.

altogether. Having one or two pieces in a category may be interpreted as an area that you are not as proficient working in. If your portfolio system calls attention to a weakness, create a more flattering system to use to accommodate your work.

DESCRIBING YOUR WORK

Putting a small description alongside your work is a great idea. You might consider writing a synopsis of the project, describing any interesting constrains or listing awards or honors your project may have won. If you are not able to present your work in person, a short description is a critical component in helping viewers understand what they are looking at and why you have included this piece in your portfolio. If you get tongue-tied during an interview, you can take a sneak peek at your description to help you get back on track.

Most art directors don't have time to read lengthy descriptions, so this text needs to be short and to the point. It goes without saying that your text needs to be typographically elegant, well designed, articulate, and well written. Your viewer's attention should be focused on your work, and your text should be less important hierarchically. The biggest mistake I see in student portfolios is that they choose a point size for their type that is either too large or small to be viewed comfortably.

PHOTOGRAPHING YOUR WORK

It takes more time to photograph your work in an environment than it does to convert a digital file to an image, but photographing your work can add a lot of interest to the piece. You can use different lenses, lighting techniques, and camera angles to help you build a narrative around your portfolio piece.

Jon Newman uses photography in a clever and flattering way in the example above to display a business card he designed for a client. The light blue background and the subject's hand helps provide contrast for the business card, so its shape and size can be identified quickly. In addition, Jon also uses a clever technique to move his viewers eyes around the page. After we see the photograph on the right, our eyes follow the arm back to the logo because we subconsciously want to identify who is holding the business card. Instead of a face, our eyes come to rest on the Princeton logo. Then we move our eyes back to the business card on the right and finish by looking at the description of the project in the lower right hand side of the page. This is a good example of how smart photography and a good eye for layout can really help you to elevate your work. Who would have thought that a simple business card and logo would make such a strong impression? Jon's spread shows that he clearly understands how to move his viewers' eyes around the page, and he takes full advantage of this knowledge.

stationary
stationery

When you photograph your portfolio pieces, make sure you set your white balance on your camera and shoot a few practice images. Open these files on your computer to verify that your camera settings are correct and that your images are coming out well lit, crisp, and clear. Sometimes images look great on the small LCD screen on the back of the camera, but appear different when viewed on a computer screen. If you need to change your settings, take a few more test shots to verify that you're getting the file type and quality that you need. Preparing for a photo shoot takes a lot of time and planning, but it's worth it to get the shot you need the first time. Here are a few tips you can use to get the shot you need.

- Think about paper, fabric, colors, and textures that you can place behind or underneath your work to make your projects pop. Keep in mind that your backgrounds don't necessarily have to be neutral by default.
- Think about what props you could use to help showcase your work. If you designed a wine label, perhaps you bring in grapes and some wine glasses to use as props or as elements to help move your viewers' eyes around the page.
- Think about lighting. If you're shooting images on a light table, make sure that you bring white poster board to bounce light, and duct tape, aluminum foil, scissors, and other items to assist you in setting up and getting the shot you need. If you're shooting outside, scout out the area in advance at different times of the day to determine when you'll get the best lighting and fewest distractions.
- Make sure you bring a few spare memory cards for your digital camera so that you won't have to stop shooting to download or delete images.
- Bring multiple pieces of the same project. Even if you need only one shot, you can sometimes create an interesting composition by stacking, spreading out, or propping up your work with similar items.
- Bring multiple lenses and filters with you in order to experiment with them during your photo shoot.
- Shoot in RAW format, so that you can go back and make corrections easily.

You should take hundreds of photographs of each of your projects and make small adjustments each time. Shoot from different angles, adjust your lighting from time to time, bracket your images by moving your f-stop up and down, experiment with different camera lenses, and take close-up images to use as detail shots as you go along. Make small adjustments as you work, and give yourself plenty of time to shoot your work and get the perfect shot.

> *"...it's critically important to have a plan for where your money will go, so that you don't wind up asking yourself where all your money went."*

It's much easier to set up your work and shoot lots of photos than it will be to drag everything back out, set the work up again, and reshoot because you didn't get the shot you needed the first time. You might have the perfect layout envisioned in your head, but when you go home and download your images, you might decide that your photos don't look as good as you thought they would. If you took plenty of photos, then you'll have plenty of options to choose from.

Great photography and a clever layout will make your work stand out in a sea of portfolios, so leave yourself plenty of time to get the shot you need. Keep a backup copy of all your images somewhere safe because you'll probably need to use them again in the future. Take the time to go through your images and name your files. Sort them into folders that allow you to reference the photos quickly. Spending a little extra time naming your files will save you considerable time searching for them when you need them again. You'd be surprised how many times I've used these type of shots to promote myself.

Creating a Monthly Budget

A Microsoft Excel document titled "Monthly Budget" is available for you to download—this process is described on page ix. A monthly budget is a useful tool to visualize your sources of income, expenses, investments, and assets. Being able to visualize where your money comes from and goes to can help you make better financial decisions on a daily basis. Having a monthly budget also gives you an indication of the amount of money you'll need to make in order to achieve financial independence. Discipline is a key ingredient of success, and a monthly budget allows you to see where your money is going.

Personal money-management expert Dave Ramsey points out, "We buy things we don't need, with money we don't have, to impress people we don't really like." Have you ever fallen into this trap before? We have all spent money for the wrong reasons at some point in our life, but it's critically important to have a plan for where your money will go, so that you don't wind up asking yourself where all your money went.

A Federal Reserve survey estimates that around 75 percent of households have at least one credit card, and the average household credit-card debt is almost $10,000. This is credit-card debt alone and does not reflect real estate mortgages, car loans, or education loans. You can probably see how easy it would be to accumulate a lot of debt in a hurry, especially if you're trying to expedite the American dream.

If you are a person who isn't squeamish about giving out your online banking passwords, then you may want to consider subscribing to an online money managing service like Mint.com. Mint's website states, "Mint brings all your financial accounts together online, automatically categorizes your transactions, lets you set budgets & helps you achieve your savings goals." Indeed, when I tested their services out I was impressed with how easy it was to see where I was spending my money and with the suggestions on how I could save more. I saw that I was eligible for a credit card with a better interest rate. I called my credit-card company and told them that I had received a better offer, and soon I was talking with a supervisor, who offered to lower my interest rate by 7 percent for the next twelve months—saving me a considerable amount of money.

Mint's services are free. It makes money by charging banks and credit cards a fee for introducing them to new customers. While I didn't end up changing my credit-card company, I was prepared to do so in order to obtain a lower interest rate. One of the features I like is that Mint lets you set up financial goals and allows you to visualize your progress more clearly. After I got the interest rate lowered on my credit-card, I set up a goal to put some rainy day money aside each month.

Using a budget is a good idea because it helps you to build good financial habits. When you first use a budget, you might feel constricted. But as you become more accustomed to budgeting, the entire process becomes second nature. You'll find that you give priority to your most important expenses first and then add your nonessential expenses afterwards. It seems silly to say, but don't forget to budget for entertainment and fun! After all, you've worked hard to get to where you are and deserve a little reward—just make sure that your reward is scaled appropriately!

Whether you prefer tracking your finances with the Excel spreadsheet available on the companion website for this book or by using a service like Mint, knowing where your money goes is a critical step in balancing your budget. Without this information at your disposal, how will you know if job offers you receive will cover your expenses? Many of my students report that their parents pay for some of their expenses, such as insurance or a campus meal plan, or even give them a small allowance or reimburse certain expenses. You should talk with your parents about their expectations to support for you after you graduate. While you may not have had to pay your own health or car insurance while you were in school, you may be asked to pay for this expense yourself after you graduate. It's often issues like this that can throw off your budget and make you go into debt. Make sure you're aware of what you'll be responsible for so that you won't be caught off guard!

Creating a PDF Portfolio

In addition to a print or web portfolio, you need to create a PDF version of your portfolio. PDF is an acronym that stands for Portable Document Format and is a format that can be accessed on many sorts of computer systems. Unlike other digital formats, you can incorporate fonts into your PDF document (meaning that they are displayed correctly on any computer system), embed multimedia and video files, and assign a password to prevent someone from editing or modifying your file. PDF documents are keyword searchable, so viewers can find the information they are looking for quickly.

When I'm designing a PDF portfolio, I take my most complex portfolio piece and my most simple portfolio piece and create a grid around these two pieces. These two portfolio pieces are likely to be the pieces that will the most difficult to fit into a grid system. By working with the two most difficult portfolio pieces first, I end up working more efficiently and save myself a great deal of time. You need to use the grid system that you create consistently and creatively. The pages in your PDF portfolio shouldn't look exactly the same, but they should all look like they are related to each other. Make sure you pay attention to typographic hierarchy and take advantage of type families (i.e., bold, regular, italic) when necessary.

I am often asked by students, "Do we need to include a description of our work?" The answer is "Yes, you should write between one and four descriptive sentences about your work." When someone is looking at your portfolio for the first time, this information will help them to understand what they are looking at, any unique constraints or project goals, if the piece has won an award, any unusual formal considerations or printing techniques, or other pertinent information that you feel makes your solution unique or especially creative. Avoid the temptation to write a long description of your work. Aim to make your comments short and sweet instead. Don't use eighty words to describe your portfolio piece when forty words will do. Your goal is to create a strong impression and make the goals of the project and outcomes understood quickly and easily.

Your PDF portfolio needs to be between 5MB and 10MB in size in order to be easily distributed via e-mail, so take the time to compress your files. Undoubtedly, you are aware that you can create PDF files from a variety of software applications. But you might not realize that recent releases of Adobe Acrobat can import and group files into what they call a "PDF Portfolio." Instead of attaching multiple files to an e-mail (e.g.,. a cover letter, school transcripts, portfolio, and résumé), with this feature you can merge your documents together and present everything in a professionally designed layout. In essence, Acrobat allows you to package your documents together in one nice and neat PDF file that is visually coherent, and one in which users can open, read, and edit your documents.

Before you package your PDF files into a PDF Portfolio, take a moment to go through your documents and delete unused objects on your art board. This may help reduce your file size. When you export a PDF document, take a moment to look over your compression settings. You may notice that there is a menu titled "Adobe PDF Preset," with the option "Smallest File Size." Select this option to compress your file and reduce its size.

You may notice a drop-down menu that says "Bicubic Downsampling to" with two numerical fields to the right. Acrobat uses these numbers to compress any images you may have embedded in your document. Take note of the settings in this field, because if you are not happy with the way your images look once your PDF document has been generated, you will probably want to play around with these numbers to achieve the level of image quality you're looking for.

Once you've reviewed the settings and are satisfied, click "Export" to generate a PDF file. You'll have to follow a few more prompts, but nothing too complicated. After your PDF file has been generated, take a moment to review it and make sure that it appears the way you intended. Sometimes the smallest things can throw you for a curve—for example, not checking the "Spreads" checkbox if you intended your document's pages to be viewed as spreads. For that reason, be sure and proofread your document.

Submitting A PDF Portfolio

Most art directors prefer to be contacted by e-mail. When you first make contact with an art director, attach a PDF document of your portfolio to the e-mail in the hope that he or she will open the document and look at your work. If you have a link to your website, then be sure to include your URL as well. If you don't hear back from them in five to ten business days, call the art director to see if you can request a meeting. Always be professional and courteous and refrain from sending the art director reminders that you haven't heard back from him or her yet. In most cases, art directors are working with tight deadlines and may not have had an opportunity to respond to your request. You need to accept that you're working on their timetable instead of yours. Be patient, but follow up if you haven't heard back after a reasonable amount of time has passed.

Some art directors consider PDF portfolios to be the first round of interviews and will only offer in-person interviews to candidates who successfully capture their attention. Make sure the work you send has flawless spelling, grammar, and execution. You might wish to limit your PDF portfolio to five to eight pieces in order to keep your file size small. Leave yourself a few "new" pieces to discuss with the art director in case you're offered an in-person interview. The pieces the art director has not seen yet will hopefully be pieces that you can spend a bit more time talking about in person. But you should make sure to include your best pieces in your PDF portfolio in order to make the strongest impression you can.

What to Say In a Letter of Interest

When you're writing an e-mail to inquire about a position, there are a few elements that you should be sure to include and some protocols you should consider using. Before sending your e-mail, make sure that your e-mail address doesn't give the wrong impression. If you're lookinforlove@yahoo.com, you should sign up for a more professional sounding e-mail address before contacting you potential employer. First impressions are lasting impressions, so keep your e-mail address and correspondence strictly professional.

Your first task is to do some research on the company's website in order to find the answers to any questions you might have before you take the time to ask someone at the company. If you ask a question that has already been obviously answered on the company's website, it may appear that you're too lazy or inept to look for or understand the information on your own.

If you're confident that your question has not been answered, your next task is to find the correct person to direct your e-mail to. If you found this position on a job message board or company website, reread the job description to see if your question has been answered in the job post. If not, these types of job posts usually have a contact person you can get in touch with to ask a question. If you looking

> *"Try to avoid using generic subjects lines like 'Hello' or 'Urgent.' Use a more descriptive subject line for your e-mail instead."*

for a job by cold-calling an agency, following up on a verbal recommendation to apply for a position, or another source, direct your question to Human Resources or to an administrative assistant, who can direct your question to the appropriate person. Don't send your e-mail to just any random person you can find and ask him or her to forward your e-mail. Doing so would distract them their duties, and they have no reason to respond to your request. It's simply more work for them. Do a little digging, and don't be afraid of picking up the phone to talk to an administrative assistant to help you get your question or request to the appropriate person.

Once you've identified the correct person to contact, you need to write a brief and concise subject line for your e-mail. If you're seeking an in-house graphic design job, then perhaps you use a subject line like "In-House Graphic Design Position" or another descriptive statement. Try to avoid generic subject lines like "Hello" or "Urgent." Use a more descriptive subject line for your e-mails instead. When someone responds to your e-mail, don't change the subject line. It will be much easier for your contact person to follow an e-mail thread if the subject line remains constant. Pick a descriptive subject line and start composing your e-mail.

Begin by introducing yourself and then get to the point quickly. Your message needs to be clear, concise, and to the point, and yet have a pleasant and polite tone. Before you send your e-mail, it's a good idea to read it again out loud, because you might catch a mistake or think of a better way to say something. Once you're happy with your e-mail, double-check it to make sure that it's free of grammatical errors, attach a copy of your PDF portfolio to it, add your e-mail address to the blind carbon copy field (BCC), and send it. I like to copy myself on these types of e-mails because it helps me keep track of who I submitted my work to and when. Here's an example of what your letter of interest might look like:

I noticed the graphic design position posted on your company website, and I would like to apply for this position. I will graduate in May from <insert your university> with a degree in Graphic Design. During my studies I completed an internship with XYZ Graphics, won numerous awards for my graphic design work, and worked with a wide variety of freelance clients.

I've looked at your company's portfolio, and I'm impressed with the diversity and quality of your agency's work. I feel that the work in my portfolio will appeal to your clients, and I am attaching a few samples of my design portfolio for you to view.

I would love an opportunity to meet with you and talk to you about the graphic design position that you are advertising, show you my design portfolio, and learn about the opportunities your company provides. Thank you in advance for your time. I'll give you a call next week to see if you have any questions or need any additional information in case I don't hear back from you this week.

Sincerely,

< insert your name>
<insert your contact information>

Check your e-mail daily after applying for a job and respond to any requests for additional information or clarifications as soon as possible. When you receive a response, read it carefully and follow the directions you are given promptly and carefully. Do your best to make your contact's job easier by anticipating the information he or she needs and make sure to give him or her this information in the format he or she requested in order to make the process go smoothly.

If things go well, and you are offered an opportunity to meet with your contact and apply for the position, make sure you confirm the interview date, time, and location in writing. This is particularly important if you've talked with your contact over the phone. You might send a quick e-mail that says, "Thank you for the opportunity of an interview at your office on Main Street. I look forward to seeing you on Thursday, June 16 at 3:30 p.m."

One of my students had lined up an interview with a company, and she was excited about the opportunity. She had practiced her interview, polished her portfolio, and was ready to knock the ball out of the park. The following day I saw her, and I asked her how the interview went. She replied, "Uhh, it was okay." I was shocked and said, "But you were so excited to meet with this company! What happened?" She replied,"I got there right at 11:30, as instructed by the secretary, but when I arrived the secretary told me that I was thirty minutes late and the art director only had fifteen minutes to talk with me."

I felt horrible for her because there was nothing she could say to prove she had been given the wrong information. If she protested too loudly, she'd look immature, and the secretary would probably say that she gave her the right information and that she was trying to hide the fact that she arrived late. If she accepted the blame, it looks as if she did not appreciate the time the art director took out of his schedule to meet and review her portfolio. There was no way the student could win—unless she was able to produce an e-mail that confirmed she had arrived at the correct time. If she had a confirmation e-mail, she could send it to the art director and apologize for the confusion and ask if there was another time that might work better with his busy schedule.

I asked my student what she did, and she said, "I tried to make the best of the situation, but I could tell the art director wasn't really into the interview. I think he was tired of waiting for me to show up and was ready to go to lunch. He looked through my portfolio, but he didn't have a whole lot to say. I can't really blame him, but it wasn't my fault. I guess I'll just keep looking because I don't think I'm likely to get a call back from them."

There's an old saying, "Hope for the best, but prepare for the worst." That seems pretty accurate statement sometimes. I truly believe that my student was given an incorrect time for her meeting, and I agree that there isn't much she could do to redeem herself in the eyes of the art director. Sadly, this student learned the hard way that she probably should have sent written confirmation of her discussion with the office secretary.

Advanced Level Checklist

☐ Decide what your postcollege plans will be and define your goals.

☐ Carefully choose your freelance clients and projects.

☐ Create a monthly budget and start recording your income and expenses.

☐ Purchase a portfolio to display your creative work.

☐ Create your senior portfolio (twenty pieces total).

☐ Create a PDF version of your portfolio (5MB to 10MB).

☐ Get your college degree.

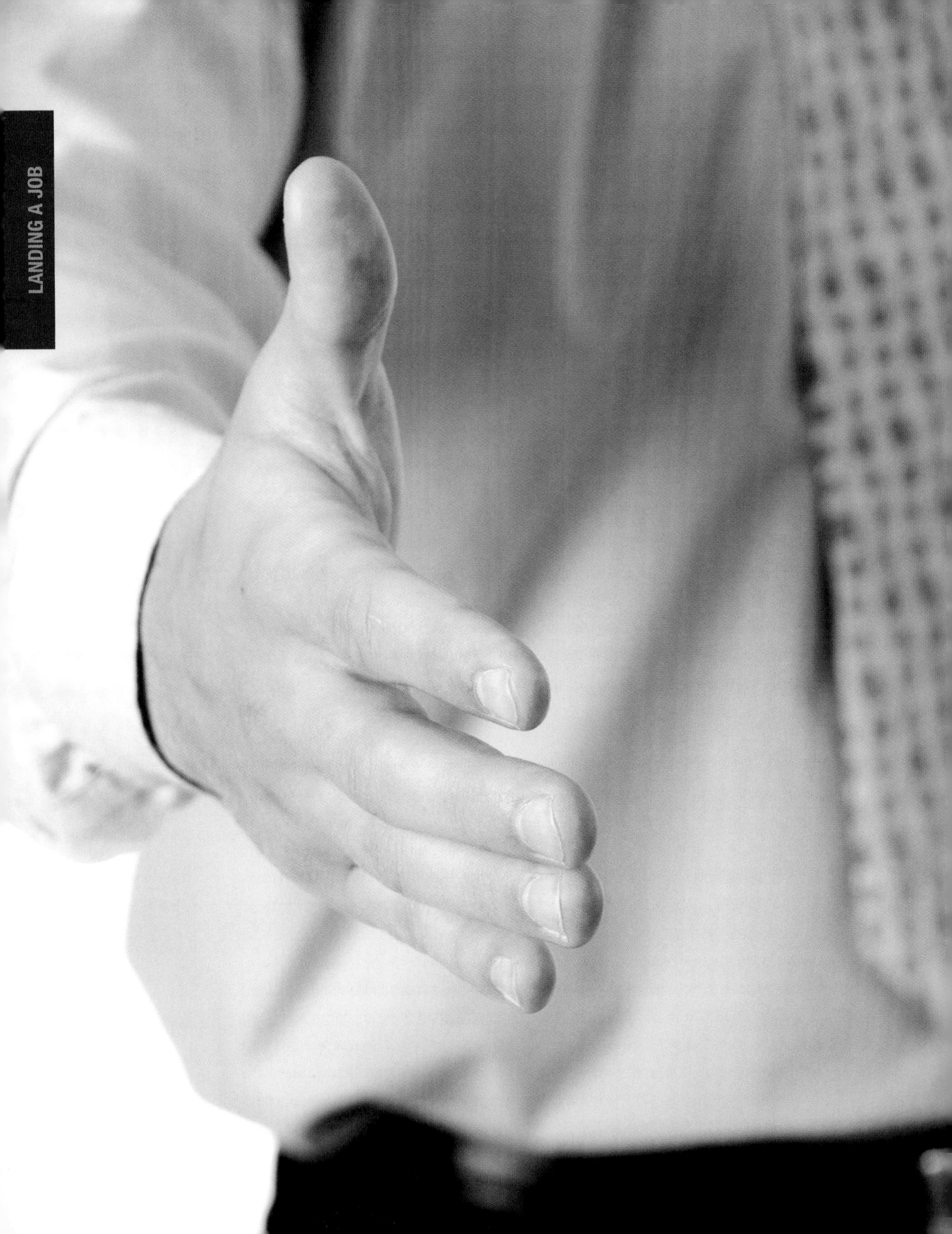

Moving Forward

Getting a Job

You should be proud of yourself for getting this far and accomplishing so much. Think about it. You started your own freelance graphic design business, photographed your work, networked with professionals, and put your portfolio together. All that's left for you to do is to land a job and enjoy the fruits of your labor.

In this chapter we're going to focus on three components that will help you accomplish this task. We're going to start by building your résumé, talk about strategies to prepare you for an interview, and discuss the art of negotiating a salary. Finding a job can be an emotional time because you are likely to face a few bumps in the road along the way. But hopefully all your hard work will payoff, and you'll land a job quickly.

One of the biggest annoyances that I hadn't considered when I started looking for my first job is that companies were interested in talking to me, but they were six to nine months away from being in a position to hire me. I believed that if I worked hard in school, developed my graphic design skills, and graduated with a degree in design I'd find a job quickly and easily. I learned that there's a big difference between finding a job and starting a career. I feel confident that each person reading this book is capable of finding a job, but finding a job to launch your career can be a bit trickier.

Before we get into the particulars, I just want to tell you from experience that I believe it's important for you to run your own race and not measure your successes and failures against those of your classmates. I had a good friend in school who graduated ahead of me and found an art director position for a design agency as soon as she graduated. I was excited for her and thought that if she could find an art director position, then I should be able to find a comparable position, too. Her accomplishment made me want to hurry up and graduate. Before I knew it, my senior year was over, and I had graduated. I was ready to hit the streets with my portfolio and show employers how creative I was. My plans quickly came crashing to a halt when I searched for graphic design job positions and didn't find anything even close to what I was hoping for.

I was crushed that I had gone to school for all this time and was unable to find a job! I couldn't understand why I was having such a hard time, while my friend had found something easily. I wondered if I had overlooked something. I called my friend, who had graduated a year ahead of me, with the hopes that I would learn what she had done to land her job. I discovered that I was doing all the same things she had done—except I didn't have the same results.

The money I received for graduation was beginning to run out, and I began to panic. What would I do if I couldn't find a job before I ran out of money? Would I have to wait tables or work at a retail store? I had been on lots of interviews, but I just didn't seem to be able to land an offer. I couldn't figure out what was going wrong, and in all honesty I was beginning to freak out.

Looking back on this experience years later, I would do two things differently. First, it was unrealistic to expect to land an art director position right out of school. I'd say the percentage of designers with no experience landing an art director position right out of school is mathematically less than predicting who will win the Super Bowl and what the final score will be at the beginning of the NFL season. The expectations I was putting on myself were far too high. Looking back twenty years later, I'm surprised that I was even given an interview! I was under qualified for many of these positions, and while I would have worked hard, the learning curve would have been steep. I'm afraid that even if I had been given a chance, I wouldn't have done a very good job.

The second thing I would change if I could go back in time is my how I wrote and formatted my résumé. Looking back at my résumé at the time, I recognize that it wasn't formatted correctly and was far too conversational. Your résumé needs to be brief and to the point, and it must frame your accomplishments in the best possible light. My résumé was not structured or focused enough to instill confidence in an employer that I had the tools and experience necessary to get the job done.

I don't want you to repeat my mistakes, so we're going to focus on how to write a résumé that will make you feel confident about your application. Writing a résumé isn't hard; it's mostly just an issue of formatting and deciding what information to include in your document.

Writing a Résumé

A résumé is a summary of the skills and experiences that are relevant to the job you are applying for. Your résumé highlights your most notable accomplishments and shows an employer why you are qualified to do a particular job. A résumé is not a biography of everything you've done, a philosophical statement, or a lengthy document. Your résumé should be exactly one page long until you get a few more years of experience under your belt.

The purpose of a résumé is to get you an interview, not to get you a job. It's function is to help you get your foot in the door to talk to someone in person. In many cases, a résumé can include more than just your work experience. You can include information about your education, extracurricular activities, leadership roles, and other experiences that are relevant to the job you are applying for.

Your résumé isn't a document that you can write and then send out a million copies at the same time. Instead your résumé needs to fit the job you are applying for. If you are applying for multiple positions at a time, it's a good idea to create slightly different versions of your résumé that are tailored to the positions your are applying for.

Similar to how you prepare a website for Search Engine Optimization, your résumé needs to be optimized using keywords from the job posting. In fact, some firms use an Applicant Tracking System (ATS) to match keywords from their job posting with keywords from an applicant's résumé. Unless you modify your résumé and incorporate some of these keywords into your résumé, then you might be eliminated from consideration before a human even looks at your document.

I found the following job posting on www.monster.com using the search term "graphic designer." Read the job posting and think about what strategy you might take if you were going to apply for this position:

GRAPHIC DESIGN POSITION: Newell Rubbermaid
Newell Rubbermaid is a global marketer of consumer and commercial products that touch the lives of people where they live, work and play. We are committed to building consumer and commercial Brands That Matter™ while leveraging the benefits of being one company: shared expertise, operating efficiencies, and a culture of innovation. Our globally recognized brands include Sharpie, Paper Mate, DYMO, EXPO, Waterman, Parker, Rolodex, IRWIN, LENOX, BernzOmatic, Rubbermaid, Graco, Calphalon, Goody, and Teutonia.

Newell Rubbermaid Décor division is seeking a Graphic Designer for its Marketing Communications team. This division's portfolio includes Levolor, Kirsch, and Amerock brands. The successful candidate will have a demonstrated ability to develop and maintain creative solutions for Marketing Communication strategies and execution. The Graphic Designer will report to the Design Manager in the Décor division.

COLLABORATION
- Work with team of designers and Design Manager in developing design solutions for Brand and Channel marketing initiatives, including point of purchase graphics, packaging, and direct mail marketing collateral.
- Work with Marketing Communications Project Managers throughout design development and execution processes to meet all deadlines, job specifications, and expectations.

BRAND STEWARDSHIP
- Maintain consistent brand guidelines and representation across all media and touch points, including print and basic Web graphics.
- Create presentations and basic support documents for brand-related standards and guidelines.

DESIGN AND LAYOUT
- Execute design from template-based design and complete revisions to existing materials, including quick turnaround projects.
- Create and review project layouts and proofs for accuracy and consistency in design specifications and brand requirements.
- Execute creative concepts and design layouts consistently and per brand requirements that meet and/or exceed project requirements.
- Collect and maintain digital files for photography, logos, and layouts.

PRE-PRESS PROCESSING
- Set up and prepare files for print production, including the creation of print-ready PDF files.
- Ensure accurate file collection and prepare files correctly to meet printer specifications, including die lines.

KEY REQUIREMENTS
- Strong creative sense of style and trends.
- Demonstrated creative conceptualizing skills and strong visual design application for print and basic Web graphics.
- Ability to work effectively and efficiently under tight deadlines; manage projects independently.
- Ability to communicate effectively with all levels of organization.
- Ability to take direction as well as make sound creative decisions based on project specifications and strategic initiatives.
- Strong organizational skills, keen attention to detail; ability to follow through and track projects and deliverables from beginning to end.
- Collaborative, upbeat demeanor, enthusiastic attitude; must work well as a team with internal clients, project managers, and business leads, as well as other members of Marketing Communications and other Newell Rubbermaid divisions.
- Bachelor's degree in Graphic Design, Marketing Communications, or equivalent experience.
- Command of typography, layout and graphics.
- Two to four years of graphic design experience in print design and basic Web graphics.
- Clear understanding of fundamental design and layout standards, print production techniques and processes; ability to accurately judge color and attend press runs a plus.
- Strong knowledge of Adobe CS5 applications and basic knowledge Microsoft Office is required.

ADDITIONAL SKILLS DESIRED
- Experience with creative design and marketing efforts for consumer goods retail industry.
- Experience in home décor and/or interior design industry
- Experience with Adobe Scene 7 media portal or similar digital asset management system.
- Experience with project management systems and software.
- Experience with Adobe LiveCycle or similar editable template system.
- Experience in a creative services department or similar environment.

The Human Resources Department at Newell Rubbermaid did a great job putting together a description of the type of candidate they are looking for. Their in-depth posting gives many clues about how you should tailor your résumé if you were going to apply for this position.

The first thing I recommend is that you copy the job posting text and go to a website like www.textalyser.net and see what words are repeated in the job posting. The results of the job posting analysis are recorded below:

Design	16 times	Brand	6 times
Experience	8 times	Project	6 times
Marketing	8 times	Print	6 times
Creative	7 times	Work	5 times
Ability to	6 times	Web graphics	3 times

The word count list above indicates words and phrases that you should try to incorporate in your résumé if possible. You can use the results of the job posting list to help you reverse engineer how you should word the accomplishments on your résumé. Chances are good that you already have similar accomplishments on your résumé because of your academic and freelance experiences. All you need to do is tweak how you describe your experiences. When I checked one of my student's résumés, here are the results that her résumé returned.

Virginia	8 times	Duties	4 times
Graphic	6 times	Collegiate	4 times
Design	5 times	Newspaper	4 times
Blacksburg	5 times	ADDY	3 times
Clients	4 times	Packaging	3 times

You can see that my student isn't emphasizing the same points in her résumé as what's being asked for in the Newell Rubbermaid job posting. While her résumé describes her experiences, she is failing to connect her experiences with the job she was applying for. Her challenge would be to tweak how she described her skills and experiences in a way that was truthful and yet emphasized her ability to successfully perform the tasks that Newell Rubbermaid describes in its job posting. With a minimum of effort you can use a text analyzer to tweak your résumé so that you are using some of the same terminology as the position your are applying for.

Your next challenge is to highlight important phrases and areas of emphasis in the job description. You want to look for words and phrases that give you clues about what items to include in your résumé and portfolio. For example, the job description mentions working in a "team environment," so try to include experiences or accomplishments that speak to your ability to excel in a team environment. It's important to be truthful with the information that you include on your résumé, but don't be bashful about touting your accomplishments and experiences.

After reading through the Newell Rubbermaid job posting, I've noted phrases (in bold below) that I think are important to consider, as well as the strategy I would take to address them. My comments are based on my own experiences working as a graphic designer.

- **Graphic Designer for its Marketing Communications team**: I think many candidates would forget to include examples of their marketing skills in their résumé. I would make a point to emphasize my marketing skills, as well as my graphic design skills.

- **Develop and maintain creative solutions**: I would emphasize a freelance project from my portfolio that won some awards and talk about my strategy for maintaining long-term business relationships with my clients.

- **Maintain consistent brand guidelines**: I would discuss how I worked within a client's branding guidelines and produced highly creative solutions without abandoning the client's branding system.

- **Accuracy and consistency**: I would make sure that the typographic system I used in my résumé was consistent, and I would double-check my grammar and spelling in all my documents and correspondence with the employer.

- **Prepare files correctly to meet printer specifications, including die lines**: I would emphasize my experiences and the familiarity with the printing process that I gained while working at a print shop early in my graphic design career.

- **Work effectively and efficiently under tight deadlines**: I would show how several projects with very tight deadlines ended up winning awards—not only can I meet deadlines, but I am capable of being creative under pressure.

I'm sure you get the idea. You take the qualities that the company is looking for and match these qualities with your experiences, skills, and accomplishments. This is why your résumé should be tailored to fit each job posting rather than a one-size-fits-all approach to building your résumé. Customizing your résumé to a job description will help you get your foot in the door and make a great impression.

HOW TO TALK ABOUT YOURSELF AND YOUR WORK

Now that you've identified some of the content in your résumé, it's time to discuss how you should talk about yourself. In its simplest form, employers want employees who will work, so talk about yourself and your accomplishments by using action verbs. Not only will action verbs communicate a sense of energy, but it makes your résumé active rather than passive.

Consider the following statement: "I designed a website for my client." While that might be an accurate statement, you've described this process very passively. Imagine that you describe the same project, but elaborated on this process more and added in a few more action verbs: "I designed a new website for my employer based on a competitive market evaluation that I completed, and the redesign website resulted in a 70 percent increase in traffic."

Do you remember how I recommended that you archive your projects and document qualitative and quantitative data at the Intermediate level? Well, now it's time to put the information you gathered to work! By including real data from the projects you worked on, you demonstrate that you don't just pull a solution out of thin air and hope that everything works out okay—you follow a project from start to completion and make sure that the end justifies the means.

Notice how action verbs—such as "troubleshoot, determine, perform, develop, promote, prioritize, and provide"—give the impression that you are a person who can get things done. No employer wants an employee who waits around to be assigned a job. When you use action verbs in your résumé, you appear to be the type of employee who will identify problems and find solutions to these problems. By backing your action verbs with facts like "a 70 percent increase in traffic," you show that you understand your client (and your company's) needs, and that your solutions have a history of being effective.

Consider the following example from my résumé: "TriAdventure Multisport Coaching and Fitness needed to promote their company and enhance visibility in the New River Valley. After completing an analysis of their audience, budget, and prior marketing efforts, I proposed a logo and website redesign as well as a T-shirt, bumper sticker, social media, and postcard campaign. As a result, TriAdventure has become one of the premiere triathlon training programs in the New River Valley." In this example, I used a very simple formula to describe my work with TriAdventure. First, I identified the problem: "TriAdventure needed to promote their company and enhance their visibility in the New River Valley." Next, I described the actions I took, I completed (action verb) an analysis and proposed (action verb) several modifications to their marketing efforts. Finally, I describe the result: "TriAdventure has become one of the premiere triathlon training programs in the New River Valley." To use this formula to write descriptions of your work, simply identify a problem, describe the actions you took, and describe the results of your actions.

By describing your accomplishments this way, you appear active and your résumé isn't a boring document where you simply list your accomplishments. Put yourself in your employer's shoes. Wouldn't you want to work with people who can help you get the job done? If your résumé is concise and interesting, chances are good that an employer will want to learn more about you. A good résumé will generate talking points in your interview because an employer will want you to elaborate on some of the items you've listed. It's easy to talk about work that you've completed rather than responding to impromptu questions that can make you feel like you're sitting in the hot seat. Your résumé can not only help you get your foot in the door but it can also help shape the direction your interview will take. This is why you need to spend some time working on your résumé and carefully crafting what you say and how you say it.

A FEW RULES OF THUMB

- Do not lie. Be sure the truth is on your side. If you worked in a group, then describe your responsibilities and credit others when it is appropriate to do so.
- Your résumé is a sales pitch, not an autobiography. Keep it brief.
- Write in a clear, concise manner and highlight your assets.
- Irrelevant information should be removed.
- Follow all instructions to a tee. If the employer asks for a cover letter, then be sure to include one.
- Do not staple, fold, or paper clip your résumé when mailing to an employer. Find an envelope that is large enough to mail your résumé flat.
- Do not use "I" or "me" repeatedly in your résumé. For example, don't say "I managed." Simply say "Managed."

> *"Don't be discouraged is you don't get a call back right away; be patient and look for other opportunities while you wait to hear back from a potential employer."*

DESIGNING YOUR RÉSUMÉ

When you begin designing your résumé, you should take the time to create a well-executed typographic system. Choose a typeface that has multiple weights and is easy to read. Choose a typeface whose style and letterforms will not distract the viewer from reading your content. Align copy using tabs, and use proper punctuation. Straight quotation marks (primes), three periods instead of an ellipsis, and a hyphen instead of en or em dashes may have worked on term papers, but take the time to properly set your résumé. An art director or designer will be looking at this document, and he or she is likely to quickly spot any typographic faux pas!

Use the mnemonic CRAP (Contrast, Repetition, Alignment, Proximity) to design your résumé. Pick a contrasting typeface or weight to highlight headers in your résumé; use repeating elements in your document (and be consistent with these elements); everything on the page should be aligned to something; and group similar items together. The CRAP graphic design rule of thumb will help you make better design decisions about your résumé, and help the reader find information on your résumé easily.

When designing your résumé, you should include your name, contact information, work experience (including your freelance experience), education, any awards, scholarships, or professional recognitions you may have won, professional affiliations, and relevant skills. Avoid including hobbies unless your hobbies are relevant to this position. When listing someone as a reference, you should always get direct permission to use a person as a reference before listing him or her—it's considered a professional courtesy to let your references know that someone may be contacting them in the near future.

When you list items on your résumé, list them in chronological order with the most recent item first and older items in descending order. Your most recent experiences are likely to be the items your employer is most interested in, but your previous experiences show the depth of your experiences. You should also include a brief description of your duties (remember to use action verbs) and any accomplishments you may have achieved during this time. See the example on the following page:

2011-2009   Research Assistant | Eye Tracking and Usability Testing Lab
Primary researcher for a symbology study. Duties included gathering logos for usability testing, developing research questions, and assisting Dr. Troy Abel in his Eye Tracking and Usability Testing (ETUT) lab.

When you're putting your information together, use headers to make finding your information easy. Many of my students have grouped their résumé information into the following categories. Use only the categories that apply.

- Educational Experience
- Work Experience
- Awards and Recognition

- Activities and Interests
- Leadership Roles
- Skills

After following a few rules of thumb, carefully crafting how you describe your accomplishments, matching your skills with the job posting, and editing your content for brevity and clarity, your résumé will be ready to be sent out to assist you with landing an interview. Don't be discouraged if you don't get a call back right away. Be patient and look for other opportunities while you wait to hear back from a potential employer. The more résumés you send out, the better your chances are of getting a call back. Actively scan job postings and respond to them quickly. When you get a call back for an interview, the real fun begins!

Preparing for an Interview

If you want to have a good interview, you need to look for ways to minimize your stress levels. Stress can make you panic, forget what you wanted to say, sweat profusely, and even make you feel sick. The key to preparing for an interview is finding ways to minimize your stress, anxiety, and fear before the interview. Researching the company, being prepared, and practicing your interview skills can help you feel confident during your interview. If you feel confident, you will probably look confident, too.

I feel that it's helpful to break things down into parts in order to understand how a process like preparing for an interview works. So I'm going to break down this chapter into three parts: Before the Interview, The Day of the Interview, and After the Interview. This way you can feel confident that you're doing all the things you need to do in order to succeed.

You have worked hard to get to this point in your life, and you should take a moment to be proud of your accomplishment. I find it helpful to remind myself that during a job interview not only am I being interviewed by a potential employer but I am interviewing the company as well. I want to enjoy my job and working with new colleagues, so finding a company where I will fit in is important to me. You might value opportunity for advancement more than the personality of the colleagues you work with, and that's perfectly fine. My point is that this your chance to find out about the company and what they'll bring to the table.

It's perfectly normal to feel excited, nervous, and a bit scared. It's also the perfect time to begin preparing for your interview and putting some of your fears to rest by familiarizing yourself with the company. As you go on more interviews, you will get more comfortable with the interview process. It's a good habit to go on any interview you can—even if you're not terribly interested in the job. This way you get a chance to practice your interview skills, and you might just stumble into an opportunity in disguise.

BEFORE YOUR INTERVIEW

Don't wait until the last minute to begin preparing for your interview. Give yourself as much time as you can to prepare. Some things, like conducting mock interviews, can happen well in advance, while other tasks may not be able to be completed weeks in advance. Do as much as you can as early as possible, so that you're not running around at the last minute and stressing yourself out.

Your interview begins the first time you make contact with the company. Make sure that you are professional and polite any time you talk to a company representative. This includes secretaries, who are essentially the gatekeepers for a company. Part of a secretary's job is to determine which requests are important and which are not. A pleasant personality and good attitude will serve you much better than a "get-it-done-for-me-now" demeanor.

Every time you communicate with anyone in the company, make sure you maintain a pleasant and professional tone. Do not ask questions that are easily answered on the company's website or that have already been addressed in the job description. If you have a question and cannot find the information you are looking for, prepare an e-mail and ask all your questions in one e-mail rather than sending multiple e-mails. Keep in mind that some of your questions may be addressed during your interview. Prioritize your questions and ask those that relate to your ability to prepare for your interview.

Mock interviews

Almost every college and university has a Career Services Center, where you can practice your interview techniques and get feedback from professionals. I highly recommend that you take advantage of these services. It's helpful to get feedback from someone who knows what to look for in an interview and might catch things that you may not see yourself. You might not realize that you say "Umm" a lot or that you don't make very good eye contact. Career Service Centers can offer advice and helpful suggestions. Don't be shy about contacting yours and scheduling an interview.

Keep in mind that the mock interview you have with a Career Service Center will be more generic than your actual interview. The interviewers probably aren't used to using graphic design terminology, don't understand what an employer might be looking for in a graphic design candidate, or don't know how to critique your portfolio. But they will be able to help you with how you present yourself and with the interview process overall. For instance, when you walked into the room, did you smile, make good eye contact, shake the interviewer's hand, and introduce yourself?

Similar to how you practice a sport and learn its rules before you play the first game, mock interviews help you familiarize yourself with the format and help you perform well when it matters most. Similar to how the details in your portfolio and résumé are important, small details in an interview can make a considerable difference. An employer will take note of a candidate with strong job interview skills, so give yourself as many advantages as you can by polishing up your interview skills.

Researching the company

It's a good idea to thoroughly search the company website and keep a list of questions that you cannot find the answers to in the process. At the end of almost every interview you will be asked, "Do you have any questions for us?" Rather than saying, "No. I think you've answered everything," you'll be able to use this opportunity to show that you took the time to research the company. This gives the impression that you're not walking into this interview blindly but making a careful and calculated decision.

When I research a company, my goal is to get a better sense about the type of environment I'll be working in. If the company lists their employees, I'll look over the list to see if I know anyone who works at the company. If I know someone who works there, then I'll contact him or her and ask a few questions about the

> *"When I'm researching a company, I try to find out how large the company is, who their clients are, the company's reputation, and their long- and short-term goals."*

work environment and their general level of happiness. You never know what information you'll learn by having a contact on the inside of a company. A friend at a company I was considering applying to once told me, "It's a decent job, but the company isn't managed very well; they tend to ignore problems until they can't be ignored any longer." I thanked my friend for this information and decided to keep looking for employment opportunities elsewhere. If you don't have a contact that you know who works for this company, try to find out whatever you can about the company's stability. If you're like me, you're not just looking for any job. You're looking for an awesome job where you can grow and contribute to a company's success.

When I'm researching a company, I try to find out how large the company is, who their customers are, the company's reputation, and any long- and short-term goals. Has the company had any recent employee layoffs? What are the backgrounds of the people I will work with? The answers to these and other questions can help indicate the focus of the company and the level of respect that this company has earned.

If the company has news, press release, or mission statement links on its website, I'll look at this information to try to learn more about the work they are the most proud of, recent awards, and new initiatives. I'm looking for information that I can use to help me learn more about the job and the environment in which I'll be working. Not only will this information help me decide if I'm a good fit for this company, but it will also help me answer the question, "Tell us why you're the perfect candidate for this job?"

Feel free to bring your research notes with you during your interview. Having notes in front of you may make you feel better. Keep your notes in your small leather portfolio and don't feel pressured to ask every single question you might have if time is running short. If the company is interested in talking with you further, there will be other opportunities to have your questions answered. For now just make sure that your major questions have been answered, give the impression that you've researched the company, and try and get a sense if this company would be a good fit for you.

Create a narrative

You should be able to walk an art director through your portfolio in approximately twenty minutes. By the end of your portfolio presentation, the art director should have a good idea about your background, creative process, and aspirations. It takes practice to weave together a narrative that connects your education, experiences, goals, and interests. Don't wait until the day of your interview to begin thinking about what you're going to say. Since you've already pored over the job description and researched the company, it's time to begin to think about your work and experiences in a way that supports your claim that you will be a good fit.

Your portfolio will consist of eight to twelve pieces. If you followed my advice of having twenty portfolio pieces to choose from, you can choose pieces that will help you tell your narrative and also address the constraints of the job description. Practice taking someone through your portfolio and ask for feedback about your presentation. Your presentation shouldn't be over in ten minutes, nor should it run over your goal of twenty minutes.

When you talk about your work, don't just talk about it in terms of "projects" you completed for your classes and clients. Instead, give your work a greater context by discussing your research, process, unexpected discoveries you made, your (or your client's) level of satisfaction with the results, obstacles that needed to be overcome, and how the project was received by the audience. Virtually every project has a bump in the road. Did you do something unique to overcome an obstacle? What did you do to exceed your client's expectations?

Depending on what you've learned about the position you're applying for, you might highlight that you're a problem solver, highly resourceful, a self-starter, or that you work well in group settings. Whatever points you decide are important to highlight about yourself, you will want your other application materials to support this claim. This, in essence, is your narrative. It's a description of how the actions you've taken and the work you've accomplished has led you to this particular moment. All you need is the opportunity to shine.

Logistical concerns

It may sound silly, but go and get a haircut or get your nails done. You're going to want to appear polished and put together. You've spent considerable time, effort, and money making your portfolio look great. Now put a little effort into looking great yourself. When you feel good about how you look, you are likely to feel great during your interview.

Avoid any major changes, and focus on small things that will make you feel good about yourself—a fresh haircut, getting your nails done, or buying a new pair of shoes. Sometimes a small change on the outside can bolster feelings of confidence and enthusiasm on the inside. Don't leave deciding what to wear to your interview until the last minute! Picking what to wear to an interview is something that many people stress out about. Choose your outfit (and try it on) a few days before your interview. This way you won't stress out about what you're going to wear the day of your interview. Your goal is to have a stress-free morning the day of your interview.

Your outfit should look professional, be ironed neatly, and should not have any holes or stains. When you're deciding on what to wear, aim for one degree nicer than what you think your interviewer will be wearing. If you suspect the person interviewing you will be wearing a button-down shirt, you should wear khaki pants and a button-down shirt with a tie or dress pants with a blouse. Keep any jewelry you decide to wear to a minimum so that it does not distract the employer from your presentation, especially if your jewelry rattles or makes noise. You should also go easy on perfume or cologne. While it's nice to meet someone who smells good, keep in mind that you are entering a place of business. It's best not to overpower your potential employer's olfactory senses.

Driving to your destination can also be a stressor. You might consider driving to your interview location a day or two early to familiarize yourself with the route you will take. As you drive, you should take mental notes of traffic patterns and construction that might cause you to be late, identify a location where you can park, and get a good idea of how long it will take to get to your destination. If you are unable to drive the route, print out driving directions or program your destination into your GPS or smart phone.

The day before your interview, iron your clothes and lay them out flat, go to the gym for a light work out in order to reduce your stress levels, eat a healthy dinner (avoiding foods that will irritate your stomach), and enjoy an activity that you find calming. Towards the evening, as your day winds down, set your alarm, go to bed at a reasonable time, and get a good night's sleep. I want you to feel like you're prepared when you wake up and not have to rush around attending to last minute details. I want you to feel excited that all your hard work has prepared you to have a really great interview and to feel relaxed and ready.

THE DAY OF THE INTERVIEW

When I get anxious, I tend to talk quickly, have difficulty focusing, and get butterflies in my stomach. You might experience a variety of other symptoms, so your first objective on the day of your interview is to be calm. Follow your usual morning rituals, leaving yourself plenty of time to get dressed, eat breakfast, and get to your appointment a little early.

Mentally prepare yourself that once you walk out the front door, your interview begins. Smile as you drive to your interview—even if you're scared to death or not feeling particularly confident. Who knows, by the time you get to your interview you might feel really good.

Arrive to your interview on time (you can sit in your car and breathe deeply and visualize success if you have some time to kill). Smile and introduce yourself when you enter the building. Greet everyone with a big smile and say "Hello" or "Good morning" when it's appropriate. As you check in, you will probably be asked to wait while the person you are meeting with is contacted. Take this time to collect your thoughts and take in your surroundings. Does this look like a place you'd enjoy coming to every day? Do the people here look happy?

When your contact arrives, greet him with a big smile and a firm handshake. When you greet someone with a smile, chances are good that you will receive a smile back. As you're walking to the location of your interview, this is a good time to make small talk with your contact. Small talk is conversation that is safe and usually geared toward superficial topics like the weather, news, or sporting events. The goal of small talk is to get your contact talking and to help put him or her at ease. While your own heart might be racing, you want the person interviewing you to feel as comfortable as you appear to be.

Once you are led to the area where the interview will take place, try to bring the conversation back to the task at hand slowly. Your twenty minutes starts once you have your contact's full attention and he or she indicates a readiness to begin. You might say something like "I really appreciate you taking the time to look at my portfolio. I know you're busy, but after reading the job description I think I'd be a great fit." After you receive a response, add in "Well, I guess you're interested in seeing some of my work! Can I show you my portfolio?"

Give your interviewer a big smile occasionally as you present your work and act interested in what he or she has to say. Sometimes you can learn a lot by listening to how someone you don't know perceives your work. Keep the mood light, but stay focused on presenting your work and trying to make a good impression.

If your interviewer would rather hold your portfolio, adapt your presentation to his or her preference and talk about the projects he or she is looking at and offer interesting tidbits about your experiences, clients, and accomplishments. Begin to weave your narrative into your presentation and adapt your presentation to the tone and mood of your interviewer. Talk about your work, highlight your achievements, and don' forget to ask questions about the company throughout your interview.

As your interview winds down, you'll have a chance to ask questions. Take advantage of this opportunity and try to learn more about the company. Try to prioritize your questions in order of importance and avoid questions with a simple "yes" or "no" answer in order to keep the conversation flowing. Here are a few questions you might consider asking at the end of your interview.

- Was there any work that you didn't see that you wish I had included in my portfolio? (e.g., ad campaign, website design, packaging)
- Was there a particular piece in my portfolio that stood out?
- What advice would you give someone who's interested in a career in graphic design? Are there any secrets to success that I should know about?

After asking a few questions to gauge how your presentation went, refer to the questions you wrote down when you researched the company and ask a few questions in order to let your interviewer know that you've done your research.

As the interview concludes, make sure you ask, "So what is your time frame for making a decision about this position? Will someone contact me or should I contact you at a specific time?" This question is to give you peace of mind about how long it will take before you can expect to hear back from the company.

Give your interviewer a firm handshake and big smile, thank him or her for the time spent with you, and say that you hope to hear back from the company soon. Your interview isn't officially over until you're back at your house. Don't let out a loud sigh, untuck your shirt, take off your high heels, or pump your fists in victory until you're back home.

AFTER YOUR INTERVIEW

After you're back home, you need to sit down and write—by hand—a thank-you note to your interviewer while the events of the day are still fresh in your mind. While this might not seem like an important step, a thoughtful hand-written note will help you keep your name on the top of the stack of candidates as the company wraps up its interviews and determines who it is going to hire. Writing a thank-you note is a way of maintaining contact with the interviewer after your interview has concluded. Even if you feel that you completely bombed at your interview, take the time to send a thank-you note. Send your note out that same day, so that it will arrive the following day—especially if the interviewer will be meeting with other candidates.

Once, when I worked as a creative director, we had several job candidates who all had about the same skill level and experience. After reviewing their applications, we decided to extend our offer to the candidate who had sent us a thank-you note, because we felt that she would be the type of person who would see a task through to completion. There was no way for us to tell if this was actually true or not, but we decided to give her a shot based on her thank-you note. We offered the her a job and all it cost her was an extra five minutes of her time and a forty-four-cent postage stamp.

A thank-you note does not have to be a particular length, but you can use it to clarify a point or provide additional information if necessary. See the sample note below, and feel free to modify it to meet your needs.

<Insert interviewer name>,
<Insert company name>

I would like to thank you for interviewing me for the <insert the name of the job you are applying for> position. I appreciate the time you spent talking with me, and I value the comments you gave me regarding my work.

I look forward to hearing from you regarding your hiring decision.

Sincerely,
<Insert your name>
<Insert your contact information>

Your final step is to repeat the entire process over again. Don't wait until you hear back from the interview before you set up your next interview—don't put all your eggs into one basket! Instead, find another position that interests you and repeat the process again until you have been hired. It can be tiresome work, but it will be worth the effort when you land a job you love. Maybe you'll get lucky and land a job on the first try, but you should expect to have to go on several interviews before getting an offer. Don't get discouraged. Don't give up, keep a positive outlook, and give each interview your best effort. Hopefully, sooner rather than later you'll have an offer on the table.

Negotiating an Offer

Negotiating an job offer can be unnerving. I dislike the process, but I understand how important it is in the grand scheme of things. It's important for companies to turn a profit, and in order to do so they try to minimize their expenses and maximize their income. When you receive a job offer, you may need to negotiate the terms of the offer. Your job is to look out for your best interests, while not negotiating so hard that the employer rescinds his offer. When you receive an offer, it is standard practice to take a few days to consider the offer before either accepting, declining, or negotiating the terms of the agreement.

Money isn't the only consideration when determining if an offer is fair. There are often benefits and perks, insurance, moving expenses, flexibility, vacation days, and so many more elements that can be negotiated. Each of these items improves the quality of your life or ensures compensation if a particular set of events were to unfold. In order to make an informed decision you'll need all the information regarding your offer. Make sure you have all the details written down and understand what is being offered. This way you can compare your offer to offers that other designers have received and make an intelligent counteroffer if appropriate. After you review the terms of your offer, you can begin to prepare for your next encounter with your contact by conducting some research. If you go to www. designsalaries.com, you can access a survey that has been put together by AIGA and Aquent that indicates what kind of salaries other designers report they are making in their area. This can be a great tool and help you determine what a competitive salary might looks like in your geographic area. Additionally, you may want to look at www.salary.com or www.indeed.com/salary to find statistics on what other professionals in your area are being paid.

It's important to search for this information using the job title you have been offered. Otherwise there may be discrepancies in the data. For example, the median salary for a "graphic designer" in Blacksburg, Virginia, is $34,000, while the median salary for a "Web designer" is $44,000. If the offer you received is for a"graphic designer," you shouldn't search using the title "Web designer." Since facts are easily checked, it's best to base your argument on the correct data.

Now that you have a ballpark salary figure in mind, you'll note that this data is a range rather than a specific amount. Some designers make more than this amount, and others make less. While you probably want to make the most money you can, it's important to take this into consideration when comparing your offer against the salary that other designers make.

Benefits are important to factor into the equation, and often benefits are worth their weight in gold. Health-care insurance and prescription plans can be expensive if you have to pay for them on your own. A good benefits packages can be worth 20 to 40 percent of your salary. Figuring out what these benefits are worth is worth the investment of your time. Many employers provide some kind of vacation pay, sick time, medical, dental, and vision insurance, educational com-pensation, holiday pay, and retirement contributions. You will need to refer to the compensation package details that your contact sent you in order to calculate the value of these items. You can use the Internet to help you determine the value of these benefits in case their value isn't immediately apparent.

I've always had the philosophy that some income is better than no income, so I've been known to take a job offer to make sure that I'm able to pay my bills. If a better offer comes along, I'll either renegotiate with my current employer or move on to greener pastures. I continued to apply for other jobs as I worked at a printing company. Before too long, I was offered a position with another company where I would make $8,000 more, but they didn't have as good a benefits package as my current employer. I decided to make a bold move and told my current employer that I had been offered anther job and if he matched the salary I would stay. He asked me what the salary was and when I told him he said he'd match the offer if I stayed. At the end of the day I got an $8,000 raise and got to continue working for the company with the better benefits package.

If you've been interviewing with other companies, call them up and tell them that you have an offer on the table. Ask if they can speed up their interview process or make you an offer. Knowing that you have another offer on the table might actually make you a more attractive candidate. If they are willing to make you an offer, you've really managed to negotiate yourself into a good position because you have gained a small amount of negotiating power.

When you've finished your research or run out of time, you need to call the company that offered you the position and let it know your decision. If you accept the terms of their offer, congratulations! If your research indicates that their offer is low, you might want to press them for a better offer.

Throughout the entire time you need to maintain a professional yet firm tone, appearing grateful for the offer, yet intent on trying to make the right decision for you and your family. It's definitely not an easy process, but pressing an employer a bit may be worth your while.

The next time you hear from your contact, he is going to give you an offer and pressure you to make a decision quickly. You contact is probably eager to wrap up the job search and move on to other duties, so you will have to gauge how much longer you can press the issue. If you agree to the terms of the new agreement, you should be prepared to sign paperwork making the terms of your employment official. It's best not to take the terms of your employment on good faith or through verbal agreement. Ask for an updated copy of the terms of your agreement and keep the documents in a safe place.

The following day, you'll need to call your contact back and accept the position, demonstrating enthusiasm, eagerness, and appreciation for the opportunity the company has given you. You've taken a big step toward establishing a career in graphic design, and you should feel very proud!

Tips From Professionals

Sometimes it's helpful to hear what other professionals have to say about their experiences as a freelance designer. I asked a few of my favorite graphic designers to share their thoughts on freelance with you. I also asked them to think about what kind of advice they wished they had received when the first started out freelancing and to share this information with you. Here's what they had to say:

JIM MOUNTJOY, CREATIVE DIRECTOR, LKM

Several creative individuals I respect and have had the opportunity to chat with have spoken of a practice they benefit from. It involves spreading out the work they have done over the past several months and critiquing not just the work, but the process that led to the work. Not surprisingly, they are hard on themselves and make notes about what to change and how. This is done diligently to see where they falter and where they fly. They recognize the connection and impact that the creative process can have on a creative product and evaluate themselves in that light. Smart.

MEAGHAN DEE, DIRECTOR, FOURDESIGN

When writing estimates, always include time for revisions. Often the edits can take just as long (or longer) than the original work. Make sure to write a clause for "additional charges" for when a client goes over the agreed-upon number of corrections. Remember to specify what work is covered by a proposal, particularly when working for a flat fee—otherwise you could get bogged down with rounds of revisions that you are completing for free.

It's easy for clients to take advantage of young freelancers. This can take many forms, from wanting you to work for free to continuously making changes that keep you behind schedule. But more than anything else, watch out for the client that wants you to compromise your design standards or your morals. Standing up to a paying client is difficult. But if you are going to freelance, it's something you need to be able to do. Now I'm not saying you shouldn't make changes to a design, but there is a point (and hopefully you will recognize it) past which your work can lose integrity. Not only should you not want to contribute to the plethora of bad designs that are floating around, but you will also lose the opportunity to have a strong portfolio piece. Beyond aesthetics, you also need to have workplace ethics. Most people have lines they wouldn't want to cross, such as designing cigarette packaging aimed at children. But what do you do when the situation is less cut and dry? Would you market unhealthy fast foods to underprivileged audiences? Would you advertise that a product can perform a function, that it cannot? Reading this, right now, it's easy to say that you wouldn't, but if your livelihood depended on your income from freelance, you might have a harder time saying no.

So, if you're considering freelancing full time or starting your own company, you might want to write down your ideals, to serve as a reminder of where you want to be. Manifestos can also help you define your design beliefs. If you want inspiration, Bruce Mau, Frank Lloyd Wright, and Post Typography all have some interesting manifestos.

BRIAN LEMEN, SENIOR GRAPHIC DESIGNER, HINGE

I've been both a freelancer and a studio designer, and I've found they share one thing in common: you can never plan too much or too early. The visual part of design is only a small portion of the process. The majority of your energy should go into planning. Whether you design for the Web, print, identity or all of the above, you need to ask yourself and your client, "Who is the audience, how will they be using or interpreting the design, and what are the business goals of the project?"

Frank Lloyd Wright wrote, "I never design a building before I've seen the site and met the people who will be using it." It's no different with graphic design.

Many designers can make a piece look great, but it's meaningless if the design doesn't accomplish its objective. Before starting a freelance project, take the time to get clear insight from the client about their audience and goals. If you are planning a website, for example, and the goal is to encourage people to register for an event, you have about three seconds to get a visitor's attention and persuade them to take action. In the planning process, a clear call to action should be reflected in the creative brief, the site map, and the initial sketches for the home page.

Review and discuss these ideas with the client before you start the visual design, as this will usually save you a lot of time in the end. Then check in with the client often to ensure that the project goals are being addressed. Remind your client to voice any changes they want to make to the plan…before it's too late. Good planning will ultimately lead to a more visually compelling and functional finished product—one that will make you proud.

ELIZABETH MEGGS, ARTIST, ILLUSTRATOR AND DESIGNER

Define your philosophies and make choices that reflect your beliefs in the long run. For example, do you have a cultural, social, or political agenda? Do you have a creative philosophy or stance? Are you willing to do work for clients whose business practices you consider unethical? Do you have beliefs about design process and typography that you want to maintain at all costs, such as embracing creative anarchy or the use of specific underlying grids? Articulate your beliefs early on and uphold them. Make choices that will elevate your creative potential.

It is far too easy to become mired in a meaningless quagmire of commercialism and accept any job that comes one's way regardless of whether or not the freelance job aligns with one's beliefs, especially when the jobs are few and far between. Some naysayers may believe that upholding one's strong philosophies is ideological to the detriment of being successful at business. But historically it is the designers who staunchly uphold their ideals who innovate and prove influential.

Instead of only accepting the woodcut print jobs clients of the day demanded, Johann Gutenberg spent thankless decades of his life perfecting typographic printing and producing the first typographically printed book, allowing knowledge to spread throughout the world. Typographic printing could ultimately be considered a chief factor fostering a long, steady decline of illiteracy, the Protestant movement of the Reformation era launched by Martin Luther, and the American and French revolutions of the late eighteenth century. If William Morris had not rejected what he considered crass mass-produced goods and tacky Victorian-era typefaces, and staunchly advocated a return to high aesthetic ideals, refined handicraft, and a revival of historically allusive fonts, the Arts and Crafts Movement likely would not have occurred.

Doing what is popular or only what clients ask for is easy. Innovators do more than that. Be smart for the long term. Have vision. Your life, talent, and education can be applied to a cause greater than fulfilling one commercial commission at a time. It is possible for one individual to change the world and make history. Why not be that person?

JD VOGT, UX LEAD, SALESFORCE

When tasked with a large project like architecting a substantial website or app, I'll often find myself a little overwhelmed. Those initial creative steps after the research has been done can be intimidating. Where should I begin? How will early decisions affect the overall design? Where do I start when the destination is unknown?

Artists run into the same indecisiveness when staring at a blank canvas—to combat it they'll create studies to help them explore the space. These studies may be drawings, thumbnails, or painted vignettes. I've found particular inspiration from the process Seurat used while creating "A Sunday Afternoon on the Island of La Grande Jatte." It's a tremendous work measuring nearly 7 feet by 10 feet and resides at the Chicago Art Institute. Go see it sometime.

Before Seurat embarked on the finished piece, he made a large number of drawings and painted panels. Many of these studies were only portions of what the final work would become—some were of dogs, some were shorelines and groups of trees, others were figures in repose. He didn't have an exact plan for how all the pieces would fit together but over the years, each study gave him a glimpse of what the whole would eventually become. Later, he'd compose the piece by bringing together the various studies he'd made, making adjustments and striking a balance. Getting the small ideas and details out of his head and into something tangible was his strategy for creating the completed piece.

In modern life, those who can lay out a detailed plan and execute it are readily admired. Our society encourages and rewards linear thinking. But as designers we're given the squishy challenge of creating something new—and hopefully "cool." Unfortunately, getting to new and cool is not a linear, repeatable process.

So when confronted with the "large canvas" problem, I've found it helpful to take the nonlinear approach that Seurat used. Instead of trying to get my head around the entire system of moving parts, I'll start with one interaction or one detail. It could be a heading, a graphical treatment, or an animation. By starting on a small, almost inconsequential piece I can put aside the initial anxieties of how it will all fit together. And once one is done, the next comes quicker, and the next. I worry less about how everything will work and instead let my intuition guide and assure me that eventually the pieces will grant a me glimpse of the whole.

KIM SPENCER, PRINCIPAL/CREATIVE DIRECTOR, PROTOZOA DESIGN

My first year in business proved to be a stern learning experience. I left my job of seven years to start my own business, and I hit the ground running. Filled with excitement and thriving on the fervor of a great client, I took the next several months to regain my creative mojo that had been drained by an uninspiring in-house department. I designed for Web, print, trade—it was exactly what I needed…until the job wrapped up.

I had a small buffer but nothing on the horizon. I had been so busy relishing my newfound independence and creativity that I neglected sales. With a family to support, I joined the local Chamber of Commerce and started on the networking circuit. As the holidays drew near we found ourselves with an empty refrigerator and bills piling up. Suddenly the excitement of being a business owner wasn't so glamorous. For nearly four months we struggled. I taught a few classes at the local university, which helped, but it was nowhere near what we needed. Desperation began to set in, and I took any job that came up. We drained all our accounts and looked into government assistance.

As my creative mojo began to wane and my spirit weakened, I received a call from a local firm. A mutual colleague had given them my name. They had a big job and needed my expertise. Hesitant to breathe a sigh of relief, my husband and I attended a local panel discussion on financial matters for creatives, and I had a breakthrough.

"Always be working on work, getting work, and invoicing work. Those are your weekly goals." During those first eight months I was absorbed into my work. Aside from family outings, I was in front of my computer. That was my mistake. I didn't take time out to attend social functions, networking events, or Chamber meetings. I wasn't getting work, and therefore, I wasn't working on work or invoicing work. It all started to fall apart.

It's a delicate cycle. You have to tear yourself away from the office. You're not going to land a job at every networking event. It's about building relationships. People have to get to know you before they will refer you. Meet people for coffee. Ask them, "What are you passionate about?" "What drives you?" You'll learn about running a business, successfully, and make some new friends while you're at it.

The good news is I now have more work than I can handle, and I'm booked for the next four months. What am I doing this week aside from working and invoicing? Meeting some folks for lunch, others for coffee, and a few more for Happy Hour. The next big job is right around the corner, but you have to get out there to find it.

NOAH SCALIN, CREATIVE DIRECTOR, ANOTHER LIMITED REBELLION

Don't ever, ever, ever do work without a signed contract in hand (and preferably a check for 50 percent up front as well). You will get burned nearly every time you forget to do this, even when it's for friends or a pro bono project! Having a signed, detailed contract means both sides know exactly what they've agreed to, giving clear limitations to a project—which prevents scope creep, unnecessary rush jobs, and hurt feelings. Be sure to include exactly what you've agreed to do (How many solutions? How many revisions?), what rights you're going to assign to the client once they've paid in full, and of course how you will be compensated (pro bono clients still need limits and can still give you nonmonetary things in return). I almost never have had to enforce a contract once it's in place. Crappy clients generally never bother to make the effort to sign one in the first place. And suddenly a rush job isn't such a rush when the burden of a commitment to pay your rush fee is spelled out and autographed by a client. Of course, it's not a guarantee against every problem that can arise, but written well and used properly a contract can prevent a good majority of the issues that come with the freelance territory. Of course, if you do have a problem after it's signed you will have the law on your side!

ASHLEY SHOEMAKER, GRAPHIC DESIGNER

Be honest with yourself and realistic about your time and energy levels before you accept a job. Can you really give the client what's wanted or needed? Will you be shuffling other freelance projects, disappointing other clients, or stealing time from your personal life? We all think we can work twenty-two hours a day, but it's simply not possible. So be sure to plan time in your schedule for things besides design —like time with friends and family, a balanced meal, or maybe even sleep.

ZACH WILLIAMS, PRINCIPAL, VENVIO

Finding clients is not only challenging but, at times quite frightening. There are essentially two approaches as a freelancer to getting projects: responding to inbound leads and proactively seeking out new work.

Responding to new leads is the easiest of the two approaches, since you already know that there is an interest by the company that has contacted you. Getting people to reach out to you can be done in a number of ways. Some of the easiest and most effective ways to get inbound leads are through referrals, having a social media presence, SEO, online advertising, and showcasing your work on popular sites such as Behance and Dribbble. The key is to be very timely with your response when someone reaches out to you. As a rule of thumb I always try to respond to someone within an hour of that lead contacting me, either by e-mail or phone. This shows that you are not only responsible, but value the prospect.

Approaching companies to do work for them has been one of the most nerve-racking things in my career. I would encourage any aspiring freelancer to change their mind-set from trying to convince prospective companies that you have something they might want to being confident that your skill set and abilities are like gold. Knowing and believing that you have one of the most valuable skill sets is the key to being confident when approaching prospective clients. They might not share the same outlook on your services as you do immediately, but by merely being confident and not devaluing your work, it will help in positioning you well with the clients you want to do work with.

With that being said, to be proactive in getting new business I recommend that you narrow your search to anywhere between five and ten companies that you want to do business with. Whether you are a Web designer or a copywriter, having a list of companies that you want to target is the first step. If you don't aim for something you won't hit anything. Instead of trying to be a pushy salesman, I would suggest that you start by introducing yourself to your prospective client. This can be done by e-mailing the right decision maker, such as a director of marketing, or sending them something in the mail. Whatever way you contact them it is smart not to push your services on them, but instead to tell them that you provide services that pertain to their company or industry, and that you would like to see if you would be a good fit for them and vice versa. I really like the idea of sending a company you want to do work with a creative piece through the mail. This will cost a little more to produce the concept and mail it, but you'll know that they signed to receive the package, and it gives you a chance to show off your creativity. If you've wowed them with your creative piece and your carefully written introduction letter, there is a good chance they will reach out to you by phone or via e-mail. If they don't reach out to you, don't be discouraged. Simply give them a call or shoot them an e-mail and ask if they received what you sent them (which you know they did) and find out if there is a time you can meet.

SOMIAH LATTIMORE, OWNER/CREATIVE DIRECTOR, STRAIGHT UP CREATIVE, LLC

Double-check your swatches. I have worked with a lot of clients over the years who have had another designer create a logo for them. While I have no problem with that—I've been burned! Chances are the client printed a two-color business card, letterhead, or envelope and loved their spot color, but you may be designing a job where their logo is produced in CMYK for the first time. Use caution because the prior designer may have discussed a different color system with your client. Take the time to have a quick discussion about swatches, and make sure you are using an updated book. If you don't have one—make friends with a local print shop and borrow theirs. Explain to your client how a spot color swatch prints differently than a solid to process swatch.

BEN CAPOZZI, ARTIST AND EDUCATOR

"Freelancer!" you might be thinking. "That's like being an 'Entrepreneur' I'll be my own boss, work for who I want, when I want, from a coffee shop in Portland, or the living room couch in my pajamas. It's gonna be awesome!"

Indeed, it can be, and with this book's help you're on the right track. But it can't be overemphasized how much you will be responsible for: Ideation. Presentation. Networking. Sales. Invoicing. Taxes. IT troubleshooting. Building new skills. Drafts, comps, and a lot of revisions.

It can be overwhelming to set the agenda to meet your clients' needs, but they'll often look to you to do just that, and you can't do this well if you're exhausted or in constant crisis mode. So be aggressive about getting out in front of it all and really be your own boss—push yourself. Hold yourself accountable. Set and measure goals, and constantly improve.

My advice is to start with a routine. Burning the midnight oil and rising midday is common for many creative types, especially when you're young; others (like me) have found great benefit in being an early riser, but regardless, you need a routine. Get up at 3 p.m. and work until midnight. Or rise at 5 a.m., scan headlines and calendar, and do client work from seven to twelve, with an open afternoon and a few hours in the evening. The schedule specifics are tweaked by you for you, but the idea of the schedule is paramount. Create it, and then firewall that time. Guard it like your life depended on it—against the most tempting offers for burgers and beer; there will never be a shortage of other things you could be doing—because your freelance life really does depend on it.

Creativity loves discipline (one of those ironic paradox truths). Your work and your business will benefit from a routine; so create one for yourself in accord with yourself, before one gets imposed on you.

GLENN SORRENTINO, ZINIO

Freelancing has ups and downs, successes and failures. The good news is that you can limit (though probably not eliminate) failure by being prepared. Here are a couple of things to remember:

01. Have (and know how to use) contracts. Don't write your own. There are many good resources out there that you can take advantage of.

02. Know how to write quote, send invoices, and keep records of your earnings. I use Billings (www.marketcircle.com/billings), which sends proposals, invoices, keeps receipts, etc. This becomes very handy during tax time.

03. Find your work flow. It's hard to stay motivated when you work at home, alone. Turning the TV on is easy, taking the dog on a walk when the sun is out, and sleeping in can seem like a perk. I prefer working in an office, away from my house. You can find local office spaces where freelancers and freshly sprouting startups share a large space and often benefit from each other's company.

Most of all, you need to have a good understanding of all of this before jumping into freelancing. If you have friends that are designers or developers that have been in the industry for a bit, have them give you mock requirements for a project, and go through the steps of proposals, work agreements, nondisclosures, etc. It'll be to your benefit.

Epilogue

Looking Back on Your Experience

I hope you enjoyed your experiences freelancing and learning about the graphic design profession outside the classroom. Undoubtedly, some of the lessons were hard, but sometimes tough lessons are the most important lessons to have learned. Like snowflakes, no two designer's experiences will be identical. As long as you managed to cross the finish line and achieve your goals it doesn't really matter which path you took to get there. The obstacles that you faced and overcame have become a catalyst for your growth as a designer.

I hope you took advantage of the opportunities that were given to you and that you received some good advice along the way. Starting a career is an exciting process, and making a living from being a creative person is quite an accomplishment. Remember how nervous you were when you worked with your very first client? It probably seems like a lifetime ago since that first client meeting. You've come far in a few short years and hopefully will continue to grow as you identify your future goals and work to realize them.

Looking back on your experiences freelancing, I hope you can see how working with clients has helped round out your educational experience, given you a means of earning money, helped you learn to balance creativity and commerce, enhanced your portfolio, taught you how to recover after failing, and provided you with the thrill of owning your own business!

You will probably continue to work with all different types of clients throughout your career, but your first clients will be some of your fondest memories. Years from now you'll look back on the work you did, and you'll be able to see how far you've come since you first started working as a designer—or cringe at some of the design decisions you made at the time!

Early in my career I received some good advice: "Always save samples of your work." And over the years I've amassed quite a collection of projects I've helped complete. Sometimes I look through this collection of work and it stirs memories of terrible clients, great colleagues, tough breaks, outstanding successes, and expensive lessons that I learned the hard way.

My parting piece of advice to you is to have fun working with your clients and helping them solve the problems that keep them up at night. You hold a unique position within your community, giving many businesses and individuals a voice and a means of reaching their audience. Not everyone can deliver these messages with clarity and creativity, so good graphic designers are worth their weight in gold to businesses who need help in this area.

When I talk to students who have graduated and joined the profession, I can't help but think how their freelancing experiences and internships have been their primary means for learning what to expect after graduating college. Without these experiences, you risk investing four years of your life without knowing what you're doing all this hard work for!

People always say that trying something and failing at it is one of the best ways to learn a lesson. If the path you followed freelancing and working with clients wasn't easy, don't throw your hands up in the air and start filling out a change-of-major form, take a minute to reflect on the lessons you learned. This kind of struggle (like the frustrations you may have experienced) is the steel on which we designers sharpen our X-Acto blades, hone our skills, and look for ways to be more efficient and effective with our time.

When I first started freelancing in college, I had no clue what I was doing, but I managed to survive. Looking back, I can see how I undervalued my graphic design skills, how I let myself get talked into taking on too much work, and was afraid of walking away from a project if it wasn't a good fit for me. These certainly weren't easy lessons to learn, even though it took me some time to gain my confidence, establish boundaries, and trust my gut when it tells me to walk away from a client. While you're in school, projects seem to last forever. It may seem that you're constantly being sent back to the drawing board to make stronger connections to your research, generate more sketches, and to polish your finishing skills. But once you step foot into professional practice you realize that there is never enough time to work on a project and that you are constantly racing against the clock. You'll wish for the good old days of college when you had more than enough time to work on your projects and wish you had three weeks to devote to a project!

Time is a commodity, and there is never enough of it to go around. Efficiency increases your profit margins and leaves you with time to enjoy your life and enrich your experiences. It's hard to teach lessons like the importance of being efficient, why attention to details are critical, and that the smallest unit of business is a relationship. These lessons aren't easy to share with others because the context for their importance is often lost in translation. While teachers can try to create scenarios where students can experience business truths for themselves, the gravity of decisions aren't usually appreciated until real rewards and consequences are attached to them.

Your experiences freelancing have given you context for the graphic design profession, challenged you to work efficiently and creatively, helped you realize how important it is to establish boundaries, and helped you grow as a designer. You undoubtedly know your strengths and weaknesses much better by having started a freelance company, gotten out of your house and into your community, and pushed yourself to become a better designer.

It is my hope that you have found a profession that fulfills and sustains you and that you continue to grow as a designer. Everyone gets better the more they practice, so don't be afraid to keep "going big and failing big," because these are the times when life is the most interesting. I hope you enjoyed this book and that it helped you navigate the waters of freelancing successfully. Cheers!

Resources

Adbusters Magazine–www.adbusters.org

A magazine of culture jammers and creatives working to change the way information flows, the way corporations wield power, and the way meaning is produced in our society.

American Institute of Graphic Arts–www.aiga.com

The oldest and largest national professional graphic design organization, committed to the promotion of excellence in graphic design.

Behance–www.behance.net

Behance is a website to showcase your work, build an online portfolio, promote yourself, sell your work, and connect with other creatives to share tips and get feedback.

Bittbox–www.bittbox.com

A website where you can obtain high-quality design freebies, tutorials, vectors, Photoshop brushes, and textures.

Boing Boing–www.boingboing.net

A directory of wonderful things.

Boxes and Arrows–www.boxesandarrows.com

A website for the task of bringing architecture and design to the digital realms.

BrushKing–www.brushking.eu

BrushKing offers a wide array of Adobe Photoshop brushes, all free for download. The site currently archives over four thousand brushes and over two hundred brush sets.

CMYK Magazine–www.cmykmag.com

A magazine featuring a quarterly art school design contest for emerging artists in art direction, copywriting, design, photography, and illustration.

Colour Lovers–www.colourlovers.com

COLOURlovers is a creative community where people from around the world create and share colors, palettes and patterns, and discuss the latest trends.

Communication Arts Magazine–www.commarts.com

A bimonthly magazine that includes the Design, Advertising, Illustration, Photography and Interactive annuals, as well as design trends, color predictions, and book reviews.

Creative Review–www.creativereview.co.uk

A website whose aim is to inspire, inform, and stimulate debate among graphic design, advertising, digital media, illustration, photography, and all other fields of visual communication worldwide.

Design Dump–www.designdump.com

The Design Dump is a website whose goal is to build a credible, valuable resource that print and Web designers can utilize on an ongoing basis.

Design Float–www.designfloat.com

A digg-like website for design-related subjects.

Design Observer–www.designobserver.com

A website that features news and critical essays on design, urbanism, social innovation, and popular culture.

Designers Revolution–www.designers-revolution.com

Graphic design resources, stock photography, vector images, and freebies available.

deviantART–www.deviantart.com

deviantART is an online community for graphic artists. The downloadable graphic design resources are from community members, and you will find vectors, brushes, textures, and more.

Eye Magazine–www.eyemagazine.com

A magazine that reviews graphic design and printed quarterly. Includes writing on graphic designers and other professionals in the art and business of visual culture.

Flickr–www.flickr.com

Online photo management and sharing application. Show off your favorite photos and videos.

Freelance Folder–www.freelancefolder.com

FreelanceFolder is a blog for entrepreneurs, freelancers, and Web-workers. This site has freelance tools, advice, resources, and more.

Freelance Switch–www.freelanceswitch.com

FreelanceSwitch is a website for freelancers from around the world. If you've got a job you need doing, you can put up a free job ad on the job board to find a professional designer, developer, blogger, photographer, illustrator, or virtually any other type of freelancer.

Graphic Artist's Guild–www.gag.org

A national union of illustrators, designers, and other creative disciplines. The Graphic Artist's Guild publishes a handbook for pricing and ethical guidelines.

GD USA Magazine–www.gdusa.com

A magazine that provides information on graphic design news, trends, people, ideas, and products from the design community.

Graphic River–www.graphicriver.net

Royalty-free stock graphics and vectors, icon sets, and Photoshop add-ons from GraphicRiver. You can sell your photographs and illustrations here and make extra money.

HOW Magazine–www.howdesign.com

A magazine that helps designers, whether they work in-house, at a design firm, or on their own, to be more creative, successful, productive, and connected.

Icograda–www.icograda.org

International Council of Graphic Design Associations is an international organization for graphic design and visual communication.

Iconfinder–www.iconfinder.com

Search through more than 150,000 free icons in an easy and efficient way.

I Love Typography–www.ilovetypography.com

A typography and fonts blog. I Love Typography has typographic inspiration, typeface reviews, interviews, and fonts.

iStockphoto–www.istockphoto.com

A website that sells royalty-free content at prices anyone can afford. You can sell your photographs and illustrations here and make extra money.

LegalZoom–www.legalzoom.com

Online legal document preparation services for estate planning, trademarks, corporations, and others.

Logo Design Love–www.logodesignlove.com

A website for graphic designers and all who love logos. Logo Design Love includes articles and resources for designers.

Lynda.com–www.lynda.com

A website where you can pay to access a vast collection of software tutorials to help you gain skills and confidence.

Mint.com–www.mint.com

Free personal finance software to assist you to manage your money, financial planning, and budget planning tools.

PDF Mags–www.pdf-mags.com

This is a website that has references from many of the PDF magazines out there.

Print Magazine–www.printmag.com

Print is a bimonthly magazine about design that places contemporary visual culture in its social, political, and historical contexts.

PSD Tuts+–www.psd.tutsplus.com

Psd Tuts+ is a blog/Photoshop site made to house and showcase some of the best Photoshop tutorials around. The site publishes tutorials that not only produce great graphics and effects but also explain the techniques behind them in a friendly, approachable manner.

Smashing Magazine–www.smashingmagazine.com

A website focused on designing and building websites. Smashing Magazine presents valuable techniques, ideas, and resources for Web designers.

Textalyser.net–www.textalyser.net

An online service that allows entry of text or a website. Displays readability analysis, including reading level, sentence length, and word counts

Thinking with Type–www.thinkingwithtype.com

A website that focuses on typographic elements and is an online resource for designers, writers, educators, and students.

Tutorial Blog–www.tutorialblog.org

A website that provides software techniques and effects. In 2008, the site began to broaden its scope to include a variety of Web and graphic design tutorials, becoming a useful resource for beginner and intermediates alike.

United States Bureau of Labor Statistics–www.bls.gov

View statistics gathered by the Business of Labor about the graphic design profession and its expected growth.

United States Small-business Administration–www.sba.gov
A website with helpful information and advice on starting a small-business. Includes advice on business planning, financing, taxes, etc.

Wired Magazine–www.wired.com
Wired provides in-depth coverage of current and future trends in technology, and how they are shaping business, entertainment, communications, science, politics, and culture.

You The Designer–www.youthedesigner.com
This website has a huge range of articles and graphic design topics.

Index

Dry transfers, 125
DSLR camera, 92–94, 148

E

Economic movements, 39, 41
Embossing, 102, 125
Employer Identification Number, 50–53
Estimate, 36
Ethics, 22; ethical issues, 10, 62,
        138–39, 141–43
Equipment,
    Beginner level, 56–60
    Intermediate level, 92–96
    Advanced level, 146–50
Estimate, 19
Executive summary, 30, 36
External factors, 29, 39
External storage device, 60
External threats, 30
External work, 86

F

Failure, 7, 9, 18, 25–27
Fear, 25
Foil stamps, 124
Fonts, 74, 94, 121
Freelancing: testing the waters, 4;
        while in school, 4

G

Gang print, 123
Gloss varnish, 124–25
Google, 14, 17
Grades, 11, 20
Graduate faculty, 164
Graduate school, 158, 164

Graphic Artists Guild, 3, 140, 142,
        145–46
Graphics tablet, 95–96

I

Ideation, 71
Inkjet printer, 58–60
Internal work, 86
Internship, 3, 92, 137–38
Interview, 191–200, 196
Invoice, 72, 88–89
IRS, 50, 108

J

Job proposal, 69, 88
Job tracking number, 117
JPG files, 94

K

Kill fee, 36, 75–76

L

Laser printer, 58–59
Letterpress, 125

M

Marketing, 14, 30, 37, 187
Master client list, 116–17, 120
Master job tracking list, 116–17, 120
Megapixels, 93
Methodology, 131–136, 135
Mission statement, 30, 103, 194
Mock interviews, 193
Mock-up, 72, 84
Monthly budget, 145–46, 171–72, 178

Strategic planning, 30

Stress, 8, 110

Stripper, 1–2

Subcontract, 37

SWOT analysis, 30–34

T

Taxes, 18, 32, 42, 49–50, 52, 88, 102, 108

Tax credit, 101

Termination policy, 75

Terms of proposal, 76

Thank-you card, 99, 150, 198

Thermography, 123–24

Time management, 9, 22, 91, 130

Time sheet, 19, 87–88, 116

Trademark law, 10

Traps: trapping color, 1–2

Trends, 20

Trial-and-error, 20

Typography, 79; typographic, 16, 168, 173; typeface, 71, 73, 82, 95, 190

U

Underpromise, 5, 37

USB drive, 60, 83

UV varnish, 123, 125

V

Varnishes, 102

Vendors, 127–29

Visual Voice, 12

W

Wacom tablet, 17

Web hosting, 53, 156

Work flow, 92, 116, 143